Lecture Notes in Computer Science 1773

Edited by G. Goos, J. Hartmanis and J. van Leeuwen

T0223244

Springer
Berlin
Heidelberg
New York
Barcelona
Hong Kong
London
Milan
Paris
Singapore
Tokyo

Gunter Saake Kerstin Schwarz
Can Türker (Eds.)

Transactions and Database Dynamics

8th International Workshop on Foundations
of Models and Languages for Data and Objects
Dagstuhl Castle, Germany, September 27-30, 1999
Selected Papers

 Springer

Series Editors

Gerhard Goos, Karlsruhe University, Germany
Juris Hartmanis, Cornell University, NY, USA
Jan van Leeuwen, Utrecht University, The Netherlands

Volume Editors

Gunter Saake
University of Magdeburg
Institute of Technical and Business Information Systems
P.O. Box 4120, 39016 Magdeburg, Germany
E-mail: saake@iti.cs.uni-magdeburg.de

Kerstin Schwarz
UBS AG
Flurstrasse 62, 8098 Zürich, Switzerland
E-mail: kerstin.schwarz@ubs.com

Can Türker
Swiss Federal Institute of Technology (ETH) Zürich
Institute of Information Systems
ETH Zentrum, 8092 Zürich, Switzerland
E-mail: tuerker@inf.ethz.ch

Cataloging-in-Publication Data applied for

Die Deutsche Bibliothek - CIP-Einheitsaufnahme

Transactions and database dynamics : selected papers / 8th International
Workshop on Foundations of Models and Languages for Data and
Objects, Dagstuhl Castle, Germany, September 27 - 30, 1999. Gunter
Saake ... (ed.). - Berlin ; Heidelberg ; New York ; Barcelona ; Hong
Kong ; London ; Milan ; Paris ; Singapore ; Tokyo : Springer, 2000
    (Lecture notes in computer science ; Vol. 1773)
    ISBN 3-540-67201-X

CR Subject Classification (1991): H.2.4, H.2, H.4

ISSN 0302-9743
ISBN 3-540-67201-X Springer-Verlag Berlin Heidelberg New York

Typesetting: Camera-ready by author, data conversion by PTP-Berlin, Stefan Sossna
Printed on acid-free paper   SPIN 10719805   06/3142   5 4 3 2 1 0

Preface

These post-proceedings contain the revised versions of the accepted papers of the international workshop *"Transactions and Database Dynamics"*, which was the eighth workshop in a series focusing on foundations of models and languages for data and objects (FoMLaDO).

Seven long papers and three short papers were accepted for inclusion in the proceedings. The papers address various issues of transactions and database dynamics:

- criteria and protocols for global snapshot isolation in federated transaction management,
- unified theory of concurrency control and replication control,
- specification of evolving information systems,
- inheritance mechanisms for deductive object databases with updates,
- specification of active rules for maintaining database consistency,
- integrity checking in subtransactions,
- open nested transactions for multi-tier architectures,
- declarative specification of transactions with static and dynamic integrity constraints,
- logic-based specification of update queries as open nested transactions, and
- execution guarantees and transactional processes in electronic commerce payments.

In addition to the regular papers, there are papers resulting from two working groups. The first working group paper discusses the basis for transactional computation. In particular, it addresses the specification of transactional software. The second working group paper focuses on transactions in electronic commerce applications. Among others, Internet transactions, payment protocols, and concurrency control and persistence mechanisms are discussed.

Moreover, there is an invited paper by Jari Veijalainen which discusses transactional aspects in mobile electronic commerce.

Acknowledgments: We are grateful to the members of the program committee and others who have reviewed the submitted papers. We are also thankful to all authors who have submitted papers to this workshop. Finally, we thank all participants of the workshop for the lively discussions.

December 1999

Gunter Saake
Kerstin Schwarz
Can Türker

Program Commitee

Catriel Beeri	The Hebrew University of Jerusalem, Israel
Philip A. Bernstein	Microsoft Corp., USA
Elisa Bertino	University of Milan, Italy
Anthony J. Bonner	University of Toronto, Canada
Yuri Breitbart	University of Kentucky, USA
Jan Chomicki	Monmouth University, USA
Stefan Conrad	University of Munich, Germany
Burkhard Freitag	University of Passau, Germany
Hele-Mai Haav	Institute of Cybernetics, Tallinn, Estonia
Michael Gertz	University of California, USA
Stefan Jablonski	University of Erlangen, Germany
Gerti Kappel	University of Linz, Austria
Holger Meyer	University of Rostock, Germany
Gunter Saake	University of Magdeburg, Germany; co-chair
Hans-Jörg Schek	ETH Zürich, Switzerland
Klaus-Dieter Schewe	TU Clausthal, Germany
Michael Schrefl	University of South Australia, Australia
Kerstin Schwarz	UBS AG Zürich, Switzerland; co-chair
Can Türker	ETH Zürich, Switzerland; co-chair
Rainer Unland	University of Essen, Germany
Jari Veijalainen	University of Jyväskylä, Finland
Gottfried Vossen	University of Münster, Germany
Roel Wieringa	University of Twente, The Netherlands

Additional Reviewers

Alfread Fent	University of Passau, Germany
Carl-Alexander Wichert	University of Passau, Germany

Table of Contents

Working Group Papers

Author Index 247

Federated Transaction Management with Snapshot Isolation

Ralf Schenkel[1], Gerhard Weikum[1], Norbert Weißenberg[2], and Xuequn Wu[3]

[1] University of the Saarland, {schenkel,weikum}@cs.uni-sb.de
[2] Fraunhofer ISST, norbert.weissenberg@do.isst.fhg.de
[3] Deutsche Telekom AG, wu@tzd.telekom.de

Abstract. Federated transaction management (also known as multida-tabase transaction management in the literature) is needed to ensure the consistency of data that is distributed across multiple, largely autono-mous, and possibly heterogeneous component databases and accessed by both global and local transactions. While the global atomicity of such transactions can be enforced by using a standardized commit protocol like XA or its CORBA counterpart OTS, global serializability is not self-guaranteed as the underlying component systems may use a variety of potentially incompatible local concurrency control protocols. The pro-blem of how to achieve global serializability, by either constraining the component systems or implementing additional global protocols at the federation level, has been intensively studied in the literature, but did not have much impact on the practical side. A major deficiency of the prior work has been that it focused on the idealized correctness criterion of serializability and disregarded the subtle but important variations of SQL isolation levels supported by most commercial database systems. This paper reconsiders the problem of federated transaction manage-ment, more specifically its concurrency control issues, with particular focus on isolation levels used in practice, especially the popular snapshot isolation provided by Oracle. As pointed out in a SIGMOD 1995 paper by Berenson et al., a rigorous foundation for reasoning about such con-currency control features of commercial systems is sorely missing. The current paper aims to close this gap by developing a formal framework that allows us to reason about local and global transaction executions where some (or all) transactions are running under snapshot isolation. The paper derives criteria and practical protocols for guaranteeing glo-bal snapshot isolation at the federation level. It further generalizes the well-known ticket method to cope with combinations of isolation levels in a federated system.

1 Introduction

1.1 Reviving the Problem of Federated Transactions

With the ever-increasing demand for information integration both within and across enterprises, there is renewed interest in providing seamless access to mul-tiple, independently developed and largely autonomously operated databases.

G. Saake, K. Schwarz, and C. Türker (Eds.): TDD '99, LNCS 1773, pp. 1–25, 2000.
© Springer-Verlag Berlin Heidelberg 2000

Such a setting is known as a database federation or heterogeneous multidatabase system. More specifically, the approach of building an additional integration software layer on top of the underlying component systems is referred to as a federated database system [13,21,8,9,10,17]. Among the challenges posed by such a system architecture is the problem of enforcing the consistency of the data across the boundaries of the individual component systems. Transactions that access and modify data in more than one component system are referred to as federated or global transactions [4,5]; for example, an electronic commerce application could require a transaction to update data in a merchant's database as well as the databases of a credit card company and a service broker that pointed the customer to the merchant and requests a provisioning fee for each sale. Providing the usual ACID properties for such federated transactions is inherently harder than in a homogeneous, centrally administered distributed database system, one reason being that the underlying component systems of a federation may employ different protocols for their local transaction management. A canonical example is the following schedule of three transactions, t_1, t_2, and t_3, that read and write data objects x, y, and z in two databases, DB_1 and DB_2, managed by two different database systems (or differently configured instances of the same database system) with different concurrency control protocols:

$$DB_1: \quad r_1(x)w_1(x) \qquad\qquad C_1\ r_2(x)w_2(x) \qquad\qquad C_2$$
$$DB_2: r_3(y) \qquad\qquad r_1(y)w_1(y)\ C_1 \qquad\qquad r_2(z)w_2(z)\ C_2\ r_3(z)C_3$$

Both local schedules, as seen by each of the two component systems alone, are serializable, but the problem is that the resulting serialization orders are incompatible from a global viewpoint. In DB_1, the serialization order requires that t_1 precede t_2, whereas in DB_2, the only possible serialization order is the one in which t_2 precedes t_3 and t_3 precedes t_1. Thus, the overall execution of the three transactions is not globally serializable and may potentially result in data inconsistencies.

These kinds of problems with regard to federated transactions have been intensively studied in the late eighties and early nineties. The proposed solutions range from imposing additional constraints on the transaction protocols of the underlying component systems to building an additional transaction manager in the federated software layer on top of the component systems to reconcile or control the underlying local executions. The most notable result in the first category probably is that global serializability is self-guaranteed if all component systems allow only conflict-serializable schedules where the commit order coincides with the serialization order [6,7,19,22], with rigorous schedules being the most important special case [6]. In the second category, the family of ticket methods [11] has been among the most promising approaches, complementing knowledge about local serialization orders with graph-cycle testing at the federation level.

All this ample work has led to interesting theoretical insights, but appears to have made little impact on the practical side. Consequently, the subject of federated transactions has not been pursued further by the research community in the last few years. The current paper aims to revive the subject, pushing it in a new and practically relevant direction. We believe that the prior work has not succeeded in the intended technology transfer because it made some fundamental assumptions that did not match the typical setting of commercial database systems and their real-life applications. Essentially, the prior work made too liberal assumptions on the recovery protocols of practically used systems, and it made too restrictive assumptions on their local concurrency control protocols:

- On the recovery side, the point that the underlying component systems are largely autonomous and therefore may not necessarily be willing to coope-rate for ensuring the atomicity of global transactions has been way overrated. Today, standardized distributed commit protocols like XA or its CORBA counterpart OTS [14] are supported by virtually all commercially relevant database systems, request brokers (TP monitors, ORBs, etc.), and even pack-aged business-object software systems. Rather than building complex reco-very protocols at the federation level, it is much easier and more manageable to rely on those protocols for global atomicity. For long-running workflow-style applications, a distributed commit protocol would admittedly incur severe performance problems, but for reasonably short federated transac-tions (e.g., the kind that arises in electronic commerce applications) it is a perfectly viable solution.
- On the concurrency control side, virtually all prior work assumed that the component systems would guarantee at least conflict-serializability for their local schedules. In real life, however, various kinds of isolation levels are provided by commercial database systems and widely used by performance-conscious application developers. These include the isolation levels of the SQL standard, such as "read committed" (known as "cursor stability" in some commercial systems), as well as vendor-specific options like Oracle's snapshot isolation feature. None of the prior work on federated transac-tion management has taken these isolation level options into account, de-spite their undebatable practical relevance. Even worse, there is generally a wide gap in the theoretical foundation of transaction management as far as such concurrency tuning options are concerned. To our knowledge, the only exceptions are the remarkable paper by Berenson et al. [2], discussing SQL-standard as well as vendor-specific isolation levels from a conceptual viewpoint without truly foundational ambitions, however, and the work by Atluri et al. [1] extending the classical serializability theory to incorporate weaker isolation levels from a formal and rather abstract viewpoint. Both papers restrict themselves to a centralized database setting.

1.2 Contribution and Outline of the Paper

The current paper aims to narrow the aforementioned gap in the foundation of transaction management, while also pursuing practically viable solutions for federated transaction management in the presence of isolation levels different from standard serializability. We essentially concentrate on concurrency control issues, disregarding recovery for the fact that standardized distributed commit

protocols like XA and OTS can ensure global atomicity across system boundaries, as discussed above. We focus on conventional types of transactions, the
key problem being their federated, heterogeneous nature, and do not address
workflow-style activities that may run for hours or days. Further note that the
problem of federated concurrency control arises even if the same database system is used for all component databases of the federation, since the system may
be configured with different isolation level options for different databases (and
transaction classes).

Our approach is largely driven by considering the capabilities of commercial systems. In particular, Oracle provides interesting options that are fairly
representative for the subtle but important deviations from the pure school of
serializability theory. Like several other commercial systems, Oracle supports
transient versioning for enhanced concurrency, and exploits versions, by means
of a timestamp-based protocol, to offer the following two isolation level options
[15,16]:

1. A transaction running under the "read committed" option reads the most
   recent versions of the requested data objects that were committed at the
   time when the read operation is issued. Note that these read accesses to
   committed versions can proceed without any locking. All updates that the
   transaction may invoke are subject to exclusive locking of the affected data
   objects, and such locks are held until the transaction's commit.
2. For transactions running under the "snapshot isolation" level, all operations read the most recent versions as of the time when the transaction began, thus ensuring a consistent view of the data through the transaction.
   A particularly beneficial special case is that all read-only transactions are
   perfectly isolated in the sense of the multiversion serializability theory [3].
   For read-write transactions, on the other hand, the sketched protocol cannot
   ensure (multiversion) serializability. In addition, Oracle performs the following check upon commit of a transaction: if any data object written by the
   transaction has been written by another, already committed transaction that
   ran concurrently to the considered one (i.e., committed after the considered
   transaction began), then the current transaction is aborted and rolled back.
   Additionally, exclusive locks are used for updates and held until the transaction's commit. If a transaction has to wait for a lock and the transaction
   holding that lock commits, the waiting transaction is aborted. This is a special case of the commit-time test, allowing prevention of concurrent writes
   before they happen.

Disallowing concurrent writes aims to provide an additional level of sanity, and
Oracle even advocates this option under the name "serializability". Nonetheless,
the protocol cannot ensure full (multiversion) serializability, with the following
schedule as a counterexample (x_i denotes the version of x generated by transaction t_i, and t_0 is a fictitious initializing transaction):

$$r_1(x_0)r_1(y_0)r_2(x_0)r_2(y_0)w_1(x_1)C_1w_2(y_2)C_2$$

The example may lead to inconsistent data, for example, violating a constraint such as $x + y < 100$ although both transactions alone would enforce the constraint. However, given that such anomalies are very infrequent in practice, the protocol is widely popular in Oracle applications.

As pointed out by Berenson et al. [2], such non-serializable isolation levels, and especially the snapshot isolation option, are extremely useful in practice, despite their lack of theoretical underpinnings. Since Oracle would obviously be a major player also in a federated database setting, we concentrate in this paper on understanding the impact of snapshot isolation for federated transaction management. In fact, the work presented here is part of a larger effort to build a federated database architecture, coined VHDBS, that currently supports Oracle and O_2 databases [23,24,12,20].

The paper's "plan of attack" proceeds in two steps, leading to the following contributions:

– We develop a formal model that allows us to reason about isolation levels in the context of federated transactions, and we derive results that relate local and global isolation levels. Since snapshot isolation exploits transient versioning, all our formal considerations are cast in a multiversion schedule framework.
– Based on these theoretical results, we develop new algorithms for federated concurrency control, to ensure global snapshot isolation or global (conflict-) serializability, whatever the application demands. The latter algorithm is based on a generalization of the ticket method to cope with component systems that provide snapshot isolation.

The rest of the paper is organized as follows. In Section 2, we introduce the basic model and notations, and we develop the theoretical underpinnings for coping with snapshot isolation in concurrent transaction executions. In Section 3, we derive results on how to relate the isolation levels in local schedules with the desired correctness criteria at the federation level, and develop an algorithm for ensuring global snapshot isolation under the assumption that all component systems guarantee local snapshot isolation. Section 4 develops a practically viable protocol to guarantee global serializability in a federated system with some component systems providing snapshot isolation, extending and generalizing the ticket method of [11]. We conclude the paper with an outlook on future work. All proofs of theorems are given in the paper's Appendix.

2   Basic Model and Notation

This section introduces the formal apparatus that is necessary for our study of snapshot isolation. We briefly introduce the notation and some results of the standard theory of (multiversion) serializability in Subsection 2.1, and then develop a formal characterization of snapshot isolation in Subsection 2.2.

2.1 Preliminaries

Definition 1 (transaction). *A transaction t_i is a sequence, i.e., total order $\ll$, of read and write actions on data objects from one or more databases, along with a set of begin and commit actions, one for each database accessed by t_i, such that all begin actions precede all read and write actions in the order $\ll$ and all commit actions follow all other actions w.r.t. $\ll$. The readset and writeset of t_i are the sets of objects for which t_i includes read and write actions, respectively.*

We denote the j-th read or write step of t_i by $a_{ij}(x)$ where x is the accessed object, or $r_{ij}(x)$ (for reads) and $w_{ij}(x)$ (for writes) when the kind of actions is relevant. When we want to indicate the database to which a step refers, we extend the notation for an action as follows: $a_{ij}^{(k)}(x)$ denotes the j-th step of transaction t_i accessing object x that resides in database DB_k. The begin and commit actions for database DB_k, explicitly denoted whenever they are relevant, are written as $B_i^{(k)}$ and $C_i^{(k)}$, respectively. □

For all transactions, we further restrict the sequence of read and write accesses to allow a write on object x only if there the transaction includes also a read on x that precedes the write in the action order $\ll$. Furthermore, we allow at most one read and at most one write on the same object within a single transaction. None of these two properties present serious restrictions of the executions that we can model; in practice, writes are usually preceded by reads, and multiple reads or writes to the same object can easily be eliminated by using temporary program variables.

Note that we do not consider partial orders within a transaction for the sake of simpler notation, although this relaxation could be incorporated in the model quite easily. Similarly, disallowing multiple reads or writes on the same object is also only a matter of notation. The only "semantically" relevant restriction of our model is that we do not consider transaction aborts and assume all transactions to be committed. This paper addresses federated concurrency control; extensions to incorporate recovery issues in the formal model would be the subject of future work.

Definition 2 (global and local transactions). *A global transaction (GT) is a transaction that accesses objects from at least two different databases. In contrast, a local transaction (LT) accesses only a single database. The projection of a global transaction t_i onto a database DB_k is the set of actions of t_i that refer to objects from DB_k, along with their corresponding order $\ll$. This projection will be referred to as a global subtransaction (GST) and denoted by $t_i^{(k)}$.* □

Note that the dichotomy between GTs and LTs is a purely syntactic one in our definition. In practice, an additional key difference is that LTs are not routed through an additional federation software layer but rather access a database directly through the native database system and nothing else.

Definition 3 (schedule, multiversion schedule, monoversion schedule). *A schedule of transactions $T = \{t_1, ...\}$ is a sequence, i.e., total order $\ll$, of the* *union of the actions of all transactions in T such that the action ordering within transactions is preserved.*

A multiversion schedule of transactions $T = \{t_1, ...\}$ is a schedule with an additional version function that maps each read action $r_i(x)$ in the schedule to a write action $w_j(x)$ that precedes the read in the order $\ll$. The read action is then also written as $r_i(x_j)$ with x_j denoting the version created by the write of t_j.

A monoversion schedule of transactions $T = \{t_1, ...\}$ is a multiversion schedule whose version function maps each read action $r_i(x)$ to the most recent write action $w_j(x)$ that precedes it (i.e., $w_j(x) \ll r_i(x)$ and there is no other write action on x in between). □

The usual correctness criterion for multiversion concurrency control is that a given multiversion schedule should be view-equivalent to a serial monoversion schedule, with view-equivalence being defined by the reads-from relation among the actions of a schedule [3,18].

Definition 4 (MVSR). *A multiversion schedule s is multiversion serializable (MVSR), if it is view-equivalent to a monoversion serial schedule.* □

Definition 5 (version order, MVSG). *Given a multiversion schedule s and an object x, a version order $\ll$ is a total order of the versions of x in s. A version order for s is the union of the version orders for all objects.*

Given a multiversion schedule s and a version order $\ll$ for s, the multiversion serialization graph for s and $\ll$, $MVSG(s, \ll)$, is the directed graph with the transactions as nodes and the following edges:

- *For each operation $r_j(x_i)$ in the schedule there is an edge $t_i \rightarrow t_j$ (WR pair).*
- *For each pair of operations $r_k(x_j)$ and $w_i(x_i)$ where i, j and k are distinct, there is an edge*
  (i) $t_i \rightarrow t_j$, if $x_i \ll x_j$ (WW pair),
  (ii) $t_k \rightarrow t_i$, if $x_j \ll x_i$ (RW pair). □

The following theorem is the most important characterization of MVSR by means of the MVSG, serving as the basis for correctness proofs of practical multiversion concurrency control protocols (see, e.g., [3]).

Theorem 1 (characterization of MVSR [3]). *A multiversion schedule s is in MVSR if and only if there exists a version order $\ll$ such that $MVSG(s, \ll)$ is acyclic.* □

When we consider only (non-serial) monoversion schedules (for which each write is preceded by a read of the same transaction) and wish to reason about their correctness, the criterion of MVSR automatically degenerates into the well-known notion of conflict-serializability (SR) [18]. This results from the restriction of the version function. So with this restriction, MVSR becomes equivalent to the standard definition of conflict-serializability (SR) based on read-write, write-write, and write-read conflicts (and the corresponding conflict-graph construction).

2.2   Formalizing the Snapshot Isolation Level (SI)

So far we have introduced the traditional apparatus of multiversion serializability. We are now ready to discuss relaxations, in the sense of isolation levels, within this model. In this paper we concentrate on the situation where an entire schedule satisfies a certain relaxed isolation level. The general case where only a specific subset of transactions tolerates a relaxed isolation level and the "rest of the schedule" should still be serializable or MVSR is the subject of future work.

Definition 6 (snapshot isolation). *A multiversion schedule of transactions* $T = \{t_1, ...\}$ *satisfies the criterion of snapshot isolation (SI) if the following two conditions hold:*

(SI-V) **SI version function**: *The version function maps each read action* $r_i(x)$ *to the most recent committed write action* $w_j(x)$ *as of the time of the begin of* t_i, *or more formally:*
$r_i(x)$ *is mapped to* $w_j(x)$ *such that* $w_j(x) \ll C_j \ll B_i \ll r_i(x)$ *and there are no other actions* $w_h(x)$ *and* C_h *(*$h \neq j$*) with* $w_h(x) \ll B_i$ *and* $C_j \ll C_h \ll B_i$.

(SI-W) **disjoint writesets**: *The writesets of two concurrent transactions are disjoint, or more formally:*
if for two transactions t_i *and* t_j, *either* $B_i \ll B_j \ll C_i$ *or* $B_j \ll B_i \ll C_j$, *then* t_i *and* t_j *must not write a common object* x.   □

SI is weaker than MVSR in the sense that it allows non-serializable schedules, for example the following:

$$r_1(x_0)r_1(y_0)r_2(x_0)r_2(y_0)w_1(x_1)w_2(y_2)C_1C_2$$

This schedule satisfies both (SI-V) and (SI-W), but it is not equivalent to a serial monoversion schedule. On the other hand, SI is not a superset of MVSR, because there are serializable multiversion schedules that are not in SI, for example

$$r_1(x_0)r_2(y_0)w_2(y_2)C_2r_1(y_2)w_1(y_1)C_1$$

This schedule is not in SI because $r_1(y)$ is mapped to $w_2(y_2)$ rather than $w_0(x_0)$, and because t_1 and t_2 are concurrent and write the same object y. It is, however, equivalent to the serial monoversion schedule

$$r_2(y)w_2(y)C_2r_1(x)r_1(y)w_1(y)C_1$$

The key point here is that this schedule uses a version function different from the SI version function.

We now characterize SI membership of a given multiversion schedule by the absence of cycles in a graph.

Definition 7 (SI version order). *The SI version order* $\ll_s$ *is the order that is induced by the order of the commit operations of the transactions that wrote the versions, or more formally:*

$$x_i \ll_s x_j :\Leftrightarrow C_i \ll C_j$$

□

Definition 8 (SI-MVSG). *The SI multiversion serialization graph SI-MVSG for a given multiversion schedule s satisfying the property (SI-V) is a directed graph with the transactions as nodes and the following edges:*

- *For each operation $r_j(x_i)$ in the schedule there is an edge $t_i \rightarrow t_j$, labeled with "x" (WR pair).*
- *For each pair of operations $r_k(x_j)$ and $w_i(x_i)$, there is an edge*
  (i) $t_i \rightarrow t_j$, if $x_i \ll_s x_j$ (WW pair),
  (ii) $t_k \rightarrow t_i$, if $x_j \ll_s x_i$ (RW pair),
  labeled with "x" in both cases.

Edges in the graph that are labeled with "x" are called x-edges. A cycle in the graph that consists completely of x-edges is called an x-cycle. □

SI-MVSG is exactly the same as the usual multiversion serialization graph MVSG defined above, extended by the edge labels. Similarly to the MVSG theorem cited in Subsection 2.1, the following theorem gives a characterization for schedules that are snapshot isolated:

Theorem 2 (Equivalence of SI and cycle-free SI-MVSG). *A multiversion schedule satisfying (SI-V) is*

a) *in MVSR, if and only if its corresponding SI-MVSG is acyclic, and*
b) *in SI, if and only if there is no object x such that the SI-MVSG has an x-cycle.* □

As an example, consider the following two schedules:

$$s1 := r_1(x_0)r_1(y_0)r_2(x_0)r_2(y_0)w_1(x_1)w_2(y_2)C_1C_2 \tag{1}$$
$$s2 := r_1(x_0)r_1(y_0)r_2(x_0)r_2(y_0)w_1(x_1)w_2(x_2)C_1C_2 \tag{2}$$

The schedule s_1 is in SI while s_2 is not (the transactions are concurrent and both write x). For both schedules, the corresponding SI-MVSG, shown in Figure 1, contains a cycle; thus neither of the two schedules is MVSR. But only the MVSG for s_2 (on the right of Figure 1) contains a cycle that consists solely of edges labeled by the same object x. So s_2 is not SI whereas s_1 is SI.

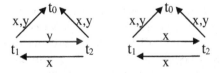

Fig. 1. SSI-MVSG for two schedules

3 Guaranteeing Global Snapshot Isolation

3.1 The Problem of Global Snapshot Isolation

The goal of this section is to derive necessary and sufficient conditions for schedules of federated transactions to be globally SI, provided that all underlying component systems generate only schedules that are locally SI. In the following, we assume that all federated transactions employ an atomic commit protocol (ACP) across the affected component systems with a conceptually centralized coordinator such that

- the relative order of the local commit operations of different global transactions is the same in all component systems (i.e., if t_i commits before t_j in DB_1, then t_i must commit before t_j in DB_2 etc. as well) and
- the local commit operations are totally ordered among all transactions, i.e., no two commit operations happen concurrently.

With these assumptions, the local commit operations of a transaction can be safely replaced by the global commit operation in all local schedules.

The following example shows that it is not at all trivial to guarantee global SI even if all component systems enforce local SI.

$$DB_1 : r_1^{(1)}(a_0)r_2^{(1)}(x_0)w_2^{(1)}(x_2) \qquad\qquad C_2\, r_1^{(1)}(x_0) \qquad\qquad\qquad C_1$$
$$DB_2 : \qquad\qquad\qquad\qquad r_2^{(2)}(y_0)w_2^{(2)}(y_2)\, C_2 \qquad\qquad r_1^{(2)}(y_2)w_1^{(2)}(y_1)\, C_1$$

In database DB_1, the subtransactions $t_1^{(1)}$ and $t_2^{(1)}$ of the two global transactions t_1 and t_2 run concurrently, so they both read from a prior transaction (here this is the fictitious, initializing transaction t_0). Only $t_2^{(1)}$ writes an object. This subschedule therefore is SI. The other subschedule, in database DB_2, is SI, too: the two subtransactions $t_1^{(2)}$ and $t_2^{(2)}$ run serially and they both read the correct values according to the SI version function. However, combining the two subschedules into a global schedule (with database superscripts omitted) yields:

$$r_1(a_0)r_2(x_0)w_2(x_2)r_2(y_0)w_2(y_2)C_2r_1(x_0)r_1(y_2)w_1(y_1)C_1$$

This schedule is not snapshot isolated: t_1 reads y from t_2 rather than t_0 (so (SI-V) does not hold), and both transactions run concurrently and both write y (so (SI-W) does not hold either). The problem lies in the fact that the local scheduler in DB_2 does not know when t_2 started at the global federation level, so it fails to assign the globally correct versions, restricting itself to local correctness. Analogous arguments hold for the consideration of global writesets versus local writesets and global concurrency versus local concurrency. The following two subsections present two algorithms that overcome these problems and guarantee that the global schedule is SI. The first, pessimistic approach, discussed in Subsection 3.2, achieves its objective by synchronizing the local begin operations of transactions (in addition to the implicit synchronization of the local commits that results from the ACP). The second, optimistic approach, discussed in Subsection 3.3., is based on testing the potential violation of global SI.

3.2   Pessimistic Approach: Synchronizing Subtransaction Begins

An idea towards a globally correct execution is to start all local subtransactions $t_i^{(k)}$ upon the first operation of the global transaction t_i. The intuition behind this is that we want all subtransactions of a global transaction to have the same start time as the global transaction in the global schedule. If we can achieve this, any violation of the SI property of the global schedule could be mapped to a corresponding violation in one of the local schedules, and the latter would be prevented by the fact that all local schedulers generate SI schedules.

The obvious way to "simultaneously" start the local subtransactions is by issuing an explicit local begin in each component system DB_k on which the transaction will possibly issue read or write operations. Unfortunately, this alone does not entirely solve the problem. It may occur that a global transaction t_1 commits while another transaction t_2 is in the process of submitting its local begin operations. If in some database the begin operation is executed before the commit of t_1 and this order is reversed in another database, global SI property can still not be guaranteed. The following part of a schedule illustrates this problem:

$$DB_1 : r_1^{(1)}(x_0)w_1^{(1)}(x_1)B_2^{(1)}\ C_1 \qquad r_2^{(1)}(x_0) \qquad\qquad C_2$$
$$DB_2 : r_1^{(2)}(y_0)w_1^{(2)}(y_1) \qquad C_1\ B_2^{(2)} \qquad r_2^{(2)}(y_1)w_2^{(2)}(y_2)\ C_2$$

This execution is not globally SI. However, both local schedules are SI, so merely adding the local begin operations did not fix the problem.

Obviously, the above problem arises because a global commit is executed in between several local begin operations of the same federated transaction. So we need to delay the commit request of a global transaction when another transaction is executing its begin operations, until all local begin operations have returned. Likewise, we have to delay the begin operations if another transaction is already in the process of committing, until the commit is finished.

With this kind of begin synchronization and the implicit synchronization by the ACP, we can now assume that all subtransactions of a global transaction t_i start at the same time B_i and end at the same time C_i in all underlying component systems. Therefore, the version functions of the various component systems are "synchronized" as well. This consideration leads us to a criterion for globally correct execution, as expressed by the following theorem.

Theorem 3. *Let s be a schedule in a federated database system whose component systems guarantee local SI for the local schedules (and with an ACP based on a conceptually centralized coordinator). If each federated transaction issues local begin operations on each potentially accessed component system and the federation level prevents global commit operations from being concurrently executed with a transaction's set of local begin operations, then s is snapshot isolated.* □

This approach is relatively easy to implement, but it has potential performance problems: At the start time of a federated transaction, it is not necessarily known which component systems the transaction may access during its execution (nor can this information be easily inferred from the transaction program). To be on the safe side, local begin operations would have to be executed in a conservatively chosen set of component systems if not even all component systems of the federation. Although each of the local begin operations is fairly inexpensive, the total overhead may incur a significant penalty in terms of the transaction throughput. Even worse, since global commit operations may have to be delayed by begin operations, there is also a potentially severe performance drawback as far as transaction response time is concerned.

3.3   Optimistic Approach: Testing for Global SI Violations

Looking again at the example in the previous Subsection 3.2, we observe a specific situation: the two transactions are concurrent in one database (DB_1), while having a reads-from relationship in the serial execution in the other database (DB_2). This type of situation is in fact the only case when global SI can be violated despite all component systems enforcing local SI. Note that the concurrent execution in one database implies that the writesets of the two transactions must be disjoint because of the local SI property. However, this concurrent execution may result in a version function that is incompatible with the version function of the second component system. Further note that in the component system where the subtransactions are concurrent, no reads-from relationship is possible between the two transactions. So it seems that all we need to do is to avoid that two transactions are a) concurrent in one database and b) have a (serial) reads-from relationship in another database. Unfortunately, the following example shows that this consideration does still not capture all relevant cases, as it disregards schedules where one transaction accesses only a proper subset of the databases accessed by the other transaction (e.g., only one out of DB_1 and DB_2):

$$DB_1 : r_1^{(1)}(a_0) \hspace{6cm} C_1$$
$$DB_2 : \hspace{2cm} r_2^{(2)}(x_0)w_2^{(2)}(x_2)C_2 r_1^{(2)}(x_2)w_1^{(2)}(x_1) \; C_1$$

This global schedule is not SI, because both transactions are concurrent and write the same object x. However, our above consideration does not capture this unacceptable case, because all operations of t_1 are strictly after those of t_2 in DB_2, and t_2 does not have any operations in DB_1. In the approach of the previous Subsection 3.2 with synchronized begin operations, such an execution would be impossible because the local begin operation of t_1 in DB_2 would make t_1 locally start before t_2 so that t_1 would read x_0 rather than x_2. However, the synchronized begin operations would have performance drawbacks that we would like to avoid in the current approach. Here, to fix the above problem, we first extend our model of a schedule by introducing additional pseudo-operations $B_i^{(k)}$ and $C_i^{(k)}$ for each transaction t_i and each database DB_k that is not accessed by t_i. The ordering of the artificial $C_i^{(k)}$ operations is such that it is compatible with all real commit operations in the other databases and arbitrary with regard to read and write operations, and the artificial $B_i^{(k)}$ operations are placed immediately before the corresponding local commit. Unlike the local begin operations of the previous Subsection 3.2, the newly introduced operations here are indeed only placeholders for the purpose of correctness reasoning about federated schedules; they do no have to be issued in the real system. The net effect of this syntactical extension is that we can now easily tell, in our model, for each pair of transactions t_i and t_j and each DB_k if $t_i^{(k)}$ fully precedes $t_j^{(k)}$, denoted $t_i^{(k)} < t_j^{(k)}$ (or more precisely: $C_i^{(k)} \ll B_j^{(k)}$), or if $t_j^{(k)}$ fully precedes $t_i^{(k)}$, or if $t_i^{(k)}$ and $t_j^{(k)}$ are concurrent, the latter being denoted as $t_i^{(k)} \| t_j^{(k)}$.

Theorem 4 (characterization of the global SI version function). *Let s be a schedule, extended in the above way, that is executed in a federated database system (using an ACP) whose component systems guarantee local SI. The version function of s, that is, the union of the version functions of the underlying local schedules, satisfies (SI-V) if and only if there are no two transactions t_i and t_j and no two databases DB_k and DB_l such that $t_i^{(k)} < t_j^{(k)}$, $t_j^{(k)}$ reads from $t_i^{(k)}$, and $t_i^{(l)} \| t_j^{(l)}$.* □

From this necessary and sufficient condition for a global schedule to satisfy (SI-V), we can further derive the following theorem that tells us when a global schedule is SI.

Theorem 5 (sufficient and necessary condition for global SI). *Let s be an extended schedule in a federated database system (using an ACP) whose component systems guarantee local SI. Then s is SI if and only if there are no two transactions t_i and t_j and no two databases DB_k and DB_l such that $t_i^{(k)} \ll t_j^{(k)}$, $t_j^{(k)}$ reads from $t_i^{(k)}$, and $t_i^{(l)} \| t_j^{(l)}$.* □

This theorem forms the basis of an algorithm to enforce global SI, under the assumption that all component systems guarantee local SI. The idea is to monitor the three conditions of the theorem and take appropriate actions at the federated level when all three are conjunctively violated for a pair of transactions. Monitoring the property whether two transactions execute serially or concurrently in one component system is straightforward. Monitoring the reads-from relationship, however, is very difficult if not infeasible in a practical system setting. The problem is that we cannot tell by merely observing the operation requests and replies at a component system's interface which version, identified by the creating transaction's number, was read by a read operation. So we need to build an actual algorithm for global SI on a coarser version of the last theorem where the reads-from condition is omitted and thus the set of allowed schedules is restricted even further.

Corollary 1 (sufficient condition for global SI). *Let s be an extended schedule in a federated database system (using an ACP) whose component systems guarantee local SI. Then s is SI if there are no two transactions t_i and t_j and no two databases DB_k and DB_l such that $t_i^{(k)} \ll t_j^{(k)}$ and $t_i^{(l)} \| t_j^{(l)}$.* □

So for global SI to hold, the situation to be disallowed is that the subtransactions of two global transactions are running concurrently in one database and serial in another one, regardless of whether one transaction reads from the other transaction or not. This leads to the following algorithm for ensuring the SI property of global schedules.

In the federation layer, we assign a unique timestamp $B_i^{(k)}$ to the subtransaction of transaction t_i in database DB_k before it issues its first operation there. This does not require any additional operation on the component system, only some bookkeeping at the federation level. When transaction t_i requests its global commit, we assign a timestamp C_i to it. In addition, we keep information about the relative execution order of subtransactions in an array R[i,j], where

$$R[i,j] = \begin{cases} serial, & \text{if there is a database } DB_k \text{ where } C_i < B_j^{(k)} \\ concurrent, & \text{if there is a database } DB_k \text{ where } B_i^{(k)} < B_j^{(k)} < C_i \\ & \quad \text{or } B_j^{(k)} < B_i^{(k)} < C_j \\ undefined, & \text{if at least one of the transactions has not yet submitted} \\ & \quad \text{any operation} \end{cases}$$

Initially, there are no transactions in the system, so R is empty. Once a transaction t_i enters the system, all the $B_i^{(k)}$ and C_i values are set to ∞, and $R[i,j] = R[j,i] = undefined$ for all active transactions t_j. Upon the first operation of transaction t_i in database DB_k, the timestamp $B_i^{(k)}$ is assigned and R is updated as follows:

```
for all transactions t_j in the system do
    if (C_j < B^i(k)) then // serial execution
                if (R[i,j] = concurrent) then abort t_i
                                else R[i,j] := R[j,i] := serial
    else if (B_j^{(k)} < B_i^{(k)}) then // concurrent execution
                if (R[i,j] = serial) then abort t_i
                                else R[i,j] := R[j,i] := concurrent
```

When transaction t_i attempts to commit, our bookkeeping needs to add "pseudo operations" for each database DB_k that t_i has not accessed at all. To do so, we set $B_i^{(k)} = C_i$ and update R as if t_i just submitted an operation to this database. If adding these pseudo operations does not force t_i to abort, we allow it to commit.

Obviously this algorithm can cause unnecessary aborts, since it does not take into account the actual reads-from relationship. However, as noted before, this is an inescapable consequence of the fact that the federation layer cannot easily observe the details of the local executions in a real-life system setting. Despite this drawback of possibly unnecessary aborts, the algorithm appears to be significantly more efficient than the begin-synchronization approach of the previous Subsection 3.2. In particular, the presented algorithm incurs overhead only for those component systems that are actually accessed, and does not delay any begin or commit requests.

3.4 Remarks On Global Snapshot Isolation with Non-SI Component Systems

In the previous two subsections we have shown how to guarantee global SI when all component systems guarantee local SI. It would, of course, also be a desirable option to enforce global SI even if some component systems may support a correctness criterion other than local SI. A particularly interesting combination would be one database supporting local SI and another database supporting standard conflict-serializability. Assume that a component system guarantees conflict-serializability in combination with the avoidance of cascading aborts (ACA). Then the first read operation of a transaction establishes a reads-from relationship that constrains the feasibility of subsequent reads if we want to guarantee that the resulting schedule is also locally SI (i.e., actually a member of the schedule class SR ∩ ACA ∩ SI). The transaction must not read any data that are committed later than at the time of that first read. Brute-force methods to enforce this constraint are conceivable (e.g., by aborting all transactions that initiate a commit between our transaction's first read and its commit), but it is very likely that they restrict the possible concurrency in an undue manner. This problem alone has discouraged us from proceeding further along these lines. In addition, one would have to ensure that the version functions of the different local schedules are compatible and that writesets of concurrent transactions are disjoint, both at the level of global transactions. Obviously, this setting calls for future research.

4 Guaranteeing Global Serializability

Although SI is a popular option in practice, there are certainly many mission-critical applications that still demand the more rigid correctness criterion of global (conflict-) serializability (SR). In this section, we study the problem of ensuring global SR in the presence of component systems that merely provide SI. We develop an algorithm that extends the well-known ticket method [6,11] so that it supports local SI schedulers, while guaranteeing global SR. In Subsection 4.1, we briefly review the standard ticket method and discuss its benefits and potential shortcomings. In Subsection 4.2, we show that, with a minor extension, the ticket method yields correct executions even when applied to local SI schedulers, but point out that this approach has certain severe drawbacks. In Subsection 4.3, we finally present a generalization of the ticket method that increases performance for applications with a large fraction of read-only (sub-) transactions.

4.1 Benefits and Potential Shortcomings of the Ticket Method

A ticket is a dedicated data object of type "counter" (or some other numerical type) in a component, used solely for the purpose of global concurrency control. Each global subtransaction must read the current value of the ticket and write back an increased value at some point during its execution (the so-called take-a-ticket operation). The ordering of the ticket values read by two global subtransaction reflects the local serialization order of the two subtransactions. A ticket graph is maintained at the federation level to detect incompatible local serialization orders. This graph has the global transactions as nodes, and there is an edge from transaction t_i to transaction t_j if the ticket of t_i is smaller than that of t_j in some component database. It has been shown in [11] that the global schedule is serializable if and only if the ticket graph does not contain a cycle, provided that all component systems generate only locally SR schedules.

This method is easy and efficient to implement; one merely needs to add the take-a-ticket operation to each subtransaction and to manage the global ticket graph, i.e., searching for cycles when a global transaction attempts to commit (or at some earlier point). Upon detecting a cycle, one (or more) of the involved transactions must be aborted. For component systems with the property of allowing only rigorous local schedules, it is not even necessary to take a ticket at all; rather the time of the commit operation can be used as an implicit ticket. So the ticket method has the particularly nice property of incurring overhead only for non-rigorous component systems, even with transactions that access both rigorous and non-rigorous component systems. This makes the ticket method a very elegant and versatile algorithm for federated concurrency control.

The ticket method has two potential problems, however. First, the ticket object may be a potential bottleneck in a component database, since all global subtransactions have to read and write the ticket. Second and much more severely, having to write the ticket turns read-only transactions into read-write transactions, thus preventing the possibility of specific optimizations for read-only (sub-) transactions (e.g., Oracle's "Set Transaction Read Only" option).

4.2   Applying the Ticket Method to SI Component Systems

The standard ticket method requires that local schedulers generate (conflict-) serializable schedules. Thus, it is not clear if the method can incorporate component systems that provide non-serializable SI schedules. Consider the effects of the additional take-a-ticket operation to the execution of global subtransactions on an SI component system. For each pair of concurrent global subtransactions on such a database, both write at least one common object, the ticket, so that one of them must inevitably be aborted to ensure local SI. The resulting local schedule is therefore trivially serializable, because it is in fact already serial, and the ordering of the ticket values of two global subtransactions reflects their local serial(ization) order. Note that this does not make the entire global transactions serial; concurrency is still feasible in other (non-SI, but SR) databases. Nevertheless, sequentializing all global subtransactions in an SI component system is a dramatic loss of performance and would usually be considered as an overly high price for global consistency.

What about local transactions on an SI component system, i.e., transactions that solely access this database and are not routed through the federation level? Those transactions do not have to take a ticket in the original ticket method (as any additional overhead for them could possibly be considered as a breach of the local database autonomy). Nevertheless, global serializability is still ensured by means of the ticket-graph testing, as cases where local transactions cause the serialization order of global transactions to be reversed would lead to local cycles and are thus detectable. Unfortunately, with SI component systems, tickets for global subtransactions alone are insufficient to detect those critical situations caused by local. An example schedule for an SI database with ticket object T, global subtransactions t_1 and t_2, and a local transaction t_3 is the following:

$$r_3(y_0)r_1(y_0)w_1(y_1)r_1(T_0)w_1(T_1)C_1r_2(x_0)r_2(T_1)w_2(T_2)C_2r_3(x_0)w_3(x_3)C_3$$

The schedule including the ticket operations is SI and even SR with the ticket operations removed, but the ticket ordering of t_1 and t_2 contradicts the serialization order of the ticket-less schedule.

A possible and in fact the only solution for this problem is to add take-a-ticket operations also to all local transactions. This can be done without modifying the application programs themselves, for example, by changing the stub code of the commit. However, there is still a major problem unsolved, as the forced serial execution on an SI component system, discussed above, would now apply to both global subtransactions and local transactions. So the resulting performance loss would involve the local transactions as well, and this is surely unacceptable in almost all cases. In the next subsection we will present a generalization of the ticket method to cope with SI databases while avoiding such performance problems for the most important case of read-only (sub-) transactions. There is, however, no panacea that can cope with the most general case without any drawbacks.

4.3 Generalizing Tickets for Read-Only Subtransactions on SI Component Systems

In this subsection, we present a generalization of the ticket method that allows read-only transactions to run as concurrently as the component systems allow them (i.e., without additional restrictions imposed by the federated concurrency control). So for application environments that are dominated by read-only transactions but exhibit infrequent read-write transactions as well, our approach reconciles the consistency quality of global serializability with a sustained high performance.

Each global subtransaction and local transaction has to be marked "read-only" or "read-write" at its beginning; an unmarked transaction is supposed to be read-write by default. A transaction that is declared as read-only before can be re-labeled as read-write at any point during its execution (with certain consequences in terms of its performance, however). A global transaction is read-only if all its subtransactions are read-only; otherwise it is a global read-write transaction. We will first discuss how to deal with read-write transactions in a rather crude, unoptimized way, and then show how read-only transactions can be handled in a much more efficient manner.

Read-Write Transactions. Our extended ticket method requires that all global read-write transactions are executed serially. That is, the federated transaction manager has to ensure that at most one global read-write transaction is active at a time. There is no such restriction, however, for global read-only transactions or for local (read-write) transactions. Each read-write subtransaction of a global read-write transaction takes a ticket as in the standard ticket method. Read-only subtransactions of read-write transactions only need to read the corresponding ticket object, as further discussed below. Note that tickets are still necessary for global read-write transactions to correctly handle the potential interference with local transactions.

Although the sequentialization of global read-write transactions appears very restrictive, it is no more restrictive than in the original ticket method if SI component systems are part of the federation. On the other hand, our generalized method is much less restrictive with regard to read-only transactions and local transactions.

Read-Only Transactions. The problem with read-only transactions is that the usual updating of ticket objects would turn them into read-write transactions, with the obvious adverse implications. A careful analysis of the possible cases, however, shows that it is sufficient if read-only (sub-) transactions merely read the ticket object.

A subtransaction's ticket value shows its position in the locally equivalent serial schedule. When a component system generates SI schedules, the ticket value that a transaction ti reads from the corresponding database DB_k depends only on the position of its first local operation $B_i^{(k)}$. The transaction reads from other transactions that were committed before $B_i^{(k)}$, so its position in the equivalent serial schedule must be behind them. Its ticket value must therefore be greater than that of all transactions that committed earlier. On the other hand, the transaction t_i does not see updates made by transactions that commit after $B_i^{(k)}$; so it must precede them in the equivalent serial schedule, hence its ticket value must be smaller than the tickets of those transactions. Thus, a feasible solution is to assign to a read-only subtransaction a ticket value that is strictly in between the value that was actually read from the ticket object and the next higher possible value that a read-write subtransaction may write into the ticket object. This approach can be implemented very easily. For example, if ticket objects are of type integer, we can restrict the actual ticket-object values to even integers with read-write subtransactions always incrementing the ticket object by two, and for read-only subtransactions we can use the odd integer that immediately follows the actually read ticket value for the purpose of building the global ticket graph. The fact that this may result in multiple read-only subtransactions with the same ticket value is acceptable in our protocol.

Figure 2 shows an example, with the ticket values that the read-write transactions write in the databases denoted by the numbers below the transaction boxes. The smaller white and black boxes denote the first operations of two read-only transactions t_W and t_B that span all three databases. Looking at the white transaction t_W in the first database, we see that its ticket value must be greater than 6 (which is the value that t_1 wrote), but smaller than 8 (which is what t_2 wrote), so a possible ticket value for t_W is 7. The tickets for the other subtransactions are assigned analogously.

Using these ticket values, we can now test if the execution of the two read-only transactions in Figure 2 leads to a globally serializable execution, i.e., a cycle-free global ticket graph. First consider the black read-only transaction t_B. In the databases DB_1 and DB_3, it starts its execution after the commit of t_2 (and t_1), so its ticket is greater than that of t_2 and t_1 (for example, the ticket of t_2 in DB_1 is 8, while that of t_B would be 9). In DB_2, t_2 had no operations, and t_B started after t_1 committed. As a result, t_B is always executed after t_1 and t_2 committed; the corresponding ticket value graph has no cycle. In an equivalent global serial schedule, t_B must be executed after t_1 and t_2.

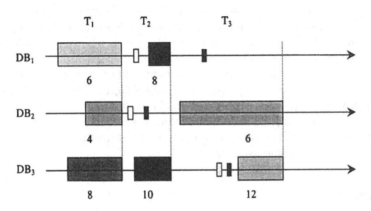

Fig. 2. Assigning a ticket value to read-only transactions

As for the white transaction t_W, it executes its first operations in DB_2 and DB_3 before t_3 committed, so its ticket value is smaller than that of t_3 in both databases. On the other hand, it makes its first operation in DB_1 before t_2 committed, but in DB_3 after t_2 committed. It is therefore possible that t_W reads values written by t_2 in DB_3 but not in DB_1, so the state of the global database seen by t_W could be inconsistent. This is captured by the ordering of the tickets of these transactions. The ticket of t_W in DB_1 is smaller than that of t_2 (7 vs. 8), while it is greater in DB_3 (11 vs. 10). The corresponding ticket graph therefore has a cycle between these two transactions which is detected when t_W attempts to commit.

Local transactions are incorporated in this protocol as before: read-write transactions need to take tickets as usual, whereas read-only transactions merely need to read the ticket object. These considerations hold for SI component systems. Our method can, however, easily be combined with standard tickets for other types of component systems, if such databases participate in the federation. For example, if some database generates schedules where the serialization order of the transactions reflects the order of their commit operations, the "implicit ticket" method [11] can be applied for this database (i.e., no explicit tickets need to be taken). In databases for which conventional (conflict-) serializability is guaranteed, all global subtransactions submit the usual take-a-ticket, whereas local transactions do not need to take a ticket as in the original ticket method.

5   Concluding Remarks

In the last few years the subject of federated transactions has been largely disregarded by the research community, despite the fact that the results from the late eighties and early nineties do not provide practically viable solutions. A major reason for this situation probably is that many application classes are perfectly satisfied with a loose coupling of database, no or very little care about mutual consistency, and possibly application-level solutions to avoid special types of severe inconsistencies. The expected proliferation of advanced applications like virtual-enterprise workflows, electronic-commerce agents and brokers, etc. should rekindle the community's interest in federations that span widely distributed, highly heterogeneous component systems while also requiring a highly dependable IT infrastructure and thus highly consistent data. The problems of federated information systems are inherently hard, but we should not give up too early and rather pursue long-term efforts towards well-founded but also practically viable solutions. This paper should be understood as a first step along these lines. In particular, we have aimed to incorporate important aspects of commercial database systems into a systematic and rigorously founded approach to federated transaction management.

References

1. V. Atluri, E. Bertino, and S. Jajodia. A Theoretical Formulation for Degrees of Isolation in Databases. *Information and Software Technology*, 39(1):47–53, 1997.
2. H. Berenson, P. Bernstein, J. Gray, J. Melton, E. O'Neil, and P. O'Neil. A Critique of ANSI SQL Isolation Levels. In M. J. Carey and D. A. Schneider, editors, *Proc. of the 1995 ACM SIGMOD Int. Conf. on Management of Data, San Jose, CA*, ACM SIGMOD Record, Vol. 24, No. 2, pages 1–10, ACM Press, 1995.
3. P. A. Bernstein, V. Hadzilacos, and N. Goodman. *Concurrency Control and Recovery in Database Systems*. Addison-Wesley, 1987.
4. Y. Breitbart, H. Garcia-Molina, and A. Silberschatz. Overview of Multidatabase Transaction Management. *The VLDB Journal*, 1(2):181–240, October 1992.
5. Y. Breitbart, H. Garcia-Molina, and A. Silberschatz. Transaction Management in Multidatabase Systems. In W. Kim, editor, *Modern Database Systems*, chapter 28, pages 573–591, ACM Press, 1995.
6. Y. Breitbart, D. Georgakopoulos, M. Rusinkiewicz, and A. Silberschatz. On Rigorous Transaction Scheduling. *IEEE Transactions on Software Engineering*, 17(9):954–960, September 1991.
7. Y. Breitbart and A. Silberschatz. Strong Recoverbility in Multidatabase Systems. In P. S. Yu, editor, *RIDE'92, Proc. of the 2nd Int. Workshop on Research Issues*

in *Data Engineering: Transaction and Query Processing, Tempe, Arizona, USA, February 2–3, 1992*, pages 170–175. IEEE Computer Society Press, 1992.

8. M. Bright, A. Hurson, and S. Pakzad, editors. *Multidatabase Systems: An Advanced Solution for Global Information Sharing*. IEEE Computer Society Press, 1994.

9. O. A. Bukhres and A. K. Elmagarmid, editors. *Object-Oriented Multidatabase Systems — A Solution for Advanced Applications*. Prentice Hall, 1996.

10. S. Conrad. *Federated Database Systems: Concepts of Data Integration*. Springer-Verlag, 1997. (In German).

11. D. Georgakopoulos, M. Rusinkiewicz, and A. Sheth. Using Tickets to Enforce the Serializability of Multidatabase Transactions. *IEEE Transactions on Knowledge and Data Engineering*, 6(1):166–180, February 1994.

12. B. Holtkamp, N. Weißenberg, and X. Wu. VHDBS: A Federated Database System for Electronic Commerce. In *Summary Proc. of the EURO-MED NET '98 Conf., Nicosia, Cyprus, March 4–7, 1998*, pages 182–189, 1998.

13. W. Litwin, L. Mark, and N. Roussopoulos. Interoperability of Multiple Autonomous Databases. *ACM Computing Surveys*, 22(3):267–293, September 1990.

14. Object Management Group, Inc. Object Transaction Service Specification 1.1, 1997.

15. Oracle Corporation. Concurrency Control, Transaction Isolation and Serializability in SQL92 and Oracle7. White Paper, 1995.

16. Oracle Corporation. *Oracle8 Concepts, Release 8.0: Chapter 23, Data Concurrency and Consistency*, 1997.

17. M. T. Özsu and P. Valduriez. *Principles of Distributed Database Systems*. Prentice Hall, 2nd edition, 1998.

18. C. Papadimitriou. *The Theory of Database Concurrency Control*. Computer Science Press, 1986.

19. Y. Raz. The Principle of Commitment Ordering, or Guaranteeing Serializability in a Heterogeneous Environment of Multiple Autonomous Resource Managers Using Atomic Commitment. In L.-Y. Yuan, editor, *Proc. of the 18th Int. Conf. on Very Large Data Bases, VLDB'92, Vancouver, Canada, August 23–27, 1992*, pages 292–312. Morgan Kaufmann Publishers, 1992.

20. R. Schenkel and G. Weikum. Experiences with Building a Federated Transaction Manager based on CORBA OTS. In S. Conrad, W. Hasselbring, and G. Saake, editors, *Proc. 2nd Int. Workshop on Engineering Federated Information Systems, EFIS'99, Kühlungsborn, Germany, May 5–7, 1999*, pages 79–94. infix-Verlag, Sankt Augustin, 1999.

21. A. P. Sheth and J. A. Larson. Federated Database Systems for Managing Distributed, Heterogeneous, and Autonomous Databases. *ACM Computing Surveys*, 22(3):183–236, September 1990.

22. W. E. Weihl. Local Atomicity Properties: Modular Concurrency Control for Abstract Data Types. *ACM Transactions on Programming Languages and Systems*, 11(2):249–283, April 1989.

23. X. Wu. An Architecture for Interoperation of Distributed Heterogenous Database Systems Database System. In R. R. Wagner and H. Thoma, editors, *Database and Expert System Applications, Proc. of the 7th Int. Conf., DEXA'96, Zurich, Switzerland, September 1996*, Lecture Notes in Computer Science, Vol. 1134, pages 688–697. Springer-Verlag, 1996.

24. X. Wu and N. Weißenberg. A Graphical Interface for Cooperative Access to Distributed and Heterogeneous Database Systems. In *IDEAS'97, Proc. of the Int. Database Engineering and Applications Symposium, Montreal, Canada, August 25–27, 1997*, pages 13–22, 1997.

Proofs of Theorems

Proof of Theorem 1

a) With the (SI-V) property as our premise and our overall assumption that each write in a transaction must be preceded by a read of the same object, the SI version order $\ll_s$ is the only version order that can render the MVSG of a schedule acyclic. The theorem then follows immediately from the standard MVSR theorem (see Subsection 2.1), because SI-MVSG contains the same edges as the ordinary MVSG.

b) **"if"**:
Assume that the schedule is not SI. Then there must be at least two concurrent transactions t_i and t_j that write the same object x. Because of the read-before-write restriction, both transactions read x before writing it, say t_i reads x_k and t_j reads x_l. By the definition of the version function, t_k must have been committed when t_i started, so $x_k \ll_s x_i$ by the definition of the SI version order $\ll_s$. The same holds for t_l and t_j, so we obtain $x_l \ll_s x_j$. Additionally, t_k must commit before t_j, because t_i reads from t_k (so t_k was committed when t_i started) and t_j runs in parallel with t_i, so it commits after the start of t_i. This yields $x_k \ll_s x_j$ and, analogously, $x_l \ll_s x_i$. The SI-MVSG now contains the edges

- $t_i \rightarrow t_j$ labeled with "x", because $r_i(x_k)$, $w_j(x_j)$ and $x_k \ll_s x_j$, and
- $t_j \rightarrow t_i$ labeled with "x", because $r_j(x_l)$, $w_i(x_i)$ and $x_l \ll_s x_i$.

But this is an x-cycle and therefore a contradiction to the precondition.

"only if":
Assume there is an x-cycle $t_{i_1} \rightarrow t_{i_2} \rightarrow ... \rightarrow t_{i_n} = t_{i_1}$ in SI-MVSG of the schedule s, $s \in SI$. If there is more than one, select one with minimal length. Without loss of generality, assume that the transactions in the cycle are renumbered such that $t_1 \rightarrow t_2 \rightarrow ... \rightarrow t_n = t_i$.

We show first that there must be one edge in this cycle that was added due to the (RW)-rule in the definition of SI-MVSG. Both the (WR)-rule and the (WW)-rule add edges from a transaction that writes an older version of x to a transaction that writes a younger version of x. Because the SI version order $\ll_s$ is defined by the commit order of the transactions, one of those edges from t_i to t_j means that t_i commits before t_j, formally $C_i \ll C_j$. But we have a cycle. This would mean that $C_1 \ll C_1$, which is a contradiction, so there must be at least one edge $t_i \rightarrow t_{i+1}$ where $C_i \gg C_{i+1}$, we choose the first such edge.

This edge was added because we have $r_i(x_l)$ and $w_{i+1}(x_{i+1})$ in the schedule, and $C_l < C_{i+1}$. We also have $C_l \ll B_i$ and there is no other commit of a transaction in between them that writes x, because t_i reads x from t_l. Putting this together, we obtain $C_l \ll B_i \ll C_{i+1} \ll C_i$. We have thus shown that C_i and C_{i+1} run concurrently. However, this does not mean that the schedule is not in SI, because t_i does not necessarily write x. The read-before-write rule means that t_{i+1} must read a version x_p of x before writing it. To show a contradiction, we now discuss the different possibilities for the transaction t_p from which transaction t_{i+1} can read.

(i)   If t_{i+1} reads from a transaction that committed before t_l, we get $C_p \ll B_{i+1} \ll C_l$. But this means that t_l and t_{i+1} are concurrent and write the same object x, so the schedule s cannot be in SI, which is a contradiction.

(ii) If t_{i+1} reads x from C_l, we have $l = p$ and $C_l \ll B_{i+1} \ll C_{i+1}$. This means that there is an x-edge in the SI-MVSG from t_l to t_{i+1} because of the (WR)-rule. But then t_l cannot be part of the cycle, or we could replace the edges $t_l \to t_i \to t_{i+1}$ by the edge $t_l \to t_{i+1}$ and would get a shorter cycle, contrary to the minimality of the selected cycle.

So we know that t_i has an incoming x-edge, and that this edge does not come from t_l, which is t_i's only incoming x-edge of (WR) type (t_i reads x only from t_l). Therefore the incoming x-edge must be an edge of type (RW) or (WW). But the definition of the SI-MVSG says that t_i must write x in order to have such an incoming edge, so we have shown that the concurrent transactions t_i and t_{i+1} both write x, which is a contradiction.

(iii) If t_{i+1} reads x from a transaction t_q that committed after t_i started, we have the ordering $C_l \ll B_i \ll C_q \ll B_{i+1} \ll C_{i+1} \ll C_i$. If t_l was not part of the cycle, we could show as before that t_i must write x, so that s would not be in SI, and t_l is on the cycle.

If there is no other transaction in between t_l and t_q that writes x, the graph contains the edges $t_l \to t_q$ (t_q reads x from t_l) and $t_q \to t_{i+1}$ (t_{i+1} reads x from t_q). If we replace the edges $t_l \to t_i \to t_{i+1}$ by the edges $t_l \to t_q \to t_{i+1}$, we get a cycle with the same length. Additionally, we can replace the edge from a larger to a smaller version ($t_i \to t_{i+1}$) by edges that respect the version order ($C_l \ll C_q \ll C_{i+1}$). As shown before there must be another version-order-reversing edge in the cycle, so we can restart the proof at the beginning. Since the cycle has finite length, we can do so only a finite number of times until one of the other cases applies.

If there is a sequence of transactions $t_{r_1}...t_{r_m}$ between t_l and t_q that write x, t_{r_1} must read x from t_l, t_{r_2} must read x from t_{r_1}, and so on, until t_q must read x from t_{r_m}. Therefore there are edges $t_l \to t_{r_1}$ and $t_{r_1} rightarrow t_{i_{j+1}}$ (because $r_{r_1}(x_l)$, $w_{i_{j+1}}(x_{i_{j+1}})$ and $x_{i_{j+1}} ll s x_l$). Now we can replace $t_l \to t_{i_j} \to t_{i_{j+1}}$ by $t_l \to t_{r_1} \to t_{i_{j+1}}$ which are edges that respect the version order, and the same argument as before applies.   □

Proof of Theorem 2

We show that the global schedule is SI by showing that both SI properties (SI-V) and (SI-W) hold for the global schedule.

(SI-V): Assume that there is a transaction t_i in the global schedule that reads a version of object x in database DB_l that another transaction t_j wrote, but that t_j is not the "right" transaction in the sense of (SI-V). Then t_j is either uncommitted, committed after the begin of t_i, or another transaction t_k wrote x and committed between the commit of t_j and the begin of t_i. But the begin and commit operations in all databases are synchronized, so if any of these three cases holds globally, it does also hold in DB_l. Therefore the local subschedule in DB_l does not satisfy (SI-V), contrary to the assumption that all local schedules are SI.

(SI-W): Assume that there are two transactions t_i and t_j in the global schedule that execute concurrently and that write an object x in database DB_l. Because the begin and commit operations in all databases are synchronized, $t_i^{(l)}$ and $t_j^{(l)}$ are executing concurrently, too. But then the local schedule is not SI, which is a contradiction.   □

Proof of Theorem 3

"There are no ..." $\Rightarrow$ **"(SI-V) holds":** Assume (SI-V) does not hold. Then there is a transaction t_i that reads a version of an object x that is either "too old" or "too new", with x being part of database DB_l. All reads and writes of x are therefore part of subtransactions in this database.

If the version is too old, t_i does not read x from the last transaction t_j that wrote x and committed before t_i started. So there must be another transaction t_k that committed in between: $C_j \ll C_k \ll B_i$, and both t_j and t_k write x. The subtransaction $t_i^{(l)}$ of transaction t_i in DB_l cannot begin before the begin of t_i itself, so $B_i \ll B_i^{(l)}$. With the ACP assumption, together this yields $C_j^{(l)} \ll C_k^{(l)} \ll B_i^{(l)}$. This means that $t_i^{(l)}$ does not read x from the last transaction that committed before $t_i^{(l)}$ started in the local database system, but this is a contradiction to DB_l guaranteeing SI for all local subtransactions.

If the version is too new, t_i reads x from a transaction t_j that was not yet committed when t_i globally started. Because the local schedulers guarantee SI, $t_j^{(l)}$ must have been committed when $t_i^{(l)}$ executed its first operation, so $C_j^{(l)} \ll B_i^{(l)}$, and therefore $t_j^{(l)} \ll t_i^{(l)}$. On the other hand, there must be at least one database DB_k where $t_i^{(k)}$ started before $t_j^{(k)}$ committed, because globally t_i started before t_j committed, so $B_i^{(k)} \ll C_j^{(k)}$. Together with $B_j^{(k)} \ll C_j^{(k)}$ and $C_j \ll C_i$ this yields $t_i^{(k)} \parallel t_j^{(k)}$, which is a contradiction.

"(SI-V) holds" $\Rightarrow$ **"There are no ...":** Assume that there are databases DB_l where $t_i^{(l)} \ll t_j^{(l)}$ and $t_j^{(l)}$ reads x from $t_i^{(l)}$, and DB_k where $t_i^{(k)} \parallel t_j^{(k)}$. Because t_j reads from t_i in DB_l, we have $B_i^{(l)} \ll C_i^{(l)} \ll B_j^{(l)}$. In database DB_k, $t_i^{(k)}$ and $t_j^{(k)}$ run concurrently, so that either $B_i^{(k)} \ll B_j^{(k)} \ll C_i^{(k)}$ or $B_j^{(k)} \ll B_i^{(k)} \ll C_i^{(k)}$. Whatever case applies, we see that $t_j^{(k)}$ begins before $t_i^{(k)}$ commits, so that the global transactions t_i and t_j run concurrently. This means that t_j reads x from a globally concurrent transaction, which is a contradiction to the version function satisfying (SI-V).   □

Proof of Theorem 4

By Theorem 3, we already know that s satisfies (SI-V). To show that s also satisfies (SI-W), we use the characterization by the SI-MVSG that we introduced in Section 2.2. The SI-MVSG of the global schedule is the union of the SI-MVSGs of the local subschedules. The SI property of the global schedule then follows immediately from the SI property of the local subschedules: If all local subschedules are SI, there is no x so that there is an x-edge in one of the local SI-MVSGs. But since an object exists in exactly one database, there is no x-edge in the global SI-MVSG, too. So by Theorem 1 the global schedule is SI.   □

Serializability, Concurrency Control, and Replication Control

Ekkart Kindler

Humboldt-Universität zu Berlin, Institut für Informatik
D-10099 Berlin, Germany
kindler@informatik.hu-berlin.de

Freie Universität Berlin, Institut für Informatik
D-14195 Berlin, Germany
kindler@inf.fu-berlin.de

Abstract. Transaction management comprises different aspects such as *concurrency control*, *recovery control*, and *replication control*. Usually, only one or at least two of these aspects are considered in theories of transaction management—the other aspects are ignored. In this paper, we propose a model of executions that allows to capture all three aspects of transaction management. Based on this execution model, we present a definition of *serializability*. Then, we show how the requirement of serializability can be decomposed into requirements that can be attributed to concurrency control, to replication control, and to recovery control, respectively. Altogether, we obtain a unified theory of transaction management, where we focus on concurrency control and replication control in this paper.

1   Introduction

Basically, a concurrent execution of some set of programs is called *serializable* if each of the programs appears as if it has been executed atomically without interference of the other programs. Therefore, the outcome of a serializable execution is the outcome of a sequential execution of the programs one after the other in some order. In this context, the programs are often called *transactions*. So, serializability provides an abstraction of atomic execution of transactions on top of a concurrent non-atomic execution of transactions in reality.

Similarly, a *consistency model* for the access to replicated data in a *distributed shared memory system* guarantees that a concurrent execution of a program appears as if there has been exactly one copy of each object though there have been many copies in reality. So, a consistency model provides an abstraction of a conventional memory on top of a distributed shared memory with replication.

For both abstractions, serializability and consistency, there exist a lot of theories. However, theories for serializability most time presuppose an underlying conventional memory, and theories for distributed shared memory systems most

G. Saake, K. Schwarz, and C. Türker (Eds.): TDD '99, LNCS 1773, pp. 26–44, 2000.

time are not interested in transactional aspects. Though there are some approaches to deal with serializability in the context of data replication, these approaches presuppose a particular memory model. For example, Bernstein et al. [2] assume that there is a fixed set of copies for each object and that copies are updated at write-time. This excludes dynamic creation of new copies, invalidation of copies, and creation of new copies on request—i.e. at write-time or at read-time.

In this paper, we propose a model for concurrent executions[1] of transactions which allows to define serializability independent of an underlying memory or consistency model. This definition does not even make a difference between replicated data and non-replicated data. There will be only one definition of serializability which applies to conventional memory as well as to multi-version serializability and serializability in replicated databases. In a second step, we will show that serializability can be split into different requirements—one concerning correct scheduling (synchronization) of access operations, one concerning consistency of accessed copies, and another concerning *recovery control*. We call the requirement concerning synchronization of access events *concurrency control* requirement and the requirement concerning consistency of accessed copies *replication control* requirement. The splitting into a concurrency control part and a replication control part helps to implement a scheduler responsible for the concurrency control part and the memory manager responsible for the replication control part independently of each other. Therefore, this splitting can be seen as an interface for correct interaction between memory managers and schedulers [6]. Moreover, the splitting provides a clearer understanding of the two abstractions *atomicity* and *consistency* mentioned above. In a sense, our model complements the approach of Schek et al. [11] which provides a unified model for specifying correctness for concurrency control and recovery control. Our model additionally includes replication control and does not require compensatable write events.

The model of concurrent executions proposed in this paper basically consists of a partial order (a *causality*) of *read* and *write* events to some objects—as usual in serializability theory (e.g. [2,5]). In addition, we represent the propagation of values between read and write operations explicitly in each execution by a so-called *data causality* [4]. This is necessary because the values returned by a read event can no longer be deduced from the order of the access events when no specific memory model is presumed. Basically, our execution model differs from the classical one by its explicit representation of the *reads-from relation*. Still, there are some differences between data causality and the classical reads-from relation which will be discussed in Sect. 2.4.

The goal of this paper, is to stipulate a discussion on the execution model and the corresponding definition of serializability. Therefore, we concentrate on the basic idea and on a careful motivation of the model rather than on its precise technical definition. The precise definitions and formal proofs of the results mentioned in this paper can be found in [8,6,7].

---

[1] In the context of concurrency control, executions are often called *histories* or *schedules*. We will use the name execution throughout this paper.

2   The execution model

In this section, we introduce and motivate our execution model which will be the formal basis for defining serializability in Sect. 3.

2.1   Events and causality

Basically, an execution consists of a set of *events* and a partial order on these events. The partial order indicates causal dependencies between the events and is therefore called *causality*. In our context, there are *read* and *write* events to some fixed set of objects and there are *commit* events.

Figure 1 shows an example of a partial order of events, which consists of three transactions: two committed transactions and one uncommitted transaction. Graphically, each event is represented by a square. An inscription represents

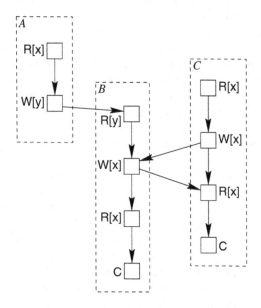

Fig. 1. A partial order of events

the type of event: R[x] stands for a read event on object x, W[x] stands for a write event on object x, and C stands for a commit event.

2.2   Transaction causality

In Fig. 1, there are three transactions which are indicated by dashed boxes. These dashed boxes, however, are not part of the formal execution model. For defining serializability, the execution model must provide some explicit information on the involved transactions and on which event belongs to which transaction.

In our execution model, we use a distinguished causality, the so-called *transaction causality*, for distinguishing different transactions and assigning events to these transactions. Figure 2 shows the transaction causality corresponding to the dashed boxes in Fig. 1. In order to distinguish transaction causality from

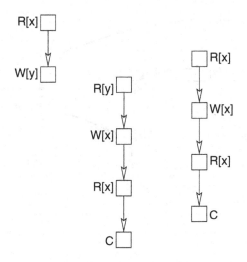

Fig. 2. Transaction causality

other causalities, we graphically represent it by arrows with a white arrow head. Note that transaction causality only represents causal dependencies within a transaction (which are represented in the code of the transaction itself). There are no transaction causalities between different transactions; but there may be other causal dependencies (for example, imposed by a transaction manger which schedules the different events of the transactions). In turn, we adopt the view that two events belong to the same transaction if and only if they are somehow connected by transaction causality.

In the rest of this paper, we will also assume that each transaction is *sequential* and has at most one commit event. This restriction, however, is not necessary but slightly simplifies the presentation of our ideas.

2.3   Data causality

As stated before, we do not presume a particular memory model on which the transactions are executed. Therefore, we cannot deduce the values returned by a read event from the order of the executed events. In the presence of different copies for the same object, it might happen that a read event returns an older value than written by an intermediate write event. For example, the read event might access an old copy. Actually, this happens in multi-version databases without doing any harm.

Therefore, we represent the propagation of values between read and write events (on the same objects) explicitly in our execution model by *data causality*. Figure 3 shows an example of data causality for the events of our previous example. Data causality is represented by bold-faced arrows. For example, we

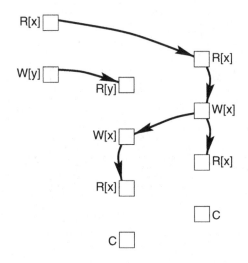

Fig. 3. Data causality

can deduce from this data causality that the read event on object y of transaction B reads the value written by transaction A. Indeed, this should not happen in a serializable execution because a committed transaction should not read a value written by an uncommitted transaction. This will be excluded in the definition of serializability but not in the execution model itself (see Sect. 3).

The read event on object x of transaction B reads the value which results from successively[2] performing the write event of transaction C on x and the write event of transaction B on x. Note that the second read event of transaction C does not read the value of the write event of transaction B, though it happens immediately before according to the causality in Fig. 1. Thus, the second read event of transaction C reads from an 'older copy' of x which is implicitly encoded in the data causality (by a split of data causality at the write event of transaction C).

Data causality must satisfy two requirements in order to have an intuitive understanding. First of all, two events which access different objects should never be related by data causality because data causality was supposed to represent the propagation of data between read and write events on the same object. Second,

---

[2] We do not claim that the read event returns a value written by a single write event. The reason is that we do not require that write events are total. Therefore, the value returned by a read event may be the outcome of a sequence of write events. See Sect. 2.4 for more details.

data causality may branch forward (which corresponds to the creation of copies) but there should be no backward branching (merge of data causality). In the latter case, we would have difficulties in interpreting the returned value of a read event as the outcome of a sequence of write events. By excluding backward branching of data causality, we need not deal with this problem. But, we will weaken this restriction in Sect. 5.

Altogether, an execution is a partial order of read, write, and commit events where two causalities are distinguished from other causalities: transaction causality and data causality. Figure 4 shows the integrated view of the execution which has been introduced step by step previously.

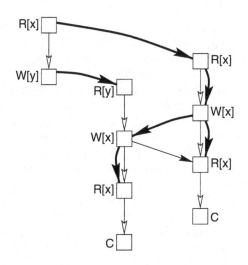

Fig. 4. An execution

2.4 Discussion

Representing an execution as a partial order of write, read, and commit events is a classical approach [2,5]. Usually, the correspondence between an event and the transaction it belongs to is represented by some index. We represent it implicitly by transaction causality. This, however, is not fundamental and does not make a big difference. We have chosen transaction causality because it nicely fits to the causality based setting.

The really new part in our execution model is data causality which explicitly represents the propagation of values between read and write events. This way, we are able to formalize serializability without presupposing a particular memory model—indeed, the memory model is in the execution itself. In particular, a single concept of serializability covers all classical definitions of serializability for conventional memory, multi-version databases, and databases with replication.

This definition of serializability formally captures all aspects of concurrency control, replication control, and recovery control.

Of course, there is a relationship between data causality and the reads-from relation: Both concepts represent how values are propagated between write and read events. However, there are some significant differences:

1. Data causality is an integral part of an execution whereas the reads-from relation is a derived concept: Given an execution and some underlying memory model, the reads-from relation can be derived. Since we are interested in a definition of serializability independent from a particular memory model, the reads-from relation can no longer be derived. Therefore, either the reads-from relation or data causality must be an integral part of the execution model.

2. Data causality is a transitive relation whereas the reads-from relation is not transitive. The transitivity of data causality has two benefits:

   First, there exists a bunch of techniques for reasoning with and about causalities which heavily exploit transitivity. For example, these techniques can be employed for verifying correctness of transaction protocols and data consistency protocols (modelled as a special kind of Petri nets [4,9]). These techniques, however, are beyond the scope of this paper.

   Second, transitivity of data causality allows not only to deal with the classical *read-write-model* (RW-model) for databases where each write operation completely overwrites previously written values. By transitivity of data causality, we can also deal with partial write operations and the *action-model* (A-model) which also allows partial write operations, atomic read-and-modify operations (e.g. increment or decrement), where a part of a previously written value is retained after the modification operation. For an example of a partial write operation, consider an object which consists of two components (e.g. a record or a tuple) and two write events such that one write event changes one component and the other write event changes the other component. Then, a read event does not return a value written by any of these write events. Rather, the read event returns a mixed value. This situation can occur in SQL transactions which update different attributes of the same tuple independently of each other and later on select this tuple. This situation is not formally captured by the reads-from relation but it is captured by data causality (cf. the situation in Fig. 4 discussed before). One might argue that we should choose the components as individual objects and deal with their consistency separately in the above example. Then, the above problem would not occur. The *granularity of replication*, however is often fixed and cannot be freely chosen. Therefore, a model of replication must properly deal with write operations which only partially change an object (called partial write operations for short).

   Data causality allows to formalize serializability not only for the RW-model but also for the A-model and, in particular, for partial write resp. update operations provided by SQL.

3. The definition of the reads-from relation for an execution makes assumptions on the underlying recovery manager. It assumes that values written by an

uncommitted transaction are ignored somehow. Data causality allows to be more explicit in this point. For example, the write event of transaction A in Fig. 4 is not ignored by transaction B—there is a data causality from the write event of transaction A to the read event on object y of transaction B. Having this clearly illegal behaviour in the execution model makes it possible to explicitly exclude it in the specification of serializability. This way, correct *recovery* is also formally captured by the definition of serializability. The relation to the approach of Schek et al. [11] will be discussed in Sect. 3.3.

Altogether, the execution model with data causality allows a definition of serializability which covers all aspects of concurrency control, replication control, and recovery. Actually, the execution model can be equipped with some more features, which will be discussed in Sect. 5. These features, however, are not relevant for understanding the basic idea of our approach.

Now, where do the executions come from? There are two answers to this question: First, an execution is an abstract representation of what is really going on when some transactions are executed by a database management system. We do not bother where the executions come from. We only define whether the execution is considered to be correct (i.e. to be serializable) or whether it is considered to be incorrect. Second, we can model a database management system by the help of a special kind of Petri nets. Each such model has a precisely defined set of executions. Then, we can use the techniques proposed in [9] for verifying that all executions of the modelled database management system are serializable. In this paper, however, we are mainly interested in the specification of serializability. We do not model and verify database management systems here (see [8] for more details on modelling and verifying database management systems).

3 Serializability

In the previous sections, we have introduced and motivated our execution model. Now, we will give a definition of serializability for this execution model. Again, we refer to [8,6] for precise definitions and rigorous proofs of the results. Here, we focus on the basic idea.

3.1 Definition

As already mentioned in the introduction, the basic idea of serializability is the following: An execution is serializable if all committed transactions can be arranged in some sequence in which they could have been executed one after the other on a conventional memory with the same outcome—i.e. in which each event reads respectively writes the same value as the corresponding event in the original execution. In particular, the values written by uncommitted transactions do not affect the committed transactions.

Now, we formulate this idea in terms of our execution model without assuming a particular underlying memory. Let us start with the requirement that write events of uncommitted transactions do not affect committed events (recovery): We say that *data causality respects commit events* if there is no data causality from a write event of an uncommitted transaction to an event of a committed transaction. In the execution from Fig. 4, data causality does not respect commit events due to the data causality from the write event of transaction A to the read event on object y of transaction B. If we add a commit event to transaction A as shown in Fig. 5, data causality respects commit events. Note that we do not fix a particular scheduling strategy in order to guarantee that data causality respects commit events. Indeed, this requirement could be implemented by quite different protocols. For example, it could be implemented by pessimistic recovery protocols (allowing strict schedules only) as well as by optimistic recovery protocols (allowing non-strict schedules, but requiring cascading aborts) [2].

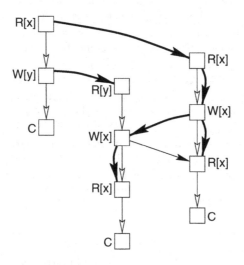

Fig. 5. A serializable execution

The execution from Fig. 5 does not only respect commit events, it is even serializable. This can be checked by arranging the committed transactions (all transactions in this example) in a linear order as shown in Fig. 6. In this linear arrangement, transaction causality and data causality are not changed—other causalities, however, have been omitted because these causalities are irrelevant for serializability. Since we did not change transaction causality and data causality, the values written and read by the events are still the same than in the original execution. In order to check serializability, we need to show that the values returned by read events in this execution (according to data causality) are the same as in a sequential execution of the events in the order of the linear arrangement on a conventional memory: We say that *data causality is compatible with the linear arrangement* if for each pair of a write event e on some object

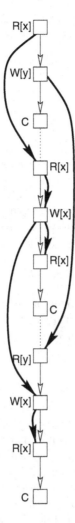

Fig. 6. A linear arrangement

x and a read or write event e' on the same object x there is a data causality from e to e' if and only if e occurs before e' in the linear arrangement. This requirement is graphically represented in Fig. 7 where a write or read event on object x is represented by $X[x]$ and the 'if-and-only-if' requirement is split into two implications. If data causality is compatible with a linear arrangement, the events write and read the same values as on a conventional memory. This can be shown by a simple induction argument on the linear arrangement which exploits the interpretation of data causality given before. A formalization of this interpretation can be found in [7].

Note that compatibility does not require that data causality goes only from top to bottom (with respect to the linear arrangement): For two read events on

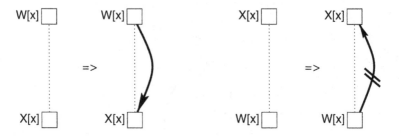

Fig. 7. Graphical representation of compatibility

the same object, data causality may run from bottom to top. But, data causality may not run from bottom to top between a write and a read event; it must run from top to bottom between a read and a write event.

Altogether, an *execution is serializable* if

1. there exists a linear arrangement of all committed transactions such that data causality is compatible with this linear arrangement and if
2. data causality respects commit events.

3.2   Serializability theorem

Similar to classical theory, we have defined serializability by the help of a linear arrangement of transactions. This kind of definition is appropriate for understanding its purpose and its intention. But, this kind of definition is not appropriate for checking whether an execution is serializable because all possible linear arrangements must be checked for 'compatibility'. In this section, we give an equivalent definition of serializability in terms of a so-called *precedence relation* which is similar to the classical *serialization graph* [2].

The precedence relation is defined on all committed transactions of an execution and says which transaction must be arranged before another transaction in a compatible linear arrangement. Since we assume that each committed transaction has exactly one commit event, we define the precedence relation on commit events. A transaction A must precede another transaction B in the following two cases:

1. There is a write event in transaction A which has a data causality to some event in transaction B. In that case, transaction B is affected by transaction A. Therefore, transaction B must be arranged after transaction A.
2. There is a read or write event e on some object x in transaction A and a write event e' on the same object x in transaction B such that there is no data causality from e' to e. In that case, transaction A is not affected by this particular write event of transaction B. Therefore, transaction B must be arranged after transaction A.

The two situations for the definition of a precedence relation from A to B are graphically represented in Fig. 8, where the required precedence is shown by dashed arrows between the corresponding commit events.

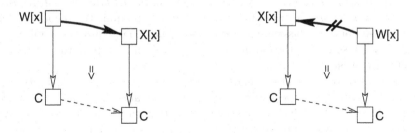

Fig. 8. The precedence relation

Now, it can be shown that an execution is serializable if and only if,

1. the precedence relation has no (non-trivial) cycles,
2. data causality respects commit events, and
3. data are correctly propagated within a single transaction; i.e. for each write event e on some object with a transaction causality to some read or write event e' on the same object there must be also a data causality form event e to event e' (cf. second read event on object x of transaction C in our example).

3.3   Discussion

Readers familiar to the classical serializability theorem might be puzzled about the three items in the equivalent characterization of serializability because there is only one (acyclicity of the serialization graph) in the classical serializability theorem. The reason is the slightly more general scope of our definition of serializability. The second item deals with the correct recovery of aborted (not committed) transactions which is ignored in classical serializability theory. The third item deals with correct propagation of values between access operation within a single transaction—this issue is also often ignored in classical approaches (or multiple access to the same object is even forbidden).

In practice, however, multiple access to the same object does occur and correct recovery is crucial for a correct operation of a database system. Of course, these issues are not ignored in implementations, but in theory. In implementations, mistakes might occur in such subtle points. Therefore, an appropriate theory should cover these points.

Usually, serializability theory starts with the definition of an *equivalence* on executions. Then, an execution is defined to be serializable if there exists an equivalent serial execution. In our definition, we do not explicitly define an equivalence on executions. Rather, we arrange the transactions in some linear order.

Since we keep data causality and transaction causality, the values written and read do not change. We rather check that the execution of the events in the linear arrangement could have been on a conventional memory (i.e. a sequentially consistent memory [10] which can be also defined for our execution model [7]). This requirement is captured by the concept of *compatibility of data causality with the linear arrangement*. This way, we need not implicitly encode the concept of an underlying classical memory in some notion of equivalence but we can explicitly represent it in the definition of compatibility (resp. in the definition of sequential consistency).

One goal of our execution model was the definition of serializability which formally captures the aspect of recovery. This was also the goal of the work of Schek et al. [11]. The difference, however, is that executions need to be expanded in [11]. Basically, each abort event is replaced by a sequence of undo events (one for each write event of the corresponding transaction) and a commit event. This expansion corresponds to a particular recovery strategy. In particular, the undo operations are supposed to be executed atomically, i.e. without interference of events of other transactions. In our approach, we only need to require that there is no data causality from an uncommitted transaction to a committed transaction. This allows for different recovery strategies. For example, a backup to the object's before-image. In contrast, Schek et al. [11] assume that each write operation can be compensated by an inverse write operation.

4   Separation of concerns

In the previous section, we have introduced two equivalent definitions of serializability. Usually, this overall requirement of serializability is guaranteed by a combination of different modules of a database management system: for example, a *scheduler*, a *memory manager*, and a *recovery manager*. The scheduler is responsible for a correct synchronization of read and write events of different transactions (concurrency control). The scheduler, however, does not deal with the propagation of values between read and write events; this is the task of the memory manager (replication control). The recovery manager guarantees correct backup for aborted or crashed transactions. Serializability defines the overall correctness for the different modules.

In this section, we split serializability into different requirements concerning different modules. If each requirement is guaranteed by the corresponding component, serializability is guaranteed for the complete database management system. The requirement concerning the scheduler basically is *conflict serializability* [2] (in its classical definition)[3] and the requirement concerning the memory manager is *weak coherence* [3,1]. Weak coherence is a much weaker consistency model than sequential consistency and, therefore, it can be implemented in a more efficient way. Most interestingly, we need not require sequential consistency

---

[3] Conflict serializability is defined in terms of the order of events and not in terms of propagated data. Therefore, conflict serializability deals with correct synchronizations of events, only—the task of a scheduler.

for the memory manager though this might be expected from the definition of serializability.

If the scheduler guarantees conflict serializability, the memory manager guarantees weak coherence on committed read and write events, and the recovery manager guarantees that data causality respects commits, serializability is guaranteed (see [8,6,7] for details).

4.1   Weak coherence

We start with a reformulation of weak coherence for our execution model (see [9,7] for details). An execution is weakly coherent if for each write event e on some object x and each read or write event e' on the same object x which happens causally after e there is also a data causality from e to e'. In the context of transactions and serializability, we only impose this requirement on events of committed transactions. Figure 9 shows a graphical representation of this requirement.

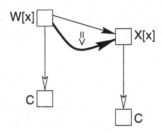

Fig. 9. Definition of weak coherence

4.2   Conflict serializability

Conflict serializability of an execution is defined by the help of the serialization graph on the committed transactions. Again, we represent the serialization graph as a relation on the commit events. Let us consider two access events e and e' on the same object and at least one is a write event. Then, there is an edge in the serialization graph from the transaction of e to the transaction of e' if e happens causally before e'. This requirement is graphically represented in Fig. 10, where an edge of the serialization graph is represented by a dotted arrow. An execution is conflict serializable if the serialization graph has no (non-trivial) cycles.

Note that the execution from Fig. 5 is not conflict serializable due to the write event on object x of transaction B which happens causally between two access events of transaction C. But, it is serializable. This shows that the splitting into several parts is stronger than serializability.

On the other hand, there may be executions which are conflict serializable but which are not serializable (e.g. because the execution is not weakly coherent). All three properties in combination, however, guarantee serializability.

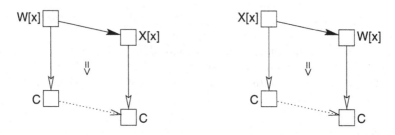

Fig. 10. Definition of the serialization graph

5   Extensions

In the previous sections, we have introduced an execution model which allows to define serializability such that the definition covers all aspects of transaction management which are relevant for correctness. The emphasis of the presentation was on the motivation and on the basic idea of the execution model. Next, we will briefly discuss some extensions of the model. These extensions have already been worked out [7] and are only omitted for simplicity in this paper.

5.1   Update causality

For simplicity, we have assumed that a write operation only modifies a single copy of an object in Sect. 2. In some situations, however, it might be necessary to propagate the value of a write event to other copies and to update these copies accordingly. To this end, we introduce a third kind of causality which is called *update causality*. It is strongly related to data causality but yet different.

Figure 11 shows an example where first some value is written to object x by event e_1. Then, the object is split into two copies (a 'left' and a 'right' one). On the left copy, a write event e_2 and a read event e_3 is performed, on the right copy two read events e_4 and e_6 are performed. The value written by e_2 is also propagated to the right copy. The update event e_5 updates the value of the right copy accordingly. Update causality is represented by arrows with a bold-faced arrow tip but non-bold-faced lines. This indicates the close relation to data causality on the one hand and its difference from data causality on the other hand. The update event on a copy is represented by a box inscribed by U[x]. Thus, the read event e_6 returns the same value as e_3; viz. the value resulting from the two write events e_1 and e_2.

Note that, in contrast to read, write, and commit events, an update event is not invoked by a transaction. Rather, an update event is invoked by the memory manager. Still, update events are present in the execution model in the same way data causality is present, in order to indicate the propagation of data. The update event precisely indicates the point at which a copy is updated. Therefore, there is a data causality and an update causality to an update event. This way, update causality in combination with update events allows a controlled way of

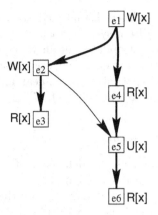

Fig. 11. Update causality

merging different values—which was not possible with data causality because data causality does not branch backwards.

Update causality even allows sequences of write events to be updated by a single update event. For an interpretation of an update of a sequence of write events, let us consider read event e_7 of Fig. 12. This read event reads the value which is the outcome of a sequential execution of the write events e_1, e_3, e_2, e_4, e_6—where e_2 and e_4 are instantaneously updated by update event e_5. Basically, we just insert the sequence of write operations of the update causality preceding the update event for the update event itself. One operational realization of update causality could be a log-file for all values written to some

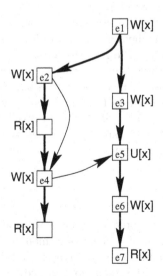

Fig. 12. Interpretation of update causality

object, which are later on updated instantaneously. Actually, we can use update causality to model recovery from system crashes by log-files.

With this interpretation of update causality, the definition of serializability can be easily transferred to this extended execution model. We only need to adapt the definition of compatibility of a linear arrangement of transactions with data causality and update causality (cf. [7]).

5.2 Compensation operations

Our execution model as well as the definition of serializability is completely *syntactical*; i.e. there are no assumptions on the value written by the write events. In particular, there are no assumptions on the relation of values written by two different write events. This corresponds to the classical point of view in serializability theory.

Sometimes, however, it is convenient—or even necessary—to have a more *semantical model* of write events. In the context of *compensating transactions*, for example, each write operation has an *inverse* that undoes the write operation. More generally, there may be a sequence of write events which undo a complete transaction. This can be formalized by an equivalence relation on sequences of write events (e.g. in an algebraic setting).

The technique of equivalent sequences of write events is orthogonal to the technique presented in our paper. Therefore, both techniques can be combined: For each read event, data causality (and update causality) defines a unique sequence of write events; the read event returns the effect of this sequence. If we additionally impose the equivalence relation on this sequence, we have a combined theory of serializability. Technically, the equivalence relation must be incorporated into the definition of compatibility of a linear arrangement with some execution (see [7] for details).

Here, we do not present the formal details of the combination of both techniques but pose the question whether a combination is worthwhile. We guess that it is for the following reason: Of course, the purely syntactical model cannot deal with semantical compensations. On the other hand, a write event inherently does not have an inverse. Therefore, a compensation based theory for recovery needs to add some artificial parameters to write events, where the additional parameter basically records the value of the object prior to the write. A combined theory allows to represent both aspects, compensation and syntactical recovery by before images, in an appropriate way.

6 Conclusion

In this paper, we have presented an execution model which allows to define serializability independently of a particular memory model. The definition of serializability captures multi-version databases as well as databases with replication. Moreover, this definition does not only cover the aspect of concurrency control but also covers the aspects of memory management and recovery.

This slightly generalized definition of serializability has the following benefits:

1. First of all, it provides a clearer understanding of the involved concepts and their relation.
2. Up to now, the definition of serializability had to be adjusted to new memory models. Our definition is independent from a specific memory model since the execution model explicitly deals with the propagation of data.
3. Since there is a single concept of serializability which covers all aspects, there is a formal correctness condition for all modules of a database system. This helps to avoid mistakes due to incorrect interplay of different modules. In particular, correctness of each module can be verified by the help of the techniques presented in [9]. The Separation Theorem guarantees the correct interplay [6].
4. The separation into requirements concerning concurrency control and replication control shows that a large range of modules can be combined with each other. Every scheduler which guarantees conflict serializability (for non-replicated data) can be combined with every memory manager which guarantees weak coherence—without further verification necessary. Though we did not introduce new algorithms or protocols for transaction management, we have indicated new combinations of protocols for schedulers and memory managers.
5. The definition of serializability does not only capture the usual read-write-model but also captures the action-model, which allows partial updates by write operations and atomic modification operations such as increment or decrement. Though partial write operations do occur in real SQL statements, partial write operations are often ignored in transaction theory.

Up to now, we have used our causality based specification technique for specifying, modelling, and verifying classical transaction protocols and for investigating the interplay between classical memory models and classical transaction models. Since these classical models are well-understood, our technique might appear to be of minor relevance for practice. However, the same techniques can be used for reasoning on new transaction models and new memory models. Since the interplay between new memory models and new transaction models is not so well-understood, our techniques might be useful in this area.

Acknowledgments

I would like to thank Ralf Schenkel and the anonymous referees for their comments on preliminary versions of this paper.

References

1. J. K. Bennet, J. B. Carter, and W. Zwaenepoel. Munin: Distributed Shared Memory Based on Type-Specific Memory Coherence. In *Proc. of the 2nd ACM SIGPLAN Symposium on Principles and Practice of Parallel Programming*, pages 168–176, ACM Press, 1990.

2. P. A. Bernstein, V. Hadzilacos, and N. Goodman. *Concurrency Control and Recovery in Database Systems.* Addison-Wesley, 1987.
3. L.M. Censier and P. Feautrier. A New Solution to Coherence Problems in Multicache Systems. *IEEE Transactions on Computers,* C-27(12), 1978.
4. D. Gomm and E. Kindler. Causality Based Proof of a Distributed Shared Memory System. In A. Bode and M. Dal Cin, editors, *Parallel Computer Architectures: Theory, Hardware, Software, Applications,* Lecture Notes in Computer Science, Vol. 732, pages 131–149. Springer-Verlag, 1993.
5. J. Gray and A. Reuter. *Transaction Processing: Concepts and Techniques.* Morgan Kaufmann Publishers, 1993.
6. E. Kindler. The Interplay of Transaction Models and Memory Models. In T. Özsu, A. Dogac, and Ö. Ulusoy, editors, *Issues and Applications of Database Technology (IADT'98), Proc. of the 3rd World Conf. on Integrated Design and Process Technology, July 6-9, 1998, Berlin, Germany,* IDPT-Vol. 2, pages 39–46, Society for Design and Process Science, 1998.
7. E. Kindler. A Classification of Consistency Models. Technical Report B99-14, Freie Universität Berlin, Institut für Informatik, October 1999.
8. E. Kindler, A. Listl, and R. Walter. A Specification Method for Transaction Models with Data Replication. Informatik-Berichte 56, Humboldt-Universität zu Berlin, March 1996.
9. E. Kindler and R. Walter. Arc-Typed Petri Nets. In J. Billington and W. Reisig, editors, *Application and Theory of Petri Nets 1996,* Lecture Notes in Computer Science, Vol. 1091, pages 289–306. Springer-Verlag, 1996.
10. L. Lamport. How to Make a Multiprocessor Computer That Correctly Executes Multiprocess Programs. *IEEE Transactions on Computers,* C-28(9):690–691, September 1979.
11. H.-J. Schek, G. Weikum, and H. Ye. Towards a Unified Theory of Concurrency Control and Recovery. In *Proc. of the 12th ACM SIGACT-SIGMOD-SIGART Symposium on Principles of Database Systems, Washington, D.C.,* pages 300–311. ACM Press, 1993.

Logical Update Queries as Open Nested Transactions

Alfred Fent, Carl-Alexander Wichert, and Burkhard Freitag

Universität Passau, Fakultät für Mathematik und Informatik
D-94030 Passau, Germany
{fent,wichert,freitag}@fmi.uni-passau.de

Abstract. The rule-based update language ULTRA has been designed for the specification of complex database updates in a modular fashion. The logical semantics of update goals is based on update request sets, which correspond to deferred basic updates in the database. The declarative character of the logical semantics leaves much freedom for various evaluation strategies, among them a top-down resolution, which can be mapped naturally onto a system of nested transactions. In this paper, we extend this operational model as follows: Not only the basic operations are performed and committed independently from the top-level transaction, but also complex operations defined by update rules. This leads to an open nested transaction hierarchy, which allows to exploit the semantical properties of complex operations to gain more concurrency. On the other hand, high-level compensation is necessary and meta information must be provided by the programmer. We present the key elements of this combination of logic-based update languages and transaction processing and propose a flexible system architecture.

1 Introduction

In [18,19] we present the rule-based update language ULTRA. In rule-based update languages as ULTRA or Transaction Logic [4,5], updates are implemented by goals, and rules can be used to define complex operations to be reused in other goals. The concept is similar to procedures/functions in classical programming languages. Thus, it is possible to build arbitrarily complex database operations in a modular fashion. In ULTRA, constructs for concurrent composition, sequential composition, and bulk updates are provided, which subsume the classical database operations. The logical semantics of an update goal with respect to a fixed database state is defined in terms of update request sets which contain insertion and deletion requests for ground EDB tuples. This semantics is declarative and does not state anything about a particular evaluation model.

In this paper we present an operational model that implements a fragment of the logical semantics in terms of open nested transactions [12,14] performed on top of a loosely coupled database system (DBS). The structure of complex operations is reflected by trees of subtransactions during the execution, and the semantics of hypothetical states is implemented using *backtrackable immediate*

G. Saake, K. Schwarz, and C. Türker (Eds.): TDD '99, LNCS 1773, pp. 45–66, 2000.

updates. This allows us to handle efficiently also non-deterministic update specifications that are possible in ULTRA and other rule-based update languages. Although non-deterministic updates are not commonplace in database systems, they are a valuable instrument when it comes to novel applications like e.g. the combination of database operations with external actions. For instance, an application that does simulation or planning for a robot needs to state only the destination of a movement without having to care about the exact path that is taken.

Our operational model features immediate updates in combination with backtracking, recovery by compensation, and nested transactions. Exploitation of additional semantical knowledge of complex operations, which correspond to subtransactions, for concurrency control and recovery is a key feature of the model. In contrast to the work presented in [17], which operated strictly at the level of basic operations and consequently used nested transactions only as rollback spheres, the additional benefits of nested transactions, like handling of long-running transactions, increased possibilities of concurrency, or more efficient compensation of complex operations are incorporated in the new model as well. The sequential program fragment and the execution strategy discussed in this paper, for instance, will lead to more inter-transaction concurrency with the possibility to soften the ACID properties [3]. Other strategies featuring parallel subtransactions may also profit with respect to intra-transaction concurrency. However, this is still a point of ongoing work. In the open nested transaction model it must be possible to issue a compensating subtransaction [10] for every committed subtransaction. These compensating (undo) transactions can be specified by the same means, i.e. using ULTRA rules, as the forward (do) operations. We identify the components that are necessary for the transactional execution of logical update queries and give a protocol for the interaction between logical evaluation and a transaction scheduler. It turns out that the logical evaluation is independent from operational aspects like the actual scheduling protocol, so we can use the results from database theory here and do not have to invent e.g. special scheduling protocols. The only requirement is that the scheduling protocol corresponds to the selected transaction model, i.e., in our case, open nested transactions. The key components of our model – logical evaluation, transaction scheduling, and external DBS – can be selected and tuned essentially independently from each other according to the requirements of the application.

An important aspect in the treatment of open nested transactions is the meta information that is needed to schedule complex operations and to compensate already committed subtransactions. Although the meta information, i.e. the data about the compatibility or conflict of complex operations and the data about how a complex operation can be compensated, is essential for a practical system, it has not received much attention yet. Compatibility information is usually assumed to exist in the form of a compatibility relation, but details on how this relation can be obtained and what must be taken into consideration are rarely addressed. The same applies to compensation, where little if anything is said about the internal structure of compensating actions, about how to pass parameters, etc. We sketch a method to declare compatibility information and show how it can be used for an actual compatibility test. We further discuss the central issues concerning compensation in our framework.

In the literature, various other logic- or rule-based update languages are presented, among them Chen's approach [6], Transaction Logic [4,5], and U-Datalog [13]. These approaches mainly deal with specification of updates, while execution is not in the main scope of investigation. In this paper, we apply results from database theory to ULTRA as one representative of such update languages. We provide a mapping between complex operations specified by logical rules and nested transactions and use nested transactions not only for backtracking, but also to increase concurrency. Furthermore, we allow high-level compensation operations, which are again specified in the logic language. As the components of our architecture can be adapted to various evaluation strategies and scheduling protocols, we are sure that the techniques described in this paper can also be applied to other rule-based update languages, if these are extended to provide the necessary additional meta information. We are also convinced that our model can be adopted for general update programs that can be combined in a modular fashion, for instance *stored procedures* in SQL [7]. The evaluation of stored procedures is simpler than the evaluation of update rules, but the technical results about scheduling and the declaration of meta information apply to both languages.

HiPAC [8], an active object-oriented database management system, also uses nested transactions for the execution of ECA rules. In contrast to the model described in this paper, the nested transactions of HiPAC only reflect the internal structure of the triggered rules and are not used to increase the possible amount of concurrency. To accomplish the requirements of the active component, e.g. coupling modes between rules, the transaction model is extended with special features like "deferred subtransactions" or "nested top transactions". Yet, the semantics of HiPAC is operationally defined based on this extended nested transaction model, while our approach combines the purely declarative semantics of ULTRA with an open-nested-transaction-based operational model. Moreover, the paradigm behind ECA rules is inherently different from that behind ULTRA rules.

The rest of the paper is organized as follows: In Section 2 we recall the key elements of the sequential fragment of the ULTRA language. We develop and discuss a new operational model in Section 3. Section 4 presents some central points concerning meta information, before Section 5 summarizes the paper and collects some research issues to be addressed in the future.

The work described in this paper has been funded by the German Research Agency (DFG) under contract number Fr 1021/3-1.

2 The ULTRA Language

ULTRA extends the syntax known from Datalog [11] by *basic update atoms*, which can be used in rule bodies. The predicates defined by rules correspond to complex update operations on the extensional database (EDB), whereas in pure Datalog they correspond to views. Presently, the technical descriptions of ULTRA are restricted to insertions $INS\ r(t_1, \ldots, t_k)$ and deletions $DEL\ r(t_1, \ldots, t_k)$ of EDB tuples as basic update atoms, although other basic operations can smoothly be integrated into the ULTRA concept. To compose multiple operations, ULTRA introduces the new connective ":" *(sequential conjunction)* besides a concurrent conjunction "," derived from the traditional conjunction used in Datalog rules. While two concurrently composed subgoals are evaluated in the same state, sequential conjunction means that the subgoal on the right refers to an intermediate state that results from the execution of updates specified by the left subgoal. Consequently, the sequential conjunction is associative but not commutative. The general form of sequential rules in the ULTRA language is

$$p(\boldsymbol{X}) \leftarrow q_1(\boldsymbol{Y_1}) : \ldots : q_n(\boldsymbol{Y_n})$$

where $p(\boldsymbol{X})$ and each $q_i(\boldsymbol{Y_i}), 1 \leq i \leq n$, is an atom as known from Datalog or a basic update atom as introduced above. An update program is a set of rules that specify a collection of complex operations in a modular fashion. In analogy to Datalog, recursive update programs are allowed and have a well-defined interpretation. A detailed description of the ULTRA syntax and semantics can be found in [19].

In the top-down- and tuple-oriented operational semantics referred to in this paper, we restrict ourselves to sequentially connected subgoals, i.e. rules of the form shown above; the extension to the full language, including concurrent conjunction and especially a bulk quantifier for the specification of set-oriented updates, is subject of our present research (cf. Section 5).

Example 1 (Bank Transfer). Here we restate the standard example of how to specify the transfer of money from one bank account to another. This classical transaction example is suitable to illustrate the new features of the operational model described below. Again, we consider only insertion and deletion as basic update operations. Read access to the database is specifiable by EDB or IDB atoms, but in order to keep the example short we avoid IDB relations (views) expressed by deductive rules. In addition to the classical syntax, we allow simple constraints to express arithmetic computations.

The update program, i.e. the program written in the ULTRA language, contains the update rules

$$transfer(Amo, Ac_1, Ac_2) \leftarrow withdraw(Amo, Ac_1) : deposit(Amo, Ac_2)$$

$$\begin{aligned} withdraw(Amo, Ac) \quad &\leftarrow account(Ac, Bal) : Amo \leq Bal : \\ & DEL\ account(Ac, Bal) : \\ & Bal' = Bal - Amo : INS\ account(Ac, Bal') \end{aligned}$$

$$\begin{aligned} deposit(Amo, Ac) \quad &\leftarrow account(Ac, Bal) : DEL\ account(Ac, Bal) : \\ & Bal' = Bal + Amo : INS\ account(Ac, Bal') \end{aligned}$$

which specify a complex operation *transfer* built from (complex) sub-operations *withdraw* and *deposit*. The latter operate on the EDB which consists of one binary relation $account(Number, Balance)$. A complex operation is considered as successful, if all sub-operations in one of its defining rules are successful. As we will see below, it makes sense to handle sub-operations as subtransactions that may even be committed independently from the top-level transaction. This leads to an *open* nested transaction hierarchy [16].

In the ULTRA system, a transaction is invoked by a top-level update goal which is submitted as a query. Evaluation has to be performed as a *(top-level) transaction* to guarantee the ACID properties [2,3]. In particular, it must be ensured that the data accessed by a transaction is not affected simultaneously by other transactions *(isolation)* and that either all changes caused by the transaction are applied to the database, or none of them at all *(atomicity)*. To achieve this, the execution of all basic update requests as well as read access to the database has to be certified by the system. If the execution of an operation could possibly compromise the ACID properties, the operation cannot be certified, so the system may decide to delay it, to abort the whole transaction, or to do something else to resolve the violation of the ACID properties.

The model-theoretic semantics of the insertion/deletion-oriented ULTRA language assigns *update request sets* to every successful update goal. These update request sets contain insertion requests $+r(t_1, \ldots, t_k)$ and deletion requests $-r(t_1, \ldots, t_k)$ for tuples of EDB relations. The solutions for a top-level query are called *possible transitions*, as they represent transitions from the given initial state to a desired final state of the transaction. Non-deterministic transactions may generate more than one possible transition. Note that the characterization of the possible transitions for an update query does not depend on a particular evaluation strategy. Before a transaction invoked by a query can be committed, one of the possible transitions must have been materialized, i.e. its update requests must have been executed and committed on the persistent EDB. However, the logical semantics does not restrict the choice of a possible transition or the time of materialization in any way.

Example 2 (Bank Transfer (Cont.)). Recall Example 1 above and consider the query $\varphi :\equiv \leftarrow transfer(1000, 88009, 88004)$. The (unique) possible transition for φ is encoded by the following update request set Δ, assuming that the accounts 88004 and 88009 have a balance of \$1000 and \$5000, respectively:

$$\Delta = \{ \ -account(88004, 1000), \ -account(88009, 5000),$$
$$+account(88004, 2000), \ +account(88009, 4000) \ \}$$

Due to space limitations, we do not describe in detail how the possible transitions are constructed using the ULTRA semantics, but refer the reader to [18]. Note that the update request sets do not express an evaluation by subtransactions. They just express the resulting changes of the accounts.

3   The Operational Model

In the ULTRA concept, the execution of a transaction consists of two types of processing: the *evaluation* of a query (for binding variables and computing the update requests) and the *application* of selected update requests to the EDB. In the architecture described in [19], execution was strictly divided into two subsequent phases doing exclusively evaluation and application, respectively. Thus, in the first phase all possible transitions of the transaction goal had to be computed without changing the physical EDB instance, and in the second phase one possible transition could be materialized. This corresponds to the logical semantics described in Section 2. However, an operational semantics completely based on deferred updates has several drawbacks (see [17] for a more detailed discussion):

First, there is a need for hypothetical reasoning when referring to intermediate states: as the operations leading to an intermediate state are known but not carried out yet, their effects on the state are not visible and thus must be computed by a reasoning component. An axiomatization of the observable effects is necessary to enable such hypothetical reasoning. Unfortunately, this is only tractable for simple basic operations like insertions and deletions.

A second practical problem results from performing a transaction in two strictly separated phases (evaluation and materialization). Such a system does not show a continuous behaviour during the evaluation and thus is not suitable to be extended by e.g. interactive components. It merely implements a batch mode, where action requests are collected to be performed later.

Finally, the standard bottom-up evaluation as proposed for the ULTRA semantics always computes all possible transitions in the evaluation phase. Especially in presence of non-deterministic specifications and much hypothetical reasoning this may lead to a lot of unnecessary work, and even small examples may not be tractable anymore.

To solve these problems we reuse the top-down left-to-right evaluation strategy well-known from Prolog and apply it to sequential ULTRA programs. During evaluation, updates are not collected for later execution, but executed immediately using database techniques. Evaluating queries in this top-down fashion results in a resolution tree, which can be mapped onto a nested transaction tree (see Fig. 1). This is a well-known fact and has been used e.g. in the model described in [17]. There, we show how subtransactions are used as rollback spheres to implement a backtracking that fits with the logical semantics.

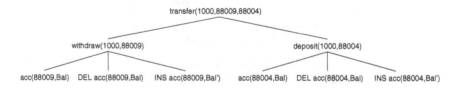

Fig. 1. Resolution tree corresponding to a nested transaction tree

Yet, using subtransactions only to aid backtracking is not satisfying. Nested transactions were invented in the database community to, among other reasons, increase the possible amount of concurrency between transactions by using the additional semantical knowledge of complex operations. This can of course also be done in the case of logical update languages as investigated in this paper. All that is needed is a scheduler for nested transactions and meta information about compatibility or conflict between the operations. The latter is discussed in Section 4.

3.1   Execution of Update Queries

In the following, we assume that P is an ULTRA program consisting of update rules as introduced in Section 2.

Definition 1 (Transactional Update Query).   *A transactional update query has the form* $\leftarrow g(c_1, \ldots, c_k)$, *where* $g(c_1, \ldots, c_k)$ *is an update atom.*

Note that the restriction of queries to only one atom is not a severe one as complex queries of the form $\leftarrow g_1(c_1) : \ldots : g_n(c_n)$ can be expressed using a new rule $query \leftarrow g_1(c_1) : \ldots : g_n(c_n)$.

Execution of transactional update queries is done by two components: a *logical evaluation* on the one hand, and a *scheduler* on the other hand. Seen as black boxes, the task of the logical evaluation is to take a transactional update query, evaluate it, and return success or failure. The task of the scheduler is to take operations (atomic goals) including special operations to begin, commit, or abort (sub-) transactions and to execute them atomically or reject them. If an operation is executed, its outcome (success or failure) and additional results (variable bindings for read operations) are returned. If it is rejected, failure is returned.

With these two components, transactional update queries can be executed as follows:

Definition 2 (Execution of Transactional Update Queries).
Logical evaluation of query $\leftarrow g(c)$:

I.1 Resolve the goal $g(c)$ against the update program P. This results in a set of (partially) instantiated rule bodies for g.

I.2 Choose one of the rule bodies, say $g_1(X_1) : \ldots : g_n(X_n)$.

I.3 Send a begin-of-transaction request to the scheduler.

I.4 For each $1 \leq i \leq n$, take the instantiated subgoal $g_i(c_i)$

   – *Send the goal $g_i(c_i)$ to the scheduler and wait for the result.*
   – *If the scheduler returns success and exactly one result, use this result to obtain an answer substitution θ_i, apply it to the subsequent subgoals $g_{i+1}, \ldots, g_n$ and continue the loop with the next subgoal.*
   – *If the scheduler returns success and more than one result, create a new choice-point. Begin a new subtransaction by sending the corresponding request to the scheduler, choose one of the results to obtain an answer substitution θ_i, and continue the loop with the next subgoal.*

- *If the scheduler returns failure but there exist unused results from a previous choice-point, force a rollback of the current subtransaction, i.e. the subtransaction created as described before. Also undo the application of the current substitution θ_i, choose another result to obtain a new substitution θ_i, apply it to the subgoals $g_{i+1}, \ldots, g_n$ and continue the loop at point I.4. A choice-point and a new subtransaction have to be created again if other untried choices are still left.*
- *If the scheduler returns failure and there is no possibility to use other variable bindings (i.e. all possible choices for θ_i failed), react on that failure by backtracking: discard the variable bindings obtained, send an abort request relative to the current (sub-) transaction to the scheduler, and either retry the current operation (i.e. continue at point I.3), choose another possible rule body (i.e. continue at point I.2), or return failure.*

I.5 *If all subgoals have succeeded, send a commit request to the scheduler. If this commit is acknowledged, return success. If the commit is rejected by the scheduler, return failure.*

Scheduling the execution of request $g(c)$:

II.1 *If a begin-of-transaction request is received, start a new (sub-) transaction.*

II.2 *If a commit request is received, test according to the scheduling protocol if this commit is possible. If so, return success as soon as the commit is executed. Otherwise, abort the current (sub-) transaction and return failure.*

II.3 *If an abort request is received, abort the current (sub-) transaction and report completion of the abort. See Section 3.3 for details.*

II.4 *If the requested operation $g(c)$ is a basic operation, schedule it according to the concurrency control protocol. If the operation may be executed, send it to the data manager for execution. Return the outcome-value obtained from the data manager together with additional results. Return failure if the data manager refused the operation or it was not allowed by the scheduling protocol.*

II.5 *If the requested operation $g(c)$ is a complex operation, schedule it according to the concurrency control protocol. If the operation may be executed, send to the logical evaluation the transactional update query $\leftarrow g(c)$ and return the outcome of this query (success/failure). Return failure if it was not allowed by the scheduling protocol.*

The scheduler has to record all actions taken together with their outcome in the persistent system log.

During logical evaluation, non-deterministic choice is necessary at points I.2 and I.4. These choices can possibly lead to failure in a goal evaluated later, as committing the subtransaction also commits the choice. We assume here that this is handled by the least common ancestor in the transaction tree of the operation which did the choice and the one which failed later, e.g. by retrying the evaluation with other choices.

The execution method described above can also deal with recursive programs. On the side of the logical evaluation, handling of recursion is a well-known issue.

On the transactional side, recursion does not pose new problems, as what the scheduler encounters is only the unfolded recursion. So the only requirement for the scheduler is that it can handle arbitrarily deep nested transactions. Note that especially conflicts between different recursively nested levels cannot occur, as in nested transactions there are no conflicts between a subtransaction and its ancestors. However, termination of recursive programs is not guaranteed in general: the behaviour depends on properties of the update program as well as on choice strategies during the evaluation. Yet, the semantics of a non-terminating program is undefined in general, and not a special problem introduced by our execution method.

The problem that a non-terminating recursive unfolding will never yield a consistent database state could be tackled by introducing a depth limit for the nested transactions. If this limit is reached, the creation of the next subtransaction will fail and backtracking will be enforced. Consequently, infinite branches in the transaction hierarchy are excluded. Note that such a solution is purely operational and destroys the theoretical universality of the recursion, having consequences also for non-recursive programs. From the practical point of view, the limit value should be high enough to support the (sequential) implementation of set-oriented updates by recursive rules.

Note that there may be various threads doing logical evaluation in the system, which may also belong to different top-level transactions that are concurrently executed. Yet, there is only *one* central scheduler, which ensures that the interleaved execution of concurrent transactions is correct, i.e. serializable.

Proposition 1. *Execution of transactional update queries as described in Definition 2 performs the updates that are required by the logical semantics of* ULTRA.
Proof (sketch): *For every update query, the* ULTRA *semantics yields one or more update request sets that capture the logical meaning of the query. To execute the query, one of the sets has to be chosen and materialized.*

Our operational model executes the updates immediately, so, if there is no logical failure during the evaluation, the "sum" of all the immediate updates corresponds to one of the update request sets of the ULTRA *semantics. If, on the other hand, a logical failure occurs, all updates done on the failing branch so far are removed from the database by aborting the corresponding subtransaction. So, failing branches cause no updates that could compromise correctness with respect to the logical semantics.*

Finally, during evaluation there are several points where non-deterministic choices are made (see I.2 and I.4 in Definition 2). If the choice results in a failing branch, its updates are removed. If, on the other hand, the choice leads to a successful branch, this corresponds to one possible transition due to the ULTRA *semantics. The only difference is that the decision to materialize this branch and not another one would have been delayed at the semantical level until all possible update request sets are known, while the operational model anticipated the choice.*

The execution of the *transfer* query φ of Example 2 is shown in Fig. 2 as a time-line diagram.

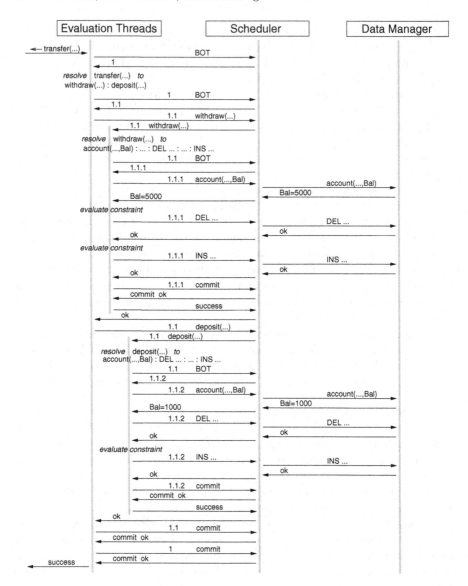

Fig. 2. Successful execution of a *transfer* query

Execution of queries in this operational model allows us to exploit concurrency between transactions not only at the level of basic operations (point II.4 in Definition 2), but also between high-level operations (point II.5). Thus, our execution model goes beyond the simple use of subtransactions for backtracking.

Proposition 2. *Interleaved executions of transactional update queries according to Definition 2 obey the ACID properties.*

Proof (sketch): *The execution of every (basic or complex) operation is controlled by the scheduler. So, if the scheduler uses a concurrency control protocol that guarantees serializability, this property is extended to the execution of transactional update queries, too.*

Note that we do not prescribe a certain scheduling protocol or method. We only require a protocol that can handle nested transactions and guarantees serializability. Whether this is done by locking, optimistic approaches, or something else is left to the scheduler.

An implication of this proposition is that every transaction in the system must be under the control of the ULTRA scheduler. Local transactions that operate directly on the database can destroy serializability of the interleaved executions. Therefore, we assume that no local transactions are executed. However, techniques developed for federated or multidatabase systems could be adopted here.

3.2   Compensation

Compensation is the key technique to enable recovery of open nested transactions. For every *do* operation that makes certain changes to the database, a corresponding *undo* operation has to be provided that removes the changes that have been committed independently of the top-level transaction. As other transactions may already have read these changes and may have made their own modifications, recovery by simply restoring the before images is not adequate. Instead, the changes to be removed are *semantically* undone by a compensating operation. Of course, the conventional restoration of a before image can be seen as a compensation method for simple basic operations.

In the extended ULTRA system, every operation must also have a corresponding *undo* operation. For basic operations, the undo actions can be assumed to be already implemented in the data manager, such that the scheduler can call them directly. Complex operations mostly can be compensated only by other complex operations. So, the scheduler must be informed which operation it must invoke (see also Section 4.1).

Undo operations must in general be provided by the programmer who wrote the corresponding *do* operation, as she knows its exact semantics and what is necessary to undo its effects. Although it would be possible for the system to generate compensation steps automatically from the structure of the compensated operation and the current database and log state, in essence this would lead to compensation only at the level of basic operations. Moreover, the compensating action may need some additional parameters that depend on the internal states of the forward action and that must be recorded by the log. In this paper we restricted ourselves to complex operations which can be compensated without providing additional parameters, i.e. all the information to compensate a complex operation $g(c)$ is contained in the arguments c. Note that this property does not hold for the basic insertions and deletions in ULTRA: to undo an insert operation, for instance, the scheduler must know whether the insertion was proper or not, i.e. if the tuple was already contained in the database before.

The crucial point with compensation is that the subtransaction corresponding to the *undo* operation must not fail. First, this is a requirement to the scheduler: it must not abort a compensating operation due to transactional conflicts. This problem can be solved with adequate scheduling protocols which allow only histories that are prefix reducible, for example based on [9,15], or by a simple retry of the aborted subtransaction. But it is also a requirement to the logical evaluation and the compensating operation itself: If the evaluation of the compensating goal fails logically, i.e. due to the logical semantics, the recovery is (currently) not possible. The programmer must be made responsible to provide compensating actions that always have a logical solution. Otherwise the system may remain in an uncertain state until recovery becomes possible or is done manually.

Definition 3 (Compensation (acc. to [10])). *An operation $p^{-1}(c')$ compensates another operation $p(c)$, iff $p(c)$: $p^{-1}(c')$ is the identity mapping, i.e. from a semantical point of view a null operation.*

3.3 Handling Logical and Transactional Failure

As shown in [17], logical failure corresponds to an abort of a subtransaction. Because changes made by committed subtransactions are visible to other transactions running concurrently in the open nested transaction model, we use compensation as described above to undo changes of committed subtransactions.

Definition 4 (Abort of Transactions). *To abort a (sub-) transaction, the scheduler proceeds as follows:*

1. *Record the beginning of the compensation in the log.*
2. *Consult the log and obtain all successful operations $g_1(c_1), \ldots, g_n(c_n)$ within the current (sub-) transaction that have been executed.*
3. *Compensate the operations $g_i(c_i), 1 \leq i \leq n$, in the reverse order, i.e. starting with operation $g_n(c_n)$ and proceeding until $g_1(c_1)$, as follows:*
4. *If $g_i(c_i)$ is a basic operation, issue the corresponding compensating operation $g_i^{-1}(c_i')$ to the data manager.*
5. *If $g_i(c_i)$ is a complex operation, send the corresponding compensating operation $g_i^{-1}(c_i')$ to the logical evaluation as a transactional update query $\leftarrow g_i^{-1}(c_i')$.*
6. *Record the execution of the compensating actions in the log, as well as the completion (commit) of the compensation when all compensating operations have been executed.*

An unsuccessful execution of the *transfer* query of Example 2 is shown in Fig. 3. The abort of subtransaction 1.1 requires the compensation of the already committed *withdraw* operation by a corresponding *deposit* operation.

A transaction which is aborted by compensation gets physically *committed* after all the compensating operations have been executed. This is necessary because changes of the *do* operations are undone by explicit compensation and not by simply restoring an old state.

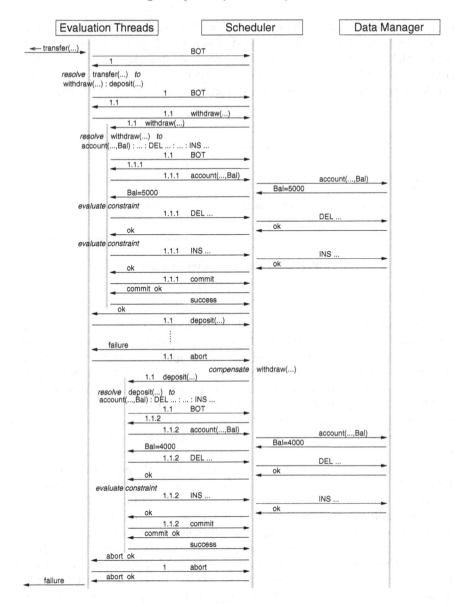

Fig. 3. Failing execution of a *transfer* query

To allow for the compensation of complex operations (labeled g_i in Definition 4 above), the corresponding high-level compensating operations (called g_i^{-1} above) must be provided by the programmer. Compensating operations can be specified by update rules just like normal complex operations.

It is important to stress the similarities between backtracking on the logical side and compensation on the transactional side. Yet, compensation with com-

plex, high-level operations introduces a new dimension since it can be seen as a
kind of high-level backtracking: instead of going back each single step that was
done with the forward operations, compensation allows to "jump back" several
steps at once. This can of course also be exploited to optimize the reasoning of
a rule-based component within a larger system architecture with this kind of
intelligent backtracking.

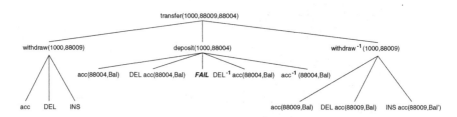

Fig. 4. Recovery by compensation

The transaction hierarchy depicted in Fig. 4 shows several examples of compensation. The failure in the *deposit* operation causes the execution of the compensating operations for the already executed operations deleting a tuple and
reading the database. The *deposit* subtransaction is committed after compensation, and the logical abort is reported to the *transfer* operation. If also *transfer*
decides to fail, i.e. to abort its transaction, the already committed *withdraw* operation must be compensated, too. This is done by executing a *deposit* operation
(see Example 3 in Section 4.1 for a discussion about compensation in our running
example).

Note that the use of compensation interferes with the argumentation of Proposition 1. There, the proof is based on the fact that failing branches do not cause
any updates on the database. This is guaranteed operationally by aborting the
subtransaction corresponding to that failing branch. Now, using compensation
failing branches do in fact cause updates which even get committed, but from the
semantical point of view, the combined effect of all theses updates is null. Nevertheless, at the operational level there are updates which are not contained in any
of the update request sets defined by the model-theoretic semantics of ULTRA.
To be able to handle this formally we are currently developing a model where the
update request objects are extended from simple sets to structured multi-sets
resembling a kind of log. This new model will facilitate reasoning about equivalence of logs and therefore will be suitable to also capture the compensation
semantics.

3.4   Architecture

The operational model described in this section can be realized in a system
architecture as depicted in Fig. 5. This reflects also the actual architecture of

our prototype system, which is implemented in the Java programming language on top of the relational database management system ORACLE. We used the prototype system to verify that our model is also suitable for the transactional execution of update queries over wide area networks like the internet. Further, we let the data manager also communicate with an external device (a virtual robot arm) instead of a database system, demonstrating the universality of the ULTRA approach.

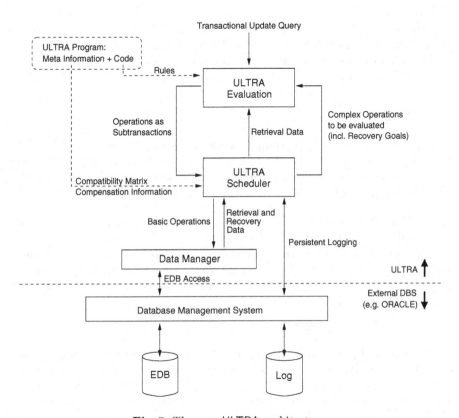

Fig. 5. The new ULTRA architecture

The responsibilities of the various components of our architecture are as follows: The external *database management system* is used as a persistent storage for EDB data as well as for logging purposes. The *data manager* executes all basic operations of the ULTRA program. The ULTRA *scheduler* is responsible for concurrency control and recovery of complex as well as basic operations. It receives requests to execute an operation, schedules them according to a nested transaction scheduling protocol, and "executes" the operation: basic operations are passed to the data manager, complex operations are forwarded to a newly created thread of the ULTRA evaluation. If compensation is necessary during recovery, the corresponding operations are generated and sent to the data manager or the evaluation, too. The ULTRA *evaluation* gets queries from the user or the scheduler. These queries are partially resolved, and the resulting subgoals are sent to the scheduler for execution. The interaction protocols of the scheduler and the evaluation have been described in detail in Sections 3.1 and 3.3.

4   Meta Information

As explained in the previous sections, the "pure" logic program, i.e. the ULTRA rules, must be enriched with additional information. On the one hand, compatibility information is needed to allow correct scheduling, on the other hand compensation information is needed for recovery.

4.1   Compensation

To enable the scheduler to do compensation as described in Sections 3.2 and 3.3, it must first be provided with the compensating operations per se, and second it must be informed about which *do* operation is undone by which *undo* operation. These two aspects of additional information are treated in the following.

Example 3 (Bank Transfer (Cont.)). As an example, let us specify the compensating rules for the operations of Example 1.

Compensating a *withdraw* is the easiest case. To undo the debit, the amount of money is simply credited back on the account. So the compensation for *withdraw*(Amo, Ac) is *deposit*(Amo, Ac). This could be declared in a meta program by the following non-ground fact:

undo(*withdraw*(Amo, Ac), *deposit*(Amo, Ac))

Undoing a *deposit* operation needs some deeper thoughts. Although one is tempted to say that, in analogy to the above, a *deposit* can be compensated by a *withdraw*, this can lead to problems. Recall that a *withdraw* operation checks for an overdraft on the account and fails if the balance would become negative. So compensation would fail logically, which must be avoided. To do so, there are two possibilities: First, the responsibility can be delegated to the scheduler, which must then ensure that the *withdraw* compensating a *deposit* does not fail logically. This essentially means that no *withdraw* operation from another transaction must have been executed between the *deposit* and its compensating *withdraw* – obviously a severe restriction. The alternative would be to provide a compensating operation that cannot fail logically, i.e. something like

$$undo\_deposit(Amo, Ac) \leftarrow account(Ac, Bal) \ : \ DEL \ account(Ac, Bal) \ : \\ Bal' = Bal - Amo \ : \ INS \ account(Ac, Bal')$$

and a declaration that *deposit* is undone by *undo_deposit*.

undo(*deposit*(Amo, Ac), *undo_deposit*(Amo, Ac))

But note that now an account may get a negative balance, which usually is forbidden. The decision whether this is nevertheless tolerable is a question of the bank's business policy. You could also imagine the policy that the balance on an account may become negative due to compensation, but that a human operator is notified if the overdraft accounts for more than, say, $5000.

Finally, the same considerations as above can be applied to the *undo* operation of a *transfer*. Again, it is either forbidden to withdraw from the target account of the transfer until the transaction finished (either successfully or with its compensation), or it is accepted that the account's balance may become negative. In the latter case, a compensation rule

$$undo\_transfer(Amo, Ac_1, Ac_2) \leftarrow undo\_deposit(Amo, Ac_2) :$$
$$deposit(Amo, Ac_1)$$

can be given along with the declaration

$$\mathsf{undo}(\, transfer(Amo, Ac_1, Ac_2), \, undo\_transfer(Amo, Ac_1, Ac_2)\,).$$

The compensation rule *undo_transfer* from Example 3 is a nice representative of an *undo* operation that also could have been generated automatically. In general, for *deterministic rules*, i.e. rules that do not require non-deterministic choice in their evaluation (see I.2 and I.4 in Definition 2), compensating operations can be generated automatically:

Proposition 3 (Generation of Compensation Rules). *Let a deterministic rule* $p(\boldsymbol{X}) \leftarrow g_1(\boldsymbol{X_1}) : \ldots : g_n(\boldsymbol{X_n})$ *be given. Then the rule*

$$p^{-1}(\boldsymbol{X}) \leftarrow g_n^{-1}(\boldsymbol{X_n}) : \ \ldots \ : \ g_1^{-1}(\boldsymbol{X_1})$$

where $g_i^{-1}, 1 \leq i \leq n$, *is the compensating operation of* g_i, *defines a compensating operation for* p.

Proof (sketch): *Leaving out the arguments, it obviously is the case that*

$$p : p^{-1} \equiv g_1 : \ldots : g_{n-1} : g_n : g_n^{-1} : g_{n-1}^{-1} : \ldots : g_1^{-1}$$

From the preconditions follows that g_n^{-1} *compensates* g_n *(for all parameter instances). Therefore, the pair* $g_n : g_n^{-1}$ *is a null operation and thus can be removed, leaving* $g_{n-1} : g_{n-1}^{-1}$ *next to each other. Now the same argument can be applied inductively, until* $g_1 : g_1^{-1}$. *As no non-deterministic choice is involved in the evaluation of* p, *no additional information is needed in compensation. So,* p^{-1} *as defined in the proposition is a compensating operation for* p.

Of course, in an actual execution the operations g_i and g_i^{-1} may be interleaved with operations from other transactions. Yet, as the scheduler guarantees serializability this interleaved execution is equivalent to a serial one, so that we may assume a serial execution as shown in the proof.

Note, however, that this works only for simple cases. In the presence of non-determinism, e.g. if an operation is defined by several rules, the undo rules may need additional tests to determine the outcome of the non-deterministic choice. This may be done by analyzing the effects that have to be compensated or with special log entries reflecting the selected rule body. But in general rules like this cannot be generated automatically and therefore must be provided by a human programmer. In a transaction abort as described in Definition 4 the system log is analyzed backwards (point 2) and so it is known which operations have been executed and must consequently be undone.

Another drawback of the automatic generation of undo rules is that the programmer may have additional semantic knowledge which the system cannot use. Recall the discussion about the compensation for *deposit* in Example 3: The solution that an overdraft on the account may be acceptable, but that a human operator must be notified cannot be deduced automatically. Things like that require a human being who is familiar with the system, its environment, business policies, etc. Moreover, there are cases where several forward steps can be undone by only one *undo* operation, but this is not known to a straight-forward generator of compensating actions. A classical example for this is a *do* operation that creates a new relation and inserts data into it. A human programmer knows that this can be undone by simply dropping the relation, while an automatically generated compensating action would delete all the inserted tuples before dropping the relation.

4.2   Compatibility Information

The second element of additional information contained in the program is information about the compatibility or conflict of complex operations. Testing the compatibility of operations is an issue in most transaction scheduling protocols. All the widely used techniques, like serialization graph testing, locking, or time-stamp based methods are founded on a notion of conflict or compatibility between operations. This central role of compatibility information is emphasized in advanced transaction models like nested transactions [1].

As the scheduler in our ULTRA system does not only handle basic operations but also complex operations specified by a programmer, it must be provided with a kind of compatibility relation between all the operations, including compensating operations and pure retrieval operations (for EDB/IDB predicates). Note that the compatibility and conflict information is used by the scheduler to decide about the serializability of an interleaved execution of concurrent transactions. So, if two operations are specified to be compatible while in reality they are not, this leads to histories that are not serializable and thus incorrect.

The needed compatibility relation can be given e.g. in the form of a compatibility matrix which contains one row/column for each (basic or complex) operation. Yet, providing such a matrix is a strenuous task as it grows quadratically in the number of operations. Moreover, as the complex operations may operate on different levels of abstraction it is necessary to take the operations' arguments into account as well.

Example 4 (Bank Transfer (Cont.)). A compatibility matrix for our banking operations *withdraw*, *deposit*, and *transfer* would state that *deposit* and *transfer* are in conflict as a *transfer* operation may fail if it was executed before a *deposit*, and succeed afterwards. Yet, the order between the two operations is only relevant if the from-account of the *transfer* is affected by the *deposit*. If the transfer's to-account is also credited by *deposit*, the order of the two operations is irrelevant. This can only be expressed when the arguments are considered, too.

As declarations with arguments cannot be accomplished easily with compatibility matrices we propose to use a simple language to specify the conditions under which operations are compatible or in conflict. This language should, on the one hand, have enough expressive power to declare the necessary conditions, typically (in)equalities of arguments or range checks. On the other hand, compatibility tests must be carried out efficiently, so the declarations must not be too complex (i.e. no full-fledged language with recursion etc.) and the conditions must be expressed only on the arguments of the operations. In particular, they must not refer to the current content of the database, as this would require a database access during compatibility check. So we can define:

Definition 5 (Compatibility Declaration). *The general form of a compatibility declaration for two (complex) operations $p(X)$ and $q(Y)$ is*

$$\mathsf{comp}(\,p(X),\,q(Y)\,) \Leftrightarrow condition(X,Y)$$

where condition(X,Y) is a boolean expression using at most the variables that appear as arguments of the predicates p and q.
The set D of all declarations of this form is called the declaration set.

Example 5 (Bank Transfer (Cont.)). Compatibility declarations for the predicates of our banking example are shown here. Note that the first arguments (the amounts of money) are irrelevant for the compatibility behaviour that only depends upon the accounts accessed.

$$
\begin{aligned}
&\mathsf{comp}(\,deposit(A, Ac),\, deposit(A', Ac')\,) && \Leftrightarrow true \\
&\mathsf{comp}(\,withdraw(A, Ac),\, withdraw(A', Ac')\,) && \Leftrightarrow Ac \neq Ac' \\
&\mathsf{comp}(\,deposit(A, Ac),\, withdraw(A', Ac')\,) && \Leftrightarrow Ac \neq Ac' \\
&\mathsf{comp}(\,deposit(A, Ac),\, transfer(A', Ac'_1, Ac'_2)\,) && \Leftrightarrow Ac \neq Ac'_1 \\
&\mathsf{comp}(\,withdraw(A, Ac),\, transfer(A', Ac'_1, Ac'_2)\,) && \Leftrightarrow Ac \neq Ac'_1 \\
&&& \wedge\ Ac \neq Ac'_2 \\
&\mathsf{comp}(\,transfer(A, Ac_1, Ac_2),\, transfer(A', Ac'_1, Ac'_2)\,) && \Leftrightarrow Ac_1 \neq Ac'_1 \\
&&& \wedge\ Ac_1 \neq Ac'_2 \\
&&& \wedge\ Ac_2 \neq Ac'_1
\end{aligned}
$$

Then, to test a pair of operations for compatibility or conflict, the scheduler only has to evaluate the condition given in the declarations about the pair. If the condition evaluates to *true*, the operation pair is compatible. If it is *false*, or there is no appropriate declaration about the pair to be checked, the scheduler must assume a conflict. Note that we allow at most one declaration for every pair of operations. As compatibility is a symmetric relation, a declaration $\mathsf{comp}(\,p(X),\,q(Y)\,)$ implies the corresponding declaration for $\mathsf{comp}(\,q(Y),\,p(X)\,)$.

Definition 6 (Compatibility Test). *Two operations $p(c)$ and $q(c')$ are compatible according to a declaration set D, iff there exists a declaration*

$$\mathsf{comp}(\,p(\boldsymbol{X}),\,q(\boldsymbol{Y})\,) \Leftrightarrow condition(\boldsymbol{X}, \boldsymbol{Y})$$

or

$$\mathsf{comp}(\,q(\boldsymbol{Y}),\,p(\boldsymbol{X})\,) \Leftrightarrow condition(\boldsymbol{X}, \boldsymbol{Y})$$

in D such that $condition(\boldsymbol{c}, \boldsymbol{c}')$ evaluates to true.

Scheduling protocols use the information about compatibility or conflict to ensure that interleaved executions are correct, i.e. serializable. The protocols generate only interleaved executions where the ordering of conflicting operations corresponds to a serial execution – whether this is done using locks, time-stamps, or other techniques does not matter here. However, it should be noted that it is safe to assume a conflict between operations per default:

Proposition 4. *Considering missing declarations as an indication of conflict as done in Definition 6 will not compromise correctness of schedules generated by a scheduling protocol.*
Proof (sketch): *If operations are considered to be in conflict the scheduling protocol only allows interleaved executions that order them according to a serial execution, i.e. some interleaved executions are considered non-serializable by the protocol and thus are not generated. Yet, the protocol still ensures that the generated schedules are serializable. In the worst case, if every pair of operations is considered to be in conflict, the resulting schedules would even be serial. Consequently, assuming a conflict if no information is given will not compromise correctness.*

Obviously, assuming a conflict may reduce the possible amount of concurrency that can be exploited by the protocol. Yet, to ensure correctness this must be tolerated.

However, since *undo* operations must also be handled by the scheduler compatibility declarations are necessary for them as well. As this again increases the number of potential declarations, adequate tool-support to aid the user would be desirable.

5   Conclusion

We presented an operational model for performing transactions specified in the ULTRA language. The model is based on open nested transactions and features exploitation of compatibility information and compensation at levels above the basic operations, which may enhance the performance in complex and distributed information systems. As far as we can see from literature, this is an innovative attempt to bring together logical specification languages and recent results in the field of transaction theory. We assume that the clear semantics of logical languages and the operational aspects of transactions can create a firm basis for a useful transaction programming environment.

Our current work includes the extension of the ideas presented above to the full ULTRA concept [19] (including concurrent conjunction and bulk updates) and their investigation at the theoretical level. In addition, the ULTRA semantics itself is extended to arbitrary basic operations. Although the scheduler and the transaction model already provide the desired flexibility, this requires some non-trivial generalizations at the semantical level of ULTRA. In parallel to the work at the semantics, we investigate how to specify and reason about the meta information which is essential to deal with the extended transaction model. Our objective is to provide tools that assist the user in the composition of the needed declarations.

References

1. C. Beeri, P. Bernstein, and N. Goodman. A Model for Concurrency in Nested Transaction Systems. *Journal of the ACM*, 36(2):230–269, 1989.

2. P. Bernstein, V. Hadzilacos, and N. Goodman. *Concurrency Control and Recovery in Database Systems*. Addison-Wesley, 1987.

3. P. A. Bernstein and E. Newcomer. *Principles of Transaction Processing*. Morgan Kaufmann, 1997.

4. A. J. Bonner and M. Kifer. An Overview of Transaction Logic. *Theoretical Computer Science*, 133(2):205–265, 1994.

5. A. J. Bonner and M. Kifer. Concurrency and Communication in Transaction Logic. In M. J. Maher, editor, *Proc. Joint Int. Conf. and Symp. on Logic Programming (JICSLP '96), Bonn, Germany*, pages 142–156, MIT Press, 1996.

6. W. Chen. Programming with Logical Queries, Bulk Updates, and Hypothetical Reasoning. *IEEE Transactions on Knowledge and Data Engineering*, 9(4):587–599, 1997.

7. C. J. Date. *A Guide to the SQL Standard*. Addison-Wesley, 1997.

8. U. Dayal, A. P. Buchmann, and S. Chakravarthy. The HiPAC Project. In J. Widom and S. Ceri, editors, *Active Database Systems — Triggers and Rules for Advanced Database Processing*, chapter 7, pages 177–206, Morgan Kaufmann, 1996.

9. H. Hasse. *A Unified Theory of Concurrency Control and Recovery of Database Transactions*, Dissertationen zu Datenbanken und Informationssystemen, Vol. 13. infix-Verlag, Sankt Augustin, 1996. (In German).

10. H. F. Korth, E. Levy, and A. Silberschatz. A Formal Approach to Recovery by Compensating Transactions. In V. Kumar and M. Hsu, editors, *Recovery Mechanisms in Database Systems*, chapter 15, pages 444–465, Prentice Hall, 1998.

11. J. W. Lloyd. *Foundations of Logic Programming*. Springer-Verlag, 2 edition, 1987.

12. N. Lynch, M. Merritt, W. Weihl, and A. Fekete. *Atomic Transactions*. Morgan Kaufmann, 1994.

13. D. Montesi, E. Bertino, and M. Martelli. Transactions and Updates in Deductive Databases. *IEEE Transactions on Knowledge and Data Engineering*, 9(5):784–797, 1997.

14. J. E. B. Moss. *Nested Transactions: An Approach to Reliable Distributed Computing*. MIT Press, 1985.

15. R. Vingralek, H. Hasse-Ye, Y. Breitbart, and H. J. Schek. Unifying Concurrency Control and Recovery of Transactions with Semantically Rich Operations. *Theoretical Computer Science*, 190(2):363–396, 1998.
16. G. Weikum and H.-J. Schek. Concepts and Applications of Multi-level Transactions and Open Nested Transactions. In A. K. Elmagarmid, editor, *Database Transaction Models for Advanced Applications*, chapter 13, pages 515–553, Morgan Kaufmann Publishers, 1992.
17. C. A. Wichert, A. Fent, and B. Freitag. How to Execute ULTRA Transactions. In *Proc. 13th Workshop on Logic Programming (WLP '98), October 6–8, 1998, Vienna, Austria*, pages 96–105, 1998. Full version also available as Technical Report MIP-9812, University of Passau, at http://daisy.fmi.uni-passau.de/publications/.
18. C. A. Wichert and B. Freitag. Capturing Database Dynamics by Deferred Updates. In *Proc. of the 1997 Int. Conf. on Logic Programming (ICLP '97). July 8 – 12, 1997, Leuven, Belgium*, pages 226–240, MIT Press, 1997.
19. C. A. Wichert, B. Freitag, and A. Fent. Logical Transactions and Serializability. In B. Freitag, H. Decker, M. Kifer, and A. Voronkov, editors, *Transactions and Change in Logic Databases*, pages 134–165, Lecture Notes in Computer Science, Vol. 1472, Springer-Verlag, 1998. Full version also available as Technical Report MIP-9807, University of Passau, at http://daisy.fmi.uni-passau.de/publications/.

Inheritance in a Deductive Object Database Language with Updates

Elisa Bertino[1], Giovanna Guerrini[2], and Danilo Montesi[1]

[1] Dipartimento di Scienze dell'Informazione
Università di Milano
Via Comelico 39/41, I20135 Milano - Italy
`{bertino,montesi}@dsi.unimi.it`

[2] Dipartimento di Informatica e Scienze dell'Informazione
Università di Genova
Via Dodecaneso 35, I16146 Genova - Italy
`guerrini@disi.unige.it`

Abstract. In this paper we introduce inheritance in deductive object databases and define an operator for hierarchically composing deductive objects with state evolution capabilities. Evolution of such objects models the expected transactional behavior while preserving many important features of deductive databases. Deductive objects can be organized in ISA schemas where each object may inherit or redefine the rules defined in other objects. The resulting inheritance mechanism handles both the deductive and the update/transactional issues. Our framework accommodates several types of inheritance such as overriding, extension, and refinement. Besides presenting the language, this paper defines its semantics and provides a description of the interpreter for the language that has been implemented.

1 Introduction

Deductive and object-oriented databases have been the focus of intense research over the last years. The former extend the mathematical foundations of relational databases towards declarative rule databases. The latter provide the modularity and encapsulation mechanisms lacking in relational databases. It is not surprising that the area of deductive object-oriented databases has been influenced, among the others, from researches in the area of databases, logic programming, artificial intelligence, and software engineering.

In our work we take the database point of view where (deductive) objects have the granularity of logical theories and extensional updates are expressed within the rule language to model methods. Cooperation among objects is supported by message passing, extending the Datalog language, as specified in [5]. The aim of this paper is to extend such an approach to accommodate different types of inheritance among objects. Thus we define a language, called Obj^{inh}-Datalog, that, in addition to the above notions, expresses simple inheritance, overriding, extension, and refinement. The resulting language supports two different cooperation mechanisms among objects: message passing and inheritance.

G. Saake, K. Schwarz, and C. Türker (Eds.): TDD '99, LNCS 1773, pp. 67–90, 2000.

An Obj^{inh}-Datalog database, indeed, consists of a set of objects that, besides cooperating through message exchanges, may also inherit predicate definitions one from another. When an object is defined as a specialization of another object, it must contain all methods of the parent object, but it can change their implementations. For each method it can keep the implementation defined in the parent object, can totally change it, or can slightly modify it, either by extending or by refining it. The language we propose provides those different possibilities on a per-rule rather than on a per-predicate basis, thus achieving a broader set of modeling options and enhancing flexibility.

We remark that our proposal focuses on inheritance mechanisms and on their use to provide a broad spectrum of modeling possibilities and to maximize code reuse. Thus, the language we consider is a very simple deductive object language with updates, from which we leave out all the features that are not relevant to the main stream of our investigation. In particular, the considered language does not support the notion of class, and inheritance relationships are defined among objects, which can thus be seen as prototypes [26]. These objects can be very useful to design methods and to verify their properties. The proposed approach can however be extended to any deductive object language providing the notion of class and inheritance relationships among classes.

The language has a two step semantics. The first step computes the bindings and collects the updates that will be performed in an *all-or-nothing* style in the second step. The resulting semantics models the traditional query-answer process as well as the transactional behavior. The advantage of this semantics is to allow a smooth integration between the declarative rule language and the updates. Indeed, no control is introduced within rules even if updates are defined in rules.

The paper is structured as follows. The language is presented in Section 2 and its semantics is given in Section 3. Section 4 shows how the language is interpreted in the prototype that has been implemented, whereas Section 5 compares our approach with related work. Finally, Section 6 concludes the work.

2   Language

The language we propose supports two fundamentally different cooperation mechanisms among objects: message passing and inheritance. When an object o sends a message m to an object o' it asks o' to solve the goal m, thus the evaluation context is switched to o'. When, by contrast, an object o inherits a method m from an object o', it simply means that the definition of m in o' is employed, but the context of evaluation is maintained to be the initial method receiver, that is, o. Thus, inheritance can be seen as message passing *without changing self.* Indeed, messages that cannot be answered using the receiver message protocol are forwarded to the parent without changing *self*; when the forwarded message is answered by executing a parent method, every subsequent message sent to *self* will be addressed to the receiver of the initial message. Hence, the context of evaluation is maintained to be the initial message receiver. The following example illustrates the difference between the two cooperation mechanisms.

Example 1. Consider an object obj_1 whose state only consists of the fact $k(a)$ without methods, and an object obj_2 whose state only consists of the fact $k(b)$ and whose only method m is defined by the rule $m(X) \leftarrow k(X)$. Consider first message passing. obj_1 may ask obj_2 to evaluate the goal $?m(X)$ (this can be accomplished by specifying in obj_1 a rule $m(X) \leftarrow obj_2 : m(X)$); the result of evaluating $?m(X)$ in obj_1 would be $X = b$ since the evaluation is performed with respect to obj_2 state. Consider now inheritance: if obj_1 inherits method m from obj_2 (this can be specified by stating $obj_1 \prec obj_2$, since method m is not defined in obj_1) the result of evaluating $?m(X)$ in obj_1 would be $X = a$ since the evaluation is performed with respect to obj_1 state. $\diamond$

In the remainder of this section, we first introduce objects and the message passing mechanism, and then we discuss how objects can be combined through inheritance.

2.1   Objects and Cooperation through Message Passing

Each real-world entity is modeled by an object. Each object has an identifier (object identifier, shortly OID) and a state. The state of an object is represented by a set of attributes, characterizing the properties of the object. The state of the object is encapsulated, that is, can only be modified by invoking operations that are associated with the object. An object communicates with other objects through message exchanges. A message may contain a request to retrieve an object attribute or to modify its state. The use of object identifiers as possible predicate arguments allows the state of an object to contain a reference to another object, and thus to express aggregation (part-of) relationships among objects, in that the value of an object attribute may be the identifier of another object.

In a conventional logic program, all facts and rules appearing in the program can be used in a deduction step. By contrast, in an Obj^{inh}-Datalog database, there exist several sets of rules and facts collected in different objects. Therefore, at each step only the facts and rules of a specific object can be used. As a consequence, a goal must be addressed to a specific object, and the refutation is executed by using only facts and rules belonging to that object, until a rule is found containing a labeled atom in its body. When such a labeled atom is found, the refutation process "moves" to the object specified by the OID labeling this atom.

An object is modeled as a set of facts and rules, where the facts represent the attribute values of an object and the rules represent the methods. Methods are used to compute derived attributes or to perform operations that modify the object state. Rules may contain both action atoms and deduction atoms in their bodies. Action atoms represent the basic mechanism supporting object state evolutions. Moreover, rule bodies may contain (deductive) atoms labeled with OIDs. The meaning of a labeled atom is to require the refutation of the atom by using the facts and rules of the object, whose OID labels the atom. Therefore, labeled atoms are the basic mechanism supporting message exchanges among objects. The object to which the message is sent can be fixed at program definition time (in which case the label is a (constant) OID) or can vary depending on the value of some object properties (in which case the label is an object-denoting variable).

The notion of object is formalized by the following definitions. We consider a many-sorted signature $\Sigma = \{\Sigma_o, \Sigma_v\}$, only containing constant symbols. Σ_o is the set of object identifiers, that is, the values used to denote objects, while Σ_v is the set of constant value symbols. The sets Σ_o and Σ_v are disjoint. We moreover consider a set of predicate symbols Π partitioned, as in Datalog, in extensional predicate symbols Π^e, and intensional predicate symbols Π^i. Both Π^e and Π^i are families of predicate symbols $\Pi^{e/i} = \{\Pi_w^{e/i}\}_{w \in S^*}$, where S^* denotes the set of all possible strings of sorts, $S = \{o, v\}$ (object identifiers and values). We denote with Π_w the set of predicate symbols $\Pi_w^e \cup \Pi_w^i$. A family of disjoint sets of variable symbols for each sort $V = \{V_o, V_v\}$ is considered. Terms in $Term = \{Term_o, Term_v\}$ are defined as usual for each sort of our language: a term is either a constant or a variable.

Definition 1. *(Deduction Atom). A deduction atom is defined as the application of a predicate symbol to terms of the appropriate sorts, that is, if $p \in \Pi_w$, $n = length(w)$ and $\forall i, i = 1 \ldots n, t_i \in Term_o$ if $w.i = o$ while $t_i \in Term_v$ if $w.i = v$, then $p(t_1, \ldots, t_n)$ is a deduction atom, also denoted as $p(\tilde{t})$.* □

Deduction atoms are partitioned in extensional deduction atoms, those built on predicates in Π^e, and intensional deduction atoms, those built on predicates in Π^i.

Update operations are expressed in our language (as in U-Datalog [24] and in $\mathcal{LDL}$ [25]), by action atoms in rule bodies.

Definition 2. *(Action Atom). An action atom is an extensional deduction atom prefixed by + (denoting insertion) or − (denoting deletion), that is, if $p(t_1, \ldots, t_n)$ is an extensional deduction atom, then $+p(t_1, \ldots, t_n)$ and $-p(t_1, \ldots, t_n)$ are action atoms.* □

Cooperation among objects in the database is supported in our language by labeled atoms. A labeled atom represents a request of evaluating the deduction atom in the object denoted by the label. Two different kinds of labeled atoms are provided. C-labeled atoms model a fixed cooperation among objects, while V-labeled ones model a cooperation depending on the value to which the variable in the label is bound. Thus, let $p \in \Pi_w, a \in \Sigma_v, obj_4 \in \Sigma_o$ and $O \in V_o$, then $obj_4 : p(a)$ is a c-labeled atom (which represents the atom $p(a)$ in the context of the -fixed- object obj_4), whereas $O : p(a)$ is a v-labeled atom. Given a substitution ϑ, assigning a value to O, $O : p(a)$ represents the atom $p(a)$ in the context of the object $O\vartheta$.

Definition 3. *(C-labeled Atom). Let $obj_h \in \Sigma_o$ be an object identifier and $p(t_1, \ldots, t_n)$ be a deduction atom, then $obj_h : p(t_1, \ldots, t_n)$ is a c-labeled atom.* □

Definition 4. *(V-labeled Atom). Let $X \in V_o$ be a variable denoting an object identifier and $p(t_1, \ldots, t_n)$ be a deduction atom, then $X : p(t_1, \ldots, t_n)$ is a v-labeled atom.* □

Having introduced all kinds of atoms that can be used in our language, we are now able to introduce the notion of rule.

Definition 5. *(Rule). A rule has the form*

$$H \leftarrow U, B, B^c, B^v$$

where:

- *H is an intensional deduction atom;*
- *$U = U_1, \ldots, U_i$ is a vector of action atoms, constituting the update part of the rule;*
- *$B = B_1, \ldots, B_w$ is a vector of deduction atoms, constituting the unlabeled part of the condition, that is, of atoms referring the object where the rule is defined;*
- *$B^c = obj_1 : B'_1, \ldots, obj_z : B'_z$ is a vector of c-labeled atoms, that is, of atoms referring specific objects;*
- *$B^v = X_1 : B''_1, \ldots, X_r : B''_r$ is a vector of v-labeled atoms, that is, atoms not referring specific objects;*
- *$X_1, \ldots, X_r$ must appear as arguments of a deduction atom in $B_1, \ldots, B_w$.*

The update part (U) and the condition part (B, B^c, B^v) cannot be both empty. H is referred to as head of the rule, while U, B, B^c, B^v constitute the body of the rule. For a rule to be safe [9] all the variables in H and all the variables in U^1 must appear in the condition part of the rule (B, B^c, B^v). □

We remark that the "," symbol in the rule bodies denotes logical conjunction, thus the order of atoms is irrelevant.

Example 2. The following is an example of Obj^{inh}-Datalog rule.

$$k(X, Y) \leftarrow -t(Z), +t(N), t(Z), p(X), obj_1 : r(Y, N), X : k(Y) \qquad \diamond$$

An object obj_j, where $obj_j \in \Sigma_o$ is the object identifier, consists of an object state and a set of methods. The object *state* EDB_j is a set of facts, that is, a set of ground extensional deduction atoms. The object state is a time-varying component, thus in the following we denote with EDB^i_j the possible states of object obj_j, i.e. EDB^i_j denotes the i-th state of object obj_j. *Methods* are expressed by rules.

Definition 6. *(Object). An object $obj_j = \langle EDB_j, IDB_j \rangle$ consists of an identifier obj_j in Σ_o, of an extensional component EDB_j, which is a set of ground extensional deduction atoms, called object state, and an intensional component IDB_j, which is a set of rules as in Definition 5, expressing methods.* □

Referring to Definition 5, we notice that action atoms cannot be labeled. Indeed, to ensure encapsulation, the updates can only refer to the object itself. Note that, as quite usual in the database field, we do not encapsulate object attributes with respect to queries. That is, the value of an object attribute can be queried from outside the object. Otherwise, forcing strict encapsulation, a number of trivial methods only returning attribute values should be written to be used in queries.

---

[1] This ensures that only ground updates are applied to the database.

2.2   Inheritance

In this section we describe the capabilities of our language for structuring information through specialization. An Obj^{inh}-Datalog database consists of a set of objects that, besides cooperating through labeled atoms, may also inherit predicate definitions from each other. Whenever an object obj_j specializes another object obj_i, the features of obj_i are inherited by obj_j; obj_j may in turn add more features, or *redefine* some of the inherited features. The redefinition of an inherited feature means that obj_j contains a feature with the same name and different definition of a feature in obj_i. The redefinition is a form of conflict between the two objects. In Obj^{inh}-Datalog, according to the object-oriented paradigm, we solve this type of conflict by giving precedence to the most specific information; therefore, the definition of a feature given in an object always takes the precedence over a definition of the same feature given in any of the objects the given object inherits from. This type of approach is called *overriding*. The specialization relationship among objects impacts not only the object structures, but also the behavior specified by the objects. Given objects obj_i and obj_j, such that obj_j inherits from obj_i, obj_j must contain all the methods of obj_i, but it can change their implementations. For each method, obj_j can keep obj_i implementation, can totally change it, or can slightly modify it. Consider a predicate p defined by one or more rules in obj_i, the following *modeling cases* may arise:

1. *simple inheritance*
   obj_j does not define predicate p; therefore, obj_j inherits p from obj_i;
2. *overriding*
   obj_j redefines predicate p, thus overriding the definition of p provided by obj_i;
3. *extension*
   obj_j extends the definition of p provided by obj_i, so that p in obj_j is defined by a set of clauses which is the union among the clauses for p in obj_i and the clauses for p in obj_j;
4. *refinement*
   obj_j refines the definition of p provided by obj_i; p results therefore to be defined in obj_j by a clause whose body is the conjunction of the bodies of clauses for p in obj_i and in obj_j, with the heads properly unified.

Note that object obj_j may provide additional predicates with respect to obj_i ones by defining predicates which are not defined in obj_i.

The above modeling possibilities offer a broad spectrum of reusing modalities to designers. In addition to single inheritance and overriding, that are usual in the object-oriented context, indeed, we support extension and refinement which offer novel and useful opportunities to refine object behavior. Both correspond to the idea of *behavioral subtyping* [18], which can be achieved in object-oriented programming languages by exploiting *super* calls or the *inner* mechanism. In particular, extension allows to handle additional cases specific to the inheriting object through the addition of clauses, whereas refinement allows to specialize the behavior by adding some conditions or actions. Note that, in some way, extension can be thought as a sort of contravariant behavior suptyping whereas refinement can be thought as a sort of covariant behavior subtyping[2].

The following example motivates the usefulness of the modeling possibilities above.

Example 3. Consider two objects obj_{person} and $obj_{student}$, such that $obj_{student}$ inherits from obj_{person}. The following are examples corresponding to each of the modeling cases above.

1. *Simple inheritance*: The rule defining a method to evaluate the age of a person, given his birth date, is the same for obj_{person} and $obj_{student}$.
2. *Overriding*: The predicate *young* of obj_{person}, returning True if the person is considered young, most likely will be redefined in $obj_{student}$. Indeed, the criteria for determining when a person is young is probably different from the criteria used for student.
3. *Extension*: Consider a predicate *intelligent* of obj_{person}, returning True if the IQ of the person is greater than a given limit. Suppose that $obj_{student}$ contains the score that a student receives on a given test. Moreover, suppose that a student is considered intelligent if either: (i) his IQ is greater than the given limit (the same for obj_{person}); or (ii) his score in the test is greater than a given limit. The predicate *intelligent* in $obj_{student}$ then results in being defined by two different rules.
4. *Refinement*: Consider a predicate that assigns a null value to all the facts in an object. The predicate *null* in $obj_{student}$ will likely refine the predicate *null* defined in obj_{person}, since the former should contain update atoms for all facts added in $obj_{student}$. $\diamond$

We remark that our goal is to support the above modeling possibilities on a per-rule rather than on a per-predicate basis, thus achieving a broader set of modeling options. Indeed, an object may retain a clause of a predicate definition from an object it inherits from, yet hiding or refining other clauses of that predicate definition. To support those modeling possibilities, a mechanism is needed to refer specific rules in an object. *Labeled rules* are then introduced. A labeled rule has the form

$$l_x : head_a \leftarrow BODY_a$$

where $l_x \in \mathcal{L}$ with $\mathcal{L}$ denumerable set of labels. All labels in a given object must be distinct. $\mathcal{L}(obj_i)$ denotes the set of labels in object obj_i.

The meaning of labeled rules can be explained as follows. Consider objects obj_i and obj_j, such that obj_j inherits from obj_i, and suppose that $l_x \in \mathcal{L}(obj_i)$,

---

[2] Note that we do not address the issue of covariant-contravariant method (signature) refinement in the paper, since we do not consider typed variables nor signature definitions for our methods.

$l_y \in \mathcal{L}(obj_j)$; then given the labeled rules

$$l_x : head_a \leftarrow BODY_a \;\; \text{rule of} \;\; obj_i$$
$$l_y : head_b \leftarrow BODY_b \;\; \text{rule of} \;\; obj_j$$

consider the following cases:

- $l_x = l_y$

  Then, rule $head_b \leftarrow BODY_b$ of obj_j *overrides* rule $head_a \leftarrow BODY_a$ of obj_i; the latter is *hidden* in obj_j. It is not possible to hide a predicate without redefining it. Therefore, if $l_x = l_y$, $head_a = head_b$, that is, the heads of the two clauses must be the same. Thus, a rule defining a predicate p in an object obj may only hide a rule defining the same predicate p in the object from which obj inherits.

- $l_x \neq l_y$

  Then, obj_j inherits rule $head_a \leftarrow BODY_a$ from obj_i. Therefore, both the rule $head_a \leftarrow BODY_a$ and the rule $head_b \leftarrow BODY_b$ can be exploited to evaluate a goal in obj_j.

Therefore, by labeling a rule with the label of a rule of the parent object *overriding* (modeling case 2 above) is realized, whereas by using a different label *extension* (modeling case 3 above) is realized.

Example 4. Given the following rules in object obj_i

$$l_1 : p(X) \leftarrow q(X)$$
$$l_2 : k(X) \leftarrow r(X)$$

if object obj_j inherits from obj_i and its IDB contains the rules

$$l_1 : p(X) \leftarrow r(X)$$
$$l_3 : k(X) \leftarrow q(X)$$

then the rule for predicate p is overridden, whereas the definition of predicate k is extended. The resulting set of rules available in obj_j is

$$l_1 : p(X) \leftarrow r(X)$$
$$l_2 : k(X) \leftarrow r(X)$$
$$l_3 : k(X) \leftarrow q(X) \qquad\qquad \diamond$$

Moreover, to express *refinement* (modeling case 4 above), a syntactic mechanism is needed that allows to specify that a rule is a refinement of a rule in the parent object. Rule bodies are thus extended to contain a special kind of atom (which we call *inh-atom*) of the form $l_x : super$. Referring to the objects and rules above, if $BODY_b$ contains the inh-atom $l_x : super$, then obj_j results in containing a single rule of the form

$$(p(\tilde{u}))\vartheta \leftarrow (BODY_a, BODY_b)\vartheta$$

where $\vartheta = mgu(\tilde{t}, \tilde{u})$, where $head_a = p(\tilde{t})$, and $head_b = p(\tilde{u})$[3]. If $head_a$ and $head_b$ cannot be unified, then p is defined in obj_j only by rule $head_b \leftarrow BODY_b$.

---

[3] We impose no condition on rule heads for refinement. That is, we do not require that $head_b$ is at least as instantiated as $head_a$. Note indeed that head refinement is not particularly meaningful in a context like ours where function symbols are not supported.

Example 5. Referring to the rules of object obj_i of Example 4 above, a refinement of the rule labeled by l_2 can be accomplished by an object obj_k, inheriting from obj_i, by the following rule:

$$l_4 : k(X) \leftarrow q(X), l_2 : super$$

In such a way, the resulting rule in obj_k will be

$$l_4 : k(X) \leftarrow q(X), r(X)$$

which is a refinement of the original rule. ◇

Labeled rules thus allow one to represent all modeling cases previously illustrated. Consider objects obj_i and obj_j, such that obj_j inherits from obj_i, and a predicate p defined in obj_i, and let us show how the different options can be realized.

1. *Simple inheritance*: It is sufficient that obj_j does not contain any clause defining p.
2. *Overriding*: For each rule defining p in obj_i, having label l_x, there must exist a rule defining p in obj_j whose label is equal to l_x.
3. *Extension*: All rules defining p in obj_j must have labels different from all the labels associated with the rules defining p in obj_i.
4. *Refinement*: In obj_j all rules defining p must contain the inh-atom $l_x : super$, where l_x is the label associated with the rule defining p in obj_i and whose body must be put in conjunction with the bodies of the rules in obj_j.

Note that through the mechanism above we can refine only some of the rules defining a predicate p, or all the rules defining it, depending on the intended behavior we want to associate with the inheriting object. Note that, moreover, when a rule labeled by l_x is refined in an inheriting object rule through an inh-atom $l_x : super$ in a rule labeled by l_y, it is also inherited by the object. To prevent this inheritance, the object must contain another rule labeled by l_x (for instance, it can simply be $l_y = l_x$).

Finally, we remark that semantically meaningful labels can be exploited to make evident which kind of behavior is being specified for a given rule. For instance, labels of rules introducing new predicates may have a *new* prefix, labels of rules extending an inherited predicate may have an *ext* prefix, and so on.

The following definitions formalize the notion of labeled rule.

Definition 7. *(Inh-Atom). An inh-atom has the form $l_x : super$ with $l_x \in \mathcal{L}$.* □

We remark that *super* is a special 0-ary predicate symbol, which cannot appear in any other kind of atoms of our language.

Definition 8. *(Labeled Rule). A labeled rule is a rule as in Definition 5, labeled by a label $l \in \mathcal{L}$; that is, a labeled rule has the form $l : r$ where r is defined as in Definition 5 extended to contain in its body, in addition to deduction, action, and labeled atoms, inh-atoms as in Definition 7.* □

By using labeled rules we are able to specify what is inherited, what is hidden, and what is refined with the clause granularity, instead of the predicate granularity. Thus, a partial overriding of a predicate is allowed.

An Obj^{inh}-Datalog database consists of a set of objects related by an inheritance hierarchy. The intensional component of each object is a set of labeled rules. Extensional facts, by contrast, are not labeled, so that only simple inheritance and overriding are supported on facts.

Definition 9. *(Database). An Obj^{inh}-Datalog database is a pair*
$$O\text{-}DB = \langle \{obj_1, obj_2, \ldots, obj_s\}, \prec \rangle$$
where:

- *$\{obj_1, obj_2, \ldots, obj_s\}$ is a set of objects according to Definition 6 such that the intensional component IDB_j of each obj_j, $1 \le j \le s$, is a set of labeled rules, as in Definition 8, whose labels are all distinct;*
- *$\prec \subseteq \Sigma_o \times \Sigma_o$ is a relation on objects representing the inheritance hierarchy. Since we consider only single inheritance, the inheritance relationship $\prec$ is a tree, that is, if objects obj_i, obj_j, obj_k $(1 \le i, j, k \le s)$ exist such that $obj_j \prec obj_i$ and $obj_j \prec obj_k$, then either $obj_i \prec obj_k$ or $obj_k \prec obj_i$.* □

Given $obj_i, obj_j \in \Sigma_o$, $obj_j \prec obj_i$ denotes that object obj_j inherits from object obj_i. Moreover, $\preceq$ denotes the partial order obtained from the non-reflexive relation $\prec$, that is, $obj_j \preceq obj_i$ denotes the relation $obj_j \prec obj_i \vee obj_i = obj_j$.

Note that we restrict ourself to single inheritance, to avoid name conflicts that will introduce unnecessary complications in the definition of the language, without bringing in any relevant issue with respect to the main focus of the paper. The approach can however be extended to multiple inheritance, by adopting one of the existing approaches to handle name conflicts, such as superclass ordering or explicit qualification.

Example 6. $\langle \{obj_1, obj_2, obj_3\}, \prec \rangle$ is an example of Obj^{inh}-Datalog database, with $obj_3 \prec obj_1$ and

$$
\begin{aligned}
EDB_1 \;=\; & q(a) \quad r(b) \quad s(obj_2) \\
IDB_1 \;=\; & l_1 : p(X) \leftarrow -q(X), q(X) \\
& l_2 : k(X, Y) \leftarrow s(X), r(Y), X : h(Y) \\
& l_3 : t(X) \leftarrow r(X) \\
& l_5 : mr(X) \leftarrow -r(X), r(X)
\end{aligned}
$$

$$
\begin{aligned}
EDB_2 \;=\; & h(b)
\end{aligned}
$$

$$
\begin{aligned}
EDB_3 \;=\; & f(b) \quad q(b) \\
IDB_3 \;=\; & l_1 : p(X) \leftarrow -q(X), f(X) \\
& l_4 : t(X) \leftarrow f(X) \\
& l_6 : mf(X) \leftarrow -f(X), f(X) \\
& l_2 : k(X, Y) \leftarrow l_2 : super, f(Y)
\end{aligned}
$$

Referring to the inheritance relationship between obj_1 and obj_3, we point out that predicate p is overridden, predicate k is refined, predicate t is extended, predicate mr is simply inherited, while predicate mf is an additional one. For what concerns the extensional component, obj_3 simply inherits facts $r(b)$ and $s(obj_2)$ from obj_1, whereas it overrides fact $q(a)$ by providing a local definition for predicate q (that is, fact $q(b)$). ◇

Note that our inheritance mechanisms based on rule labeling offer a number of alternatives with respect to redefinition of predicates (e.g. partial overriding, rule addition, rule refinement). Such alternatives could not be supported at the rule level if labeled rules were not provided. Our mechanism obviously requires that rule labels are visible in subclasses, thus requiring that predicate definitions not be encapsulated with respect to subclasses. However, note that some solutions can be devised to the problem of encapsulation. Our language could easily be extended to support both labeled and un-labeled rules, with a traditional overriding model on a per-predicate basis for some predicates. In such a way, when defining a class, the user can decide whether to encapsulate a predicate definition with respect to subclasses (by not labeling the rules defining it) or to let its definition be visible to subclasses, in which different choices can be adopted for inherited rules.

We also point out that overriding of extensional facts is supported in our model. However, since extensional facts are not labeled, on the extensional side overriding works on a per-predicate basis. This means that is not possible to inherit a fact on a predicate and to override another fact on the same predicate. We took this decision since requiring fact labeling seems an unnecessary burden for the user, given that the sophisticated mechanisms provided for rules (useful for code reuse) does not seem very useful at the data level.

We finally remark that we do not consider here the issue of dynamically creating and deleting objects from the database, which thus consists of a fixed set of cooperating objects. This possibility can obviously be added to the language, but the deletion of objects from which other objects inherit must be handled carefully (as in all prototype-based languages).

2.3 Queries

An important requirement of our language is to model both queries typical of deductive databases, as well as queries typical of object-oriented databases. In deductive databases, a query (goal) has usually the form $?p_1(\tilde{t}_1), \ldots, p_n(\tilde{t}_n)$ ($n \geq 1$) where each $p_i(\tilde{t}_i)$ ($1 \leq i \leq n$) is a deductive atom. The meaning of such query is to find all substitutions for the variables in the query so that the conjunction of predicates $p_1(\tilde{t}_1), \ldots, p_n(\tilde{t}_n)$ has the truth value True. On the other hand, in object-oriented databases, queries are usually addressed to a specific object, in form of messages. To support all above querying modalities, two different types of queries are defined:

1. *Conjunction of deduction atoms*: The meaning of this type of query is to find all solutions satisfying the query, independently from the objects where the deduction atoms, appearing in the query, are defined.

2. *Conjunction of object-labeled deduction atoms*: The meaning of this type of query is to find all solutions satisfying the query starting from the objects whose OIDs appear in the query. Note, however, that an object may need to send messages to other objects in order to answer the query.

Note that, whenever a query of the first type is issued, the objects on which the query applies may not be related by inheritance relationships. We refer to Obj^{inh}-Datalog queries as *transactions* to emphasize that, since update methods can be invoked, they do not only return sets of bindings but they can also modify the database state. However, updates are not defined in the query but only in the object methods (expressed by rules).

Definition 10. *(Transaction). A transaction has the form*

$$? \, B, B^c$$

where

- $B = B_1, \ldots, B_w$ *is a vector of deduction atoms, that is, they refer to any object of the object database,*
- $B^c = obj_1 : B'_1, \ldots, obj_z : B'_z$ *is a vector of c-labeled atoms, that is, they refer to specific objects,*

and B and B^c cannot be both empty.   □

Note that no updates are explicitly stated in the transaction because each object uses its own methods (rules) to manipulate the object state.

Example 7. Examples of transactions are $T_1 = obj_3 : k(X, Y), obj_1 : t(Y)$ and $T_2 = p(X)$.   ◇

3   Semantics

The semantics of Obj^{inh}-Datalog language is given in two steps. The first step is called *marking phase* and the second one *update phase*. The first step is similar to the query-answer since it computes the bindings for the query and collects the updates. Updates are not executed in this phase. They are executed, if there are not complementary updates, in the second phase altogether, modeling the expected transactional behavior.

3.1   Marking Phase Semantics

In this section we model the behavior of a transaction execution. We formalize the rules for evaluating a call taking into account the different options for behavior inheritance we support.

A transaction may contain two kinds of atoms: labeled and unlabeled ones. The labeled atoms must be refuted in the object whose identifier labels the atom, while for unlabeled atoms a refutation is searched for in any object in the object database.

The behavior of a predicate call in an object depends on the labels of the rules defining the predicate in that object as well as on the inheritance hierarchy. In case of overriding, the notion of *most specific behavior* is applied, that is, each object inherits a predicate from the closest ancestor in the hierarchy that contains a definition for that predicate. By contrast, in the case of extension, an object may inherit the union of the definition of a predicate in all its ancestors in the hierarchy. In case of refinement, finally, the rule obtained by combining the rule in the most specific object with the referred rules in its ancestors is exploited.

The combination of those mechanisms results in the following rule for evaluating a call. Consider a transaction $T = p(\tilde{t})$ to be evaluated in an object obj_i belonging to a database $\langle\{obj_1, \ldots, obj_s\}, \prec\rangle$. The evaluation of T proceeds according to the criteria outlined below:

1. if $p \in \Pi^e$ is an extensional atom:
   a) if p is locally defined in obj_i, then the definition in obj_i is used;
   b) the definition in the closest ancestor of obj_i that defines p is used, otherwise;
2. if $p \in \Pi^i$ is an intensional atom:
   a) if p is locally defined in obj_i, then the definition in obj_i is used; moreover, if p is also defined in an ancestor obj_j of obj_i, and the labels of the rules for p in obj_i and in obj_j are different, then the p definition of obj_j is used as well;
   b) if p is not locally defined in obj_i, then the definition in the closest ancestor of obj_i that defines p is used;
   c) if p is locally defined in obj_i (or defined in an ancestor obj_j of obj_i, and not overridden), and its definition is a refinement (that is, is a rule containing inh-atoms), then the refined definition for p is used.

Labeled atoms are evaluated by simply changing the evaluation context to the object denoted by the label. Action atoms are evaluated by simply adding the action to the appropriate update set.

The operational semantics of Obj^{inh}-Datalog is given below. For any database $O\text{-}DB = \langle\{obj_1, \ldots, obj_s\}, \prec\rangle$ and transaction T, we denote by $O\text{-}DB \vdash_{\vartheta,S} T$ the fact that there is a derivation sequence of T in $O\text{-}DB$ with answer ϑ and collecting a tuple of update sets S. We reserve the symbol ϵ to denote the empty (identity) answer, whereas $\vartheta\vartheta'$ denotes the composition of substitutions ϑ and ϑ'. Moreover, let S and S' be s-tuples of update sets, $S \cup S'$ denotes the componentwise union of update sets, that is, $(S \cup S') \downarrow i = S \downarrow i \cup S' \downarrow i$, for all i, $1 \leq i \leq s$. A set of updates $\{u_1, \ldots, u_n\}$ is consistent if it does not contain complementary updates (i.e. $+p(a)$ and $-p(a)$). A tuple of update sets S is consistent if all its component update sets are consistent, that is, if for all i, $1 \leq i \leq s$, in $S \downarrow i$ there are no complementary updates.

The derivation relation is defined by rules of the form

$$\frac{Assumptions}{Conclusion} Conditions$$

asserting the *Conclusion* whenever the *Assumptions* and *Conditions* hold. *O-DB* $\vdash_{\vartheta,S} T$ is a finite successful derivation of T in *O-DB* that computes ϑ and collects S. A successful derivation is computed as a sequence of derivation steps. Each derivation step is performed according to the rules in Fig. 1.

The index i denotes the current context, that is, the object of the database in which the computation is being carried on. It is not present in the first rule, and in the *Conclusion* of rules 2 and 3, modeling the fact that a query is issued against the whole database, and the selection of the evaluation context depends on the query.

Rule 1 models the semantics of queries, which are conjunctions of two subqueries, in terms of the semantics of the subqueries. Rules 2 and 3 model queries which are deduction atoms and object-labeled deduction atoms, respectively, according to the meaning introduced in Section 2.3. For object-labeled deduction atoms in queries the evaluation context is set to the object labeling the atom (Rule 3), while for unlabeled deduction atoms a refutation is looked for in any object of the database (Rule 2). Rule 4 models the semantics of action atoms (the atom is simply added/removed to the set of updates related to the current object). Rule 5 handles the empty conjunction, that is, an empty rule body. Rules 6 and 7 handle c-labeled atoms and v-labeled atoms, respectively, modeling the change of evaluation context. Rule 8 handles extensional atoms: conditions (a) and (b) are related to the two possibilities for evaluating extensional atoms in presence of inheritance hierarchies: the fact is locally defined in the current object or it is simply inherited from a most specific ancestor of its. Rule 9 handles intensional atoms:

- Condition (a) refers to the case of a predicate which is defined locally to the current object (either a new predicate definition, or overriding) and to the case of predicate extension; it states that all the local rules and each rule for predicate p in ancestors of object obj_i whose label does not appear in a more specific ancestor of obj_i, or in obj_i itself, can be used in the refutation.
- Condition (b) handles simple inheritance, that is, it considers the case in which the current object does not provide a definition for the predicate in the goal. In this case, the definition for that predicate in the most specific ancestor obj_j of the current object is employed.
- Condition (c) models refinement. It considers a rule which is applicable for refutation (as the ones in the cases above) and solves the inh-atoms in it. This means looking for the rule labeled by l_y (where l_y is the label of the inh-atom $l_y : super$) in the most specific object obj_k from which the object obj_j (containing the rule we are solving) inherits, and then substituting the inh-atom with the body T''' of that rule, properly instantiated.

Finally, Rule 10, which is similar to Rule 1, handles conjunctions in rule bodies.

The operational semantics of an Obj^{inh}-Datalog database *O-DB* is defined as the set of ground atoms, for which an Obj^{inh}-Datalog *proof* exists. These ground atoms are constrained by the set of ground updates their deduction collects, that is, $S\vartheta$. The semantics of an Obj^{inh}-Datalog database consists of atoms of the form $H \leftarrow \bar{U}$, where H is a ground atom (either intensional or extensional) and

$$(1) \quad \frac{\langle\{obj_1,\ldots,obj_s\},\prec\rangle \vdash_{\vartheta,S} T_1 \qquad \langle\{obj_1,\ldots,obj_s\},\prec\rangle \vdash_{\vartheta',S'} T_2\vartheta}{\langle\{obj_1,\ldots,obj_s\},\prec\rangle \vdash_{\vartheta\vartheta',S\cup S'} T_1,T_2} \quad CONS$$

$$(2) \quad \frac{i,\langle\{obj_1,\ldots,obj_s\},\prec\rangle \vdash_{\vartheta,S} p(\tilde{t})}{\langle\{obj_1,\ldots,obj_s\},\prec\rangle \vdash_{\vartheta,S} p(\tilde{t})} \quad 1 \leq i \leq s$$

$$(3) \quad \frac{i,\langle\{obj_1,\ldots,obj_s\},\prec\rangle \vdash_{\vartheta,S} p(\tilde{t})}{\langle\{obj_1,\ldots,obj_s\},\prec\rangle \vdash_{\vartheta,S} obj_i : p(\tilde{t})}$$

$$(4) \quad \frac{}{i,\langle\{obj_1,\ldots,obj_s\},\prec\rangle \vdash_{\epsilon,S} \oplus p(\tilde{t})} \quad S \downarrow i = \{\oplus p(\tilde{t})\}, \ S \downarrow k = \emptyset, \forall k = 1\ldots s, k \neq i$$

$$(5) \quad \frac{}{i,\langle\{obj_1,\ldots,obj_s\},\prec\rangle \vdash_{\epsilon,\emptyset} \square}$$

$$(6) \quad \frac{j,\langle\{obj_1,\ldots,obj_s\},\prec\rangle \vdash_{\vartheta,S} p(\tilde{t})}{i,\langle\{obj_1,\ldots,obj_s\},\prec\rangle \vdash_{\vartheta,S} obj_j : p(\tilde{t})}$$

$$(7) \quad \frac{i,\langle\{obj_1,\ldots,obj_s\},\prec\rangle \vdash_{\vartheta,S} T \qquad j,\langle\{obj_1,\ldots,obj_s\},\prec\rangle \vdash_{\vartheta',S'} p(\tilde{t})\vartheta}{i,\langle\{obj_1,\ldots,obj_s\},\prec\rangle \vdash_{\vartheta\vartheta',S\cup S'} T,X : p(\tilde{t})} \quad COND_7$$

$$(8) \quad \frac{}{i,\langle\{obj_1,\ldots,obj_s\},\prec\rangle \vdash_{\vartheta,\emptyset} p(\tilde{t})} \quad p \in \Pi^e$$

if one of the following conditions holds:
(a) $p(\tilde{s}) \in obj_i$, $mgu(\tilde{s},\tilde{t}) = \vartheta$;
(b) $p(\tilde{s}) \in obj_j$, $i \neq j$, $mgu(\tilde{s},\tilde{t}) = \vartheta$, $obj_i \preceq obj_j$ and $\forall obj_k$ such that $obj_i \preceq obj_k \prec obj_j \nexists$ in obj_k an extensional fact which unifies with $p(\tilde{t})$.

$$(9) \quad \frac{i,\langle\{obj_1,\ldots,obj_s\},\prec\rangle \vdash_{\sigma,S} T\vartheta}{i,\langle\{obj_1,\ldots,obj_s\},\prec\rangle \vdash_{\sigma\vartheta,S} p(\tilde{t})} \quad p \in \Pi^i$$

if one of the following conditions holds:
(a) $l_x : p(\tilde{s}) \leftarrow T \in obj_j$, $mgu(\tilde{s},\tilde{t}) = \vartheta$, $obj_i \preceq obj_j$, T does not contain inh-atoms, and $\forall obj_k$ such that $obj_i \preceq obj_k \prec obj_j$ and $l_y : p(\tilde{u}) \leftarrow T' \in obj_k$, $l_x \neq l_y$;
(b) $l_x : p(\tilde{s}) \leftarrow T \in obj_j$, $i \neq j$, $mgu(\tilde{s},\tilde{t}) = \vartheta$, T does not contain inh-atoms, $obj_i \preceq obj_j$ and $\forall obj_k$ such that $obj_i \preceq obj_k \prec obj_j \nexists r$ in obj_k whose head unifies with $p(\tilde{t})$;
(c) $l_x : p(\tilde{s}) \leftarrow T' \in obj_j$, $l_y : super \in T'$, $T' \setminus l_y : super = T''$, $l_y : p(\tilde{u}) \leftarrow T''' \in obj_k$, $(\forall obj_p$ such that $obj_i \preceq obj_p \prec obj_j$ and $l_y : p(\tilde{w}) \leftarrow T' \in obj_p$, $l_x \neq l_y)$, $obj_j \prec obj_k$ and not exists obj_h such that $obj_j \prec obj_h$ and $obj_h \prec obj_k$, and $mgu(\tilde{s},\tilde{u}) = \vartheta^*$, $mgu(\tilde{s}\vartheta^*,\tilde{t}) = \vartheta$, $T = T''\vartheta^*,T'''\vartheta^*$.

$$(10) \quad \frac{i,\langle\{obj_1,\ldots,obj_s\},\prec\rangle \vdash_{\vartheta,S} A_1 \qquad i,\langle\{obj_1,\ldots,obj_s\},\prec\rangle \vdash_{\vartheta',S'} A_2\vartheta}{i,\langle\{obj_1,\ldots,obj_s\},\prec\rangle \vdash_{\vartheta\vartheta',S\cup S'} A_1,A_2} \quad CONS$$

With: $\oplus \in \{+,-\}$, $CONS$ is $S\vartheta\vartheta' \cup S'\vartheta\vartheta'$ consistent, $COND_7$ is $obj_j = X\vartheta \wedge CONS$.

Fig. 1. Rules defining the derivation relation

$\bar{U}$ are updates. The presence of the atom $H \leftarrow \bar{U}$ in the semantics means that H is true and that its evaluation causes the execution of the updates $\bar{U}$.

Definition 11. *(Operational Semantics). The operational semantics of an Obj^{inh}-Datalog database O-DB is defined as the set*

$$\mathcal{O}(O\text{-}DB) = \{A \leftarrow \bar{U} \mid O\text{-}DB \vdash_{\vartheta,S} T, A = T\vartheta, \bar{U} = \bar{U}_1 \cup \ldots \cup \bar{U}_s,$$
$$\text{each } \bar{U}_i, \ 1 \le i \le s, \text{ is the conjunction of } obj_i : u_{i_j}\vartheta,$$
$$\text{for } u_{i_j} \in S \downarrow i\}$$

$\square$

Example 8. Referring to the Obj^{inh}-Datalog database $O\text{-}DB$ of Example 6 and to transactions T_1 and T_2 of Example 7, the following holds:

- $O\text{-}DB \vdash_{\vartheta_1,\emptyset} T_1$ with $\vartheta_1 = \{X/obj_2, Y/b\}$;
- $O\text{-}DB \vdash_{\vartheta_2,S_2} T_2$ with $\vartheta_2 = \{X/a\}$, $S_2 = \langle\{-q(X)\}, \emptyset, \emptyset\rangle$
  and
  $O\text{-}DB \vdash_{\vartheta_2',S_2'} T_2$ with $\vartheta_2' = \{X/b\}$, $S_2 = \langle\emptyset, \emptyset, \{-q(X)\}\rangle$.

The Obj^{inh}-Datalog proofs for those transactions are shown in Fig. 2 and Fig. 3, respectively. $\diamond$

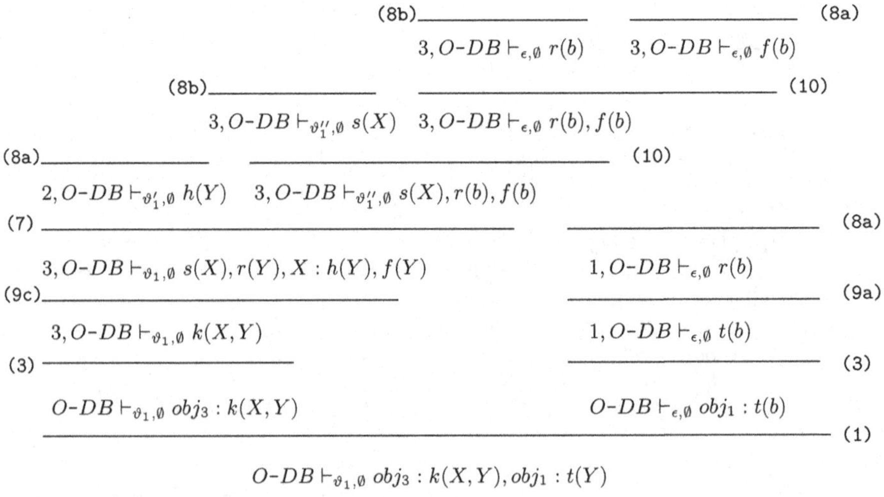

$$\vartheta_1' = \{Y/b\} \quad \vartheta_1'' = \{X/obj_2\} \quad \vartheta_1 = \vartheta_1'\vartheta_1'' = \{Y/b, X/obj_2\}$$

Fig. 2. Obj^{inh}-Datalog proof for transaction T_1 of Example 7

$$(4) \; \frac{}{1, O\text{-}DB \vdash_{\epsilon, S_2} -q(X)} \qquad\qquad \frac{}{1, O\text{-}DB \vdash_{\vartheta_2, \emptyset} q(X)} \; (8a)$$

$$\frac{}{1, O\text{-}DB \vdash_{\vartheta_2, S_2} -q(X), q(X)} \; (10)$$

$$\frac{}{1, O\text{-}DB \vdash_{\vartheta_2, S_2} p(X)} \; (9a)$$

$$\frac{}{O\text{-}DB \vdash_{\vartheta_2, S_2} p(X)} \; (2)$$

$$(4) \; \frac{}{3, O\text{-}DB \vdash_{\epsilon, S_2'} -q(X)} \qquad\qquad \frac{}{3, O\text{-}DB \vdash_{\vartheta_2', \emptyset} f(X)} \; (8a)$$

$$\frac{}{3, O\text{-}DB \vdash_{\vartheta_2', S_2'} -q(X), f(X)} \; (10)$$

$$\frac{}{3, O\text{-}DB \vdash_{\vartheta_2', S_2'} p(X)} \; (9a)$$

$$\frac{}{O\text{-}DB \vdash_{\vartheta_2', S_2'} p(X)} \; (2)$$

$$\vartheta_2 = \{X/a\} \quad S_2 = \langle \{-q(X)\}, \emptyset, \emptyset \rangle \quad \vartheta_2' = \{X/b\} \quad S_2' = \langle \emptyset, \emptyset, \{-q(X)\} \rangle$$

Fig. 3. Obj^{inh}-Datalog proof for transaction T_2 of Example 7

3.2 Update Phase Semantics

As we have said, in the marking phase updates are collected and their consistency is checked but they are not executed. The most common approach to introduce updates in declarative rules is that updates (very often defined in rules bodies) are executed as soon as they are evaluated [20]. Under this assumption the evaluation of a rule is performed in a sequence of states and thus the declarativeness of the query part is lost. Under the marking and update phases, the first phase is declarative and preserve this property for the query part while accommodating update specification that are executed altogether in the update phase. This allows one to express within this semantics the transactional behavior where all or none of the updates must be executed. At logical level, this semantics avoids to undo updates that form a transaction. Indeed, updates collected with the marking phase must be executed in the update phase and it is not possible that some of them will be undone due to the checking in former phase. Let us now see the update phase semantics.

First of all we define the semantics of a query T with respect to an Obj^{inh}-Datalog database $O\text{-}DB$. First we note that database systems use a default set-oriented semantics, that is, the query-answering process computes a set of answers. We denote with $Set(T, O-DB)$ the set of pairs (bindings and updates) computed as answers to the transaction T.

$$Set(T, O\text{-}DB) = \{\langle \vartheta, \hat{u} \rangle \mid O\text{-}DB \vdash_{\vartheta,S} T, \hat{u} = S\vartheta\}$$

We now define a function which takes a set of ground updates, the current extensional components of the objects constituting the database and returns the new extensional components.

Definition 12. *Let $EDB_1^{i_1}, \ldots, EDB_s^{i_s}$ be the current extensional components of the objects constituting the database and $u_1, \ldots, u_s$ be a s-tuple of consistent sets of ground updates. Then the new databases $EDB_1^{i_1+1}, \ldots, EDB_s^{i_s+1}$ are computed by means of the function $\Delta : \mathcal{EC} \times \mathcal{U} \to \mathcal{EC}$ as follows:*

$$\Delta(\langle EDB_1^{i_1}, \ldots, EDB_s^{i_s} \rangle, \langle u_1, \ldots, u_s \rangle) = \langle EDB_1^{i_1+1}, \ldots, EDB_s^{i_s+1} \rangle$$

where each $EDB_j^{i_j+1}$, with $j = 1 \ldots s$, is computed from $EDB_j^{i_j}$ and u_j as

$$(EDB_j^{i_j} \setminus \{p(\tilde{t}) \mid -p(\tilde{t}) \in u_j\}) \cup \{p(\tilde{t}') \mid +p(\tilde{t}') \in u_j\}$$

where $\mathcal{EC}$ denotes all possible s-tuples of extensional components (i.e. of sets of facts) and $\mathcal{U}$ denotes all possible s-tuples of updates sets. □

The update phase semantics models as observable property of a transaction the *set of answers*, the *object states* and *the result of the transaction* itself. It is called $Oss = \langle Ans, State, Res \rangle$ where Ans is the set of answers, $State$ is an s-uple constituted by the extensional components of objects in the database and Res is the transactional result, that is, either Commit or Abort. The set of possible observables Oss is OSS.

Definition 13. *Let $O\text{-}DB^{i}$[4] be an Obj^{inh}-Datalog database, with EDB^i the tuple of current object states and $O - IDB$ the tuple of method sets of objects. The semantics of a transaction is denoted by function $\mathcal{S}_{O-IDB}(T) : \mathcal{EC} \to OSS$.*

$$\mathcal{S}_{O-IDB}(T)(EDB^i) = \begin{cases} Oss^{i+1} & \text{if } OK \\ \langle \emptyset, EDB^i, Abort \rangle & otherwise(inconsistency) \end{cases}$$

where $Oss^{i+1} = \langle \{\vartheta_j \mid \langle \vartheta_j, \hat{u}_j \rangle \in Set(T, O\text{-}DB_i)\}, EDB^{i+1}, Commit \rangle$, EDB^{i+1} is computed by means of $\Delta(EDB^i, \bar{u})$. The condition OK expresses the fact that all the components of the tuple of sets $\bar{u} = \bigcup_j \hat{u}_j$ are consistent, that is, there are no complementary ground updates on the same object. □

Note that, according to the above definition, in Obj^{inh}-Datalog the abort of a transaction may be caused by a transaction that generates an update set with complementary updates on the same atom in the same object (both the insertion and the deletion of the atom). In this case the resulting object state would depend on the execution order of updates, so we disallow this situation by aborting the transaction. In such a way we ensure that the defined semantics is deterministic.

---

[4] Here we denote with $O\text{-}DB^i$ the Obj^{inh}-Datalog database to emphasize that we consider object states EDB^i at time i.

Example 9. Referring to the object database of Example 6, and to transaction T_2 of Example 7, whose answers have been computed in Example 8

$$\Delta(\langle EDB_1, EDB_2, EDB_3\rangle, \langle\{-q(a)\}, \emptyset, \{-q(b)\}\rangle) = \langle EDB'_1, EDB_2, EDB'_3\rangle$$

with

- $EDB'_1 = \{r(b), s(obj_2)\}$ and
- $EDB'_3 = \{f(b)\}$.

Moreover,

$$\mathcal{S}_{IDB}(EDB, T_2), \langle\{\{X/a\}, \{X/b\}\}, EDB', Commit\rangle. \qquad \diamond$$

Note that the update phase semantics specified in [24] for U-Datalog handles transactions composed from atomic transactions, as the ones we support, through the sequence ("$;$") operator. That semantics can trivially be extended to Obj^{inh}-Datalog, by taking into account that tuples of object states and tuples of update sets must be considered rather than a single database state and a single update set.

4 Obj^{inh}-Datalog Interpreter

A prototype implementation of the Obj^{inh}- Datalog language has been developed at the University of Genova, using KBMS1, a knowledge base management system developed in HP laboratories at Bristol [21]. The language of KBMS1, kbProlog, is an extension of Prolog with modularization facilities, declarative update operations and persistence support. The implementation of the language has been realized in two steps: (*i*) development of a translator from Obj^{inh}-Datalog to U-Datalog; (*ii*) development of a bottom-up interpreter for U-Datalog. The bottom-up interpreter for U-Datalog handles updates with a non-immediate semantics and provides the transactional behavior. The use of a bottom-up evaluation strategy ensures termination. The choice of implementing Obj^{inh}-Datalog via a translation in U-Datalog is due to the fact that the definition and implementation of Obj^{inh}-Datalog is part of a project which aims at developing an enhanced database language, equipped with an efficient implementation. Several optimization techniques for U-Datalog have been developed [4] that will lead to an optimized U-Datalog interpreter and therefore to an optimized Obj^{inh}-Datalog interpreter.

An alternative implementation might realize a "direct" interpreter for Obj^{inh}-Datalog, adapting one of the several evaluation techniques developed for deductive databases to object deductive databases (so taking into account message passing, object state evolution and method inheritance). This is a possible issue for future investigation. Our prototype is based on the following steps: (*i*) an Obj^{inh}-Datalog program OP is translated into an Obj-U-Datalog [5] program OP', that is, inheritance relationships are eliminated and each object is extended so that it explicitly contains its structural and behavioral information (thus, flattening the inheritance hierarchy); (ii) the Obj-U-Datalog program OP' is translated into a U-Datalog program UP; (iii) each Obj^{inh}-Datalog query OQ is first of all translated in a U-Datalog query UQ, and then executed against the program UP using the U-Datalog interpreter. In what follows, we describe each step.

Step 1: Flattening the inheritance hierarchy This step makes explicit the set of facts and rules available for refutation in each object of the object database. Consider an object obj_j whose direct parent object is object obj_i.

- EDB_j^f is obtained from EDB_j as follows

$$EDB_j^f = EDB_j \cup \{ \, p(\tilde{c}) \mid p \in \Pi^e, \tilde{c} \text{ tuple of constants in } \Sigma, \ p(\tilde{c}) \in EDB_i^f,$$
$$EDB_j \text{ does not contain any fact on predicate } p\}$$

- IDB_j^f is obtained from IDB_j as follows
    - IDB_j^f contains all the rules of IDB_j, whose bodies are modified by solving the inh-atoms in rule bodies;
    an inh-atom $l_x : super$ is solved by replacing it with the body of the rule labeled by l_x in the parent object obj_i, after having properly unified the rule heads and applied the obtained mgu to the rule body[5];
    - IDB_j^f contains all rules of IDB_i^f whose labels do not appear in $\mathcal{L}(obj_j)$.

The flattening process described above is recursively applied starting from the objects roots of the inheritance hierarchy (that is, the objects obj_j such that $\not\exists \ obj_i \ obj_j \prec obj_i$), and visiting the inheritance tree in a top-down style till the leaves of the tree are reached.

At the end of the flattening process, the Obj^{inh}-Datalog rules are transformed in Obj-U-Datalog rules by omitting the rule labels.

Step 2: Translation of facts and rules The translation from Obj-U-Datalog to U-Datalog is simple. For each object $obj_i \in O\text{-}DB$, for each predicate p of arity n defined in obj_i we have a corresponding predicate p of arity $n+1$ defined in U-Datalog DB. The argument added to each predicate refers to the object in which the predicate is defined. The extensional component of an object obj_i, i.e. EDB_i, is translated as follows. For each fact in EDB_i, $p(\tilde{a})$, with $\tilde{a}$ tuple of constants, we have a fact $p(obj_i, \tilde{a})$ in DB. The extensional database of the U-Datalog program consists of the union of the translation of the extensional components of each object.

The intensional rules are translated as follows. Consider the rule, defined in object obj_i,

$$p(\tilde{X}) \leftarrow B_1(\tilde{Y}_1), \dots, B_k(\tilde{Y}_k), obj_1 : B_{k+1}(\tilde{Y}_{k+1}), \dots, obj_n : B_{k+n}(\tilde{Y}_{k+n}),$$
$$X_1 : B_{k+n+1}(\tilde{Y}_{k+n+1}), \dots, X_p : B_{k+n+p}(\tilde{Y}_{k+n+p}).$$

---

[5] If the rule heads cannot be unified, the inh-atom is simply removed from the IDB_j^f rule body.

This rule is translated in the following U-Datalog rule:

$$p(obj_i, \tilde{X}) \leftarrow B_1(obj_i, \tilde{Y}_1), \ldots, B_k(obj_i, \tilde{Y}_k), B_{k+1}(obj_1, \tilde{Y}_{k+1}), \ldots,$$
$$B_{k+n}(obj_n, \tilde{Y}_{k+n}), B_{k+n+1}(X_1, \tilde{Y}_{k+n+1}), \ldots, B_{k+n+p}(X_p, \tilde{Y}_{k+n+p}).$$

The intensional database of the U-Datalog program consists of the union of the translations of all the rules of the intensional component of each object.

Step 3: Translation of transactions A transaction is translated in the conjunction of the translation of (eventually labeled) atoms that constitute it. A labeled atom $obj_i : p(\tilde{X})$ is translated in a U-Datalog atom $p(obj_i, \tilde{X})$. An unlabeled atom $p(\tilde{X})$ in a transaction, that -as we have seen- is interpreted as a transaction directed to the whole database, is translated in $p(O, \tilde{X})$, where O is a new variable. Note that in this way we obtain in the solution not only the instances of $p(\tilde{X})$ satisfied by the database, but also the objects in which such instances were found.

Example 10. The U-Datalog program resulting from the translation of the object database of Example 6 is the following.

$$EDB \;=\; \begin{array}{llll} q(obj_1, a) & r(obj_1, b) & s(obj_1, obj_2) & h(obj_2, b) \\ f(obj_3, b) & q(obj_3 b) & r(obj_3, b) & s(obj_3, obj_2) \end{array}$$

$$IDB \;=\; \begin{array}{l} p(obj_1, X) \leftarrow -q(obj_1, X), q(obj_1, X) \\ k(obj_1, X, Y) \leftarrow s(obj_1, X), r(obj_1, Y), h(X, Y) \\ t(obj_1, X) \leftarrow r(obj_1, X) \\ mr(obj_1, X) \leftarrow -r(obj_1, X), r(obj_1, X) \\ p(obj_3, X) \leftarrow -q(obj_3, X), f(obj_3, X) \\ k(obj_3, X, Y) \leftarrow s(obj_3, X), r(obj_3, Y), h(X, Y), f(obj_3, Y) \\ t(obj_3, X) \leftarrow q(obj_3, X) \\ t(obj_3, X) \leftarrow f(obj_3, X) \\ mr(obj_3, X) \leftarrow -r(obj_3, X), r(obj_3, X) \\ mf(obj_3, X) \leftarrow -f(obj_3, X), f(obj_3, X) \end{array}$$

Moreover, the transactions of Example 7 are translated as follows:

- $T_1 = k(obj_3, X, Y), t(obj_1, Y);$
- $T_2 = p(O, X).$ $\diamond$

5 Related Work

Several research proposals attempt to combine object-orientation, databases, and logical languages. There are different orthogonal dimensions along which the approaches to the integration of the deductive and object paradigms may be classified. A survey of those proposals can be found in [5].

Most of the approaches do not consider state evolution of deductive objects. More precisely, the characterization of objects as logic theories, coming from object-oriented extensions of logic programming, does not account for any notion of state. McCabe suggests that the change of state for an instance can be simulated by creating new instances [22]. Other proposals simulate state changes by using *assert* and *retract* but this approach lacks any logical foundation. In [10] intensional variables are introduced to keep trace of state changes without side effects. In other proposals, multi-headed clauses are used for similar purposes. However, the notion of updating object state does not fit well in object-oriented extensions of logic programming. In addition, also approaches developed in the database field, like e.g. [13,14,19], do not consider state evolution. Many of the approaches [1,14,8], moreover, do not consider the behavioral component of objects, that is, methods. We think that this is an important issue because it overcomes the dichotomy between data and operations of the relational model.

Few proposals moreover, deal with behavioral inheritance and overriding. In addition to [2,19,22], these topics have been addressed in [7,11,15]. All these proposals extend F-logic [17] (or F-logic variations) with behavioral inheritance. In F-logic, indeed, only structural inheritance is directly captured. For behavioral inheritance, the non-monotonic aspects introduced by the combination of overriding and dynamic binding are modeled only indirectly by means of an iterated fixpoint construction. Moreover, in F-logic, only ground data expressions, that is, values resulting from the application of a method, and not method implementations, can be inherited along the inheritance hierarchy.

In GuLog [11] overriding and conflicts arising from multiple inheritance are investigated, in a model similar to F-logic. In GuLog, however, the schema and instance levels are separated. In ORLog [15] overriding and withdrawal of properties are supported. Withdrawal is used to prevent the inheritance of some properties in subclasses. It can thus result in non-monotonic inheritance of signatures. A reasonable use of that mechanism is for preference specification for conflict resolution in case of multiple inheritance. In [7] Bugliesi and Jamil also deal with the behavioral aspects of deductive object languages. Their language, moreover, also allows dynamic subclassing, that is, the definition of inheritance relationships through rules on schemas (which are not allowed in GuLog and ORLog). Dynamic subclassing raises non-monotonicity problems and leads to the introduction of a notion of i-stratification to guarantee the existence of a unique stable model. All these proposals, however, despite of their differences, deal with overriding on a per-predicate basis and do not consider any form of state evolution[6].

A finer granularity of rule composition is offered by languages supporting embedded implication [3,12,23]. Embedded implication allows one to realize also some of the other features of our language (such as message passing and conservative inheritance), but does not account for all of them (for instance, overriding). We remark, moreover, that our way of supporting such features is very closely related to the basic modeling notions of the object paradigm. This makes it easier to develop rule sets and to reuse them.

---

[6] Actually, state evolution can be accommodated in F-Logic through Transaction logic [6], as discussed in [16]. Also in this case, however, predicate inheritance and overriding work on a per-predicate basis.

6   Conclusions

We have proposed an approach to express inheritance in deductive object databases. Deductive object databases are based on deductive objects that can change state. Cooperation among objects is defined by inheritance and message passing. Several types of inheritance have been investigated and a formal operational semantics for the language is given. This semantics models objects with the granularity of theory, updates, methods, message passing, and inheritance as well as transactional behavior. Finally, a prototype has been implemented and a sketch of the interpreter for Obj^{inh}-Datalog is provided.

Our main direction of future work concerns the investigation of the applicability of the proposed approach to other deductive object languages with updates (such as Transaction F-Logic) and to other declarative object models that allows to specify dynamic aspects.

Acknowledgments

We wish to thank the anonymous reviewers for their useful comments that helped us a lot in improving both the technical content and the presentation of the paper. The comments and suggestions emerged during the discussion at the workshop were also very useful.

References

1. S. Abiteboul and P. Kanellakis. Object Identity as a Query Language Primitive. In *Proc. of the ACM SIGMOD Int. Conf. on Management of Data*, pages 159–173, 1989.
2. S. Abiteboul, G. Lausen, H. Uphoff, and E. Waller. Methods and Rules. In *Proc. of the ACM SIGMOD Int. Conf. on Management of Data*, pages 32–41, 1993.
3. M. Baldoni, L. Giordano, and A. Martelli. Translating a Modal Language with Embedded Implication into Horn Clause Logic. In R. Dyckhoff, H. Herre, and P. Schroeder-Heister, editors, *Proc. Fifth Int'l Workshop on Extensions of Logic Programming*, Lecture Notes in Computer Science No. 1050, pages 19–33, 1996.
4. E. Bertino and B. Catania. Static Analysis of Intensional Databases in U-Datalog. In *Proc. of the Fifteenth ACM SIGACT-SIGMOD-SIGART Symposium on Principles of Database Systems*, pages 202–212, 1996.
5. E. Bertino, G. Guerrini, and D. Montesi. Towards Deductive Object Databases. *Theory and Practice of Object Systems*, 1(1):19–39, Spring 1995. Special Issue: Selected Papers from ECOOP '94.
6. A. Bonner and M. Kifer. An Overview of Transaction Logic. *Theoretical Computer Science*, 133(2):205–265, 1994.
7. M. Bugliesi and H. M. Jamil. A Stable Model Semantics for Behavioral Inheritance in Deductive Object Oriented Languages. In *Proc. Fifth Int. Conf. on Database Theory*, pages 222–237, 1995.
8. F. Cacace, S. Ceri, S. Crespi-Reghizzi, L. Tanca, and R. Zicari. Integrating Object-Oriented Data Modelling with a Rule-Based Programming Paradigm. In *Proc. of the ACM SIGMOD Int. Conf. on Management of Data*, pages 225–236, 1989.

9. S. Ceri, G. Gottlob, and L. Tanca. *Logic Programming and Databases*. Springer-Verlag, 1990.

10. W. Chen and D. S. Warren. Objects as Intensions. In *Proc. Fifth Int. Conf. on Logic Programming*, pages 404–419, The MIT Press, 1988.

11. G. Dobbie and R. W. Topor. A Model for Sets and Multiple Inheritance in Deductive Object-Oriented Systems. *Journal of Intelligent Information Systems*, 4(2):193–219, 1995.

12. B. Freitag. Extending Deductive Database Languages by Embedded Implications. In A. Voronkov, editor, *Proc. Int'l Conf. on Logic Programming and Automated Reasoning*, Lecture Notes in Computer Science No. 642, pages 84–95, 1992.

13. B. Freitag. Representing Objects as Modules in Deductive Databases. In U. Geske and D. Seipel, editors, *Proc. Second ICLP-Workshop on Deductive Databases and Logic Programming*, pages 41–56, 1994.

14. S. Greco, N. Leone, and P. Rullo. COMPLEX: An Object-Oriented Logic Programming System. *IEEE Transactions on Knowledge and Data Engineering*, 4(4):344–359, August 1990.

15. H. M. Jamil and L.V.S. Lakshmanan. A Declarative Semantics of Behavioral Inheritance and Conflict Resolution. In *Proc. Int. Logic Programming Symposium*, pages 130–144, 1995.

16. M. Kifer. Deductive and Object Data Languages: A Quest for Integration. In *Proc. Fourth Int. Conf. on Deductive and Object-Oriented Databases*, Lecture Notes in Computer Science No. 1013, pages 187–212, 1995.

17. M. Kifer and G. Lausen. F-Logic: A Higher-Order Language for Reasoning about Objects, Inheritance, and Schema. In *Proc. of the ACM SIGMOD Int. Conf. on Management of Data*, pages 134–146, 1990.

18. G. Leavens and W. Weihl. Reasoning about Object-Oriented Programs that use Subtypes. In *Proc. Fifth Int. Conf. on Object-Oriented Programming: Systems, Languages, and Applications joint with Fourth European Conference on Object-Oriented Programming*, pages 212–223, 1990.

19. Y. Lou and Z. M. Ozsoyoglu. LLO: An Object-Oriented Deductive Language with Methods and Methods Inheritance. In *Proc. of the ACM SIGMOD Int. Conf. on Management of Data*, pages 198–207, 1991.

20. S. Manchanda and D. S. Warren. A Logic-based Language for Database Updates. In J. Minker, editor, *Deductive Databases and Logic Programming*, pages 363–394, Morgan-Kaufmann Publishers, 1987.

21. J. Manley, A. Cox, K. Harrison, M. Syrett, and D. Wells. KBMS1 A User Manual. Information System Centre Hewlett-Packard Laboratories, March 1990.

22. F.G. McCabe. *Logic and Objects*. PhD thesis, University of London, November 1988.

23. D. Miller. A Logical Analysis of Modules in Logic Programming. *Journal of Logic Programming*, 6(1–2):79–108, 1989.

24. D. Montesi, E. Bertino, and M. Martelli. Transactions and Updates in Deductive Databases. *IEEE Transactions on Knowledge and Data Engineering*, 9(5):784–797, 1997.

25. S. Naqvi and S. Tsur. *A Logical Language for Data and Knowledge Bases*, Vol. 2. Computer Science Press, 1989.

26. R. Smith, M. Lentczner, W. Smith, A. Taivalsaari, and D. Ungar. Prototype-Based Languages: Object Lessons from Class-Free Programming (Panel). In *Proc. Ninth Int. Conf. on Object-Oriented Programming: Systems, Languages, and Applications*, pages 102–112, 1994.

Specifying Distributed and Dynamically Evolving Information Systems Using an Extended Co-nets Approach

Nasreddine Aoumeur*

Otto-von-Guericke-Universität Magdeburg
Institut für Technische und Betriebliche Informationssysteme
Postfach 4120, D–39016 Magdeburg, Germany
aoumeur@iti.cs.uni-magdeburg.de

Abstract. The Co-nets approach that we are developing is an object-oriented (OO) specification model based on a formal and complete integration of OO concepts and constructions into an appropriate variant of algebraic Petri nets. Interpreted in rewriting logic, the approach is particularly tailored for specifying and validating advanced information systems as distributed, autonomous yet cooperative components. However, in spirit of most existing conceptual models, the Co-nets approach requires that all system aspects have to be known during its specification and fixed at once; a fact going in contrast to reality where most systems, due to different changes in business and law factors, have to change their behaviour in unexpected way during their long life-span. With the objective to overcome this crucial limitation, we present in this paper first steps towards an appropriate extension of Co-nets approach for naturally dealing with specification evolution. The main ideas are based on, first, distinguishing between a rigid, fixed object behaviour part and a modifiable one. Second, besides usual transitions and places, we introduce the notions of meta-places and meta-transitions for dynamically governing the modifiable behaviour. Third, we propose for meta-transitions two-steps (i.e. meta- and object levels) valued rewriting rules.

1 Introduction

Present-day information systems are becoming more and more complex in size and more especially in space. For their crucial specification / validation phase, there is an overwhelming need for more appropriate object-oriented conceptual models [19]. Indeed, in contrast to (mostly sequential) existing OO specification models which conceive such systems as community of objects, advanced models have to conceive them rather as fully distributed, autonomous yet cooperative components. Each component has to be regarded at least as a hierarchy of classes with different forms of inheritance (i.e. simple, multiple, with overriding), object composition, and aggregations. Distribution in such components has to be reflected by a true intra- as well as inter-object concurrency, and by exhibition of

---

* This work is supported by a DAAD scholarship.

G. Saake, K. Schwarz, and C. Türker (Eds.): TDD '99, LNCS 1773, pp. 91–111, 2000.

different forms of communication including synchronous and asynchronous ones. Autonomy, which has to be coupled with close cooperation, should particularly be reflected by an encapsulation of proper features in each component and by the existence of explicit interfaces for interacting such components.

Besides these challenges, the capability of specifying evolving aspects in such systems is also of crucial importance. In fact, due to the very long life-span (usually several years) of these systems, which is subject to changes of laws as well as market pressure, advanced conceptual models also have to be *semantically* rich enough for naturally capturing this dynamic, runtime evolution. Such evolution must be achieved without resorting to conceive (from scratch) new systems or modifying in ad-hoc manner their corresponding implementation—which lost the essence and crucial relevance of the specification phase.

For tackling these issues, there are some ongoing approaches including, for instance, distributed temporal logic (DTL) [10] with TROLL language [15] and Real-time Object Specification Logic (ROSL) [4] with ALBERT II language [9].

Besides these more property-oriented formal frameworks, we are developing a *multi-paradigm* approach referred to as CO-NETS. It soundly combines ideas from object orientation [21] modularity and system interconnection [12,1], high level Petri nets [14], and rewriting logic [17]. The main features of our approach [2,3] for adequately specifying and validating advanced information systems as fully distributed, autonomous yet cooperative components may be summarized as follows:

- We conceive a class as a *module* with a hidden part including structure as well as behaviour, and an observed part, including structural as well as behavioural aspects. The observed part is used as interface for interacting with the environment and other classes. In each class, object states are modeled as terms with identity and gathered into an appropriate (object) place, while with each method-invocation a corresponding (message) place is associated. Transitions reflect the body of such methods (i.e., effect of messages on object state to which they are sent); where appropriate splitting /recombination of object states are allowed for a full exhibition of intra- as well as inter-object concurrency.
- An incremental construction of components, as a hierarchy of classes, using simple and multiple inheritance (with redefinition, associated polymorphism and dynamic binding), object composition and aggregation. Such components behave (i.e., their general transition form) with respect to an appropriate *intra-component* evolution pattern that naturally supports intra- as well as inter-object concurrency. Moreover, due to the possibility of splitting/ recombining of object states, the modeling of different forms of inheritance neither necessitates any complex formalization nor it suffers from the well-known inheritance anomaly problem [16].
- For interacting different components and thereby constructing more complex systems as cooperative components, an adequate *inter-component* interaction pattern is proposed; it enhances concurrency and preserves encapsulated (i.e. hidden) features of each of the interacting component.

- By interpreting CO-NETS behaviour in rewriting logic, rapid-prototyping may be generated. This can be achieved either using rewrite techniques in general [8] or current implementation of the MAUDE language [5] particularly.

The main focus of the present paper is to enhance the CO-NETS approach to deal with dynamic, runtime changes in a very comprehensible but nevertheless well-founded way. In some detail, our approach to dynamic modification— as a natural extension of the just mentioned CO-NETS features— may be explained as follows:

- Following the approach of [20,6] to specify evolving behaviour in information systems, we assume that not all object behaviour is subject to change. That is, some object behaviour part is rigid, fixed forever reflecting *minimal properties* of the modeled application. On the other sides, due to our modeling of inheritance using splitting / recombination of object states at a need, incremental extensions of given specification by introducing new messages and new behaviour (as subclasses) *do not affect* in any way the already running behaviour. As a result of this, we make a clear distinction between specification *extension* and behaviour modification. The extension, as we mentioned, is rigorously handled at the object level. For coping with the behaviour modification as a change in method bodies (i.e., the effect of messages on object states) we propose a meta-object level.
- Besides the usual object and message places and transitions, we introduce in each component new constructions for capturing this behaviour modification. We referred them to as *meta-places* and *meta-transitions*, respectively. Each meta-place, associated with a given component, is containing as tokens appropriate *behaviour* which may be assigned to a given (meta-)transition at the *runtime* (i.e. at the moment of firing this transition). More precisely, token components in meta-places are conceived as tuples composed of: transition identifiers, input tokens and created tokens with their respective places and conditions for firing the associated transition. Henceforth, from the fact that such tokens can be created, deleted or modified using transitions as in usual places, the behaviour modification is straightforwardly achieved. Meta-transitions are defined as *non-instantiated* transitions. Their input arcs, output arcs, and conditions are just specific *variables*. Therefore, only at the time of their firing that they receive appropriate instantiation and thereby corresponding behaviour from the meta-place.
- For semantically and correctly interpreting the intended behaviour of this meta-object level, we propose an appropriate (and just one) *inference rule* that we called *meta-rule*. This rule allows to propagate the abstract behaviour from the meta-object level (i.e. meta-places and meta-transitions) to the usual object level (i.e. places and transitions). At the firing time, the meta-rule effect consists in transforming a meta-transition to a usual transition, such that the behaviour precisely comes from the meta-place.

The remainder of this paper will be organized as follows. In section 2, we review main aspects of the CO-NETS approach using a simplified account specification.

In section 3, we discuss how behaviour modification is syntactically and semantically handled by extending CO-NETS. We conclude this paper by some remarks and future work.

2   The CO-NETS Approach: An Overview

The CO-NETS approach is a new form of object-oriented Petri net-based model more tailored to the specification and rapid-prototyping of distributed information systems [3].

2.1   CO-Net: Template and Class Specification

This section deals with the modelling of the basic concepts of the object-oriented paradigm, namely objects, templates, and classes. We first present the structure, or what is commonly called the object signature templates [11]. Then we describe how specification templates and classes are specified.

Template Signature Specification. The template signature defines the structure of the object states and the form of operations that have to be accepted by such states. Basically, in the CO-NETS approach, we follow the general object signature proposed for MAUDE [18]. Object states are regarded as terms —precisely as a tuple— and messages as operations sent or received by objects. However, apart from these general conceptual similarities, and in order to be more close to the aforementioned information system requirements, the OO signature that we propose can informally be described as follows:

- The object states are terms of the form

$$\langle Id|atr_1 : val_1, ..., atr_k : val_k, at\_bs_1 : val'_1, ..., at\_bs_{k'} : val'_s \rangle$$

  where
  - Id is an observed object identity taking its values from an appropriate abstract data type OId;
  - $atr_1, .., atr_k$ are the local, hidden from the outside, attribute identifiers having as actual values respectively $val_1, .., val_k$.
  - The observed part of an object state is identified by $at\_bs_1, ..., at\_bs_s$ and their associated actual v alues are $val'_1, ..val'_s$.
  - Also, we assume that all attribute identifiers (local or observed) range their values over a suitable sort denoted AId, while their associated values are ranged over the sort $Value$ with $OId < Value$ (i.e. OId as subsort of $Value$) in order to allow object valued attributes.
  - In contrast to the indivisible object state proposed in MAUDE, which avoids any form of intra-object concurrency, we introduce a powerful axiom, called splitting / recombination axiom that permits to split (resp. recombine) the object state as needed. This axiom can be described as follows:

$\langle Id|attrs_1{}^1, attrs_2\rangle = \langle Id|attrs_1\rangle \oplus \langle Id|attrs_2\rangle$. As we present in more detail later, first, it allows us to exhibit intra-object concurrency[2]. Second, it provides a meaning to our notion of observed attributes by allowing separation between intra- and inter-component evolution. Third, it allows us to drastically simplify the conceptualization of inheritance.

- In addition of conceiving messages as terms —that consist of message name, the identifiers of the objects the message is addressed to, and, possibly, parameters— we make a clear distinction between internal, local messages and the external as imported or exported messages. Local messages allow to evolve object states of a given class, while the external ones allow communication between different classes by exclusively using their observed attributes.

Following these informal descriptions and some ideas from [18], the formal description of the object states as well as the class structures are given using an OBJ [13] notation.

obj Object-State **is**
sort AId .
subsort OId < Value .
subsort Attribute < Attributes .
subsort Id-Attributes < Object .
subsort Local-attributes External-attributes < Id-Attributes .
protecting Value OId AId .
op _:_ : AId Value → Attribute .
op _,_ : Attribute Attributes → Attributes [associ. commu. Id:nil] .
op ⟨_|_⟩ : OId Attributes → Id-Attributes .
op _⊕_ : Id-Attributes Id-Attributes →
            Id-Attributes [associ. commu. Id:nil] .
vars Attr: Attribute ; Attrs$_1$, Attrs$_2$: Attributes ; I:OId .
eq1 $\langle I|attrs_1\rangle \oplus \langle I|attrs_2\rangle = \langle I|attrs_1, attrs_2\rangle$.
eq2 $\langle I|nil\rangle = I$
endo.

obj Class-Structure **is**
protecting Object-state, s-atr$_1$,...,s-atr$_n$, s-arg$_{11,1}$,.., s-arg$_{l1,l1}$,
            ...,s-arg$_{i1,1}$,...,s-arg$_{i1,i1}$ ...
subsort Id.obj < OId .
subsort Mes$_{l1}$, Mes$_{l2}$,...,Mes$_{ll}$ < Local_Messages .
subsort Mes$_{e1}$, Mes$_{e2}$,...,Mes$_{ee}$ < Exported_Messages .
subsort Mes$_{i1}$, Mes$_{i2}$,...,Mes$_{ii}$ < Imported_Messages .
sort Id.obj, Mes$_{l1}$, . . . ,Mes$_{ip}$.
(* **local attributes** *)
op $\langle$_|atr$_1$: _,...,atr$_k$: _$\rangle$: Id.obj s-atr$_1$ ...s-atr$_k$
      → Local-Attributes.

---

[1] $attr_i$ stands for a simplified form of $atr_{i1} : val_{i1}, ..., atr_{ik} : val_{ik}$.
[2] In the sense that two messages sent to the same object and acting on different attributes can be performed (i.e. rewritten) in parallel by splitting the two parts using this axiom.

(* observed attributes *)
op $\langle \_|atrbs_1 :, ..., atrbs_{k'} : \_ \rangle$: Id.obj s-atbs$_1$ ...s-atbs$_{k'}$
    $\rightarrow$ External-Attributes.
(* local messages *)
op ms$_{l1}$: s-arg$_{l1,1}$ ...s-arg$_{l1,l1}$ $\rightarrow$ Mes$_{l1}$ . ...
(* export messages *)
op ms$_{e1}$: s-arg$_{e1,1}$ ...s-arg$_{e1,e1}$ $\rightarrow$ Mes$_{e1}$ . ...
(* import messages *)
op ms$_{i1}$: s-arg$_{i1,1}$ ...s-arg$_{i1,i1}$ $\rightarrow$ Mes$_{ip}$ . ...
endo.

Example 1. We present a very simplified **Account** description, where each account that we can withdraw, deposit in or increase its interest is characterized by: its identifier as a composite of a number with bank name, its balance, a minimal limit of the balance, interest content, corresponding bank name and the account holder (identity). Following the afore described template signature, the corresponding account signature takes the following form, where all data types like **nat**, **money**, and **string** are assumed to be algebraically specified elsewhere.

```
obj Account is
 extending Object-State .
 protecting money nat   string   Id.Bank  Id.Holder  interest .
 sort Id.Account  Account  .
 sort OPEN-AC  WITHDRW  DEPOSIT  INTRS .
 subsort Id.Account < OId .
 (* the Account object state declaration *)
 op ⟨_|No : _, bk : _, Hd : _, bal : _, Lmt : _, Ints : _⟩: Id.Account nat Id.bank
 Id.Holder money   money   Interest→ Account .
 (* Messages declaration *)
 op OpenAc : Id.Account   Id.Bank   nat   string→ OPEN-AC (* open a new account *)  .
 op Wdw : Id.Account   money → WITHDWR . (* withdraw a given sum *)
 op Dep : Id.Account   money → DEPOSIT . (* deposit a given sum *)
 op IncI : Id.Account   interest → INTRS . (* increase the interest *)
 vars H : Id.Customer .
 vars C : Id.Account .
 vars W, D , L : money .
 vars I, NI : Interest . (* these variables will be used in the associated net *)
endo.
```

Template and Class Specification. On the basis of the template signature, we define the notion of template specification as a CO-NET and the notion of class as a marked CO-NET. Given template signature, the associated CO-NET structure, can informally be described as follows:

– The places of the CO-NET are precisely defined by associating with each message generator one place that we called message place. Henceforth, each message place is containing message instances of a specific form which are addressed to object states— and not yet performed. In addition to these message places, we associate with the object sort one object place that has to contain the current object states of this class. We also note that places associated with external messages will be drawn with bold circles.

– The CO-NET transitions reflect the effect of messages on the object states to which they are addressed. Also, we make distinction between local transitions that reflect the object states evolution and the external ones modeling the interaction between different classes. Input (resp. output) arcs are annotated by the input (resp. created) tokens. Both arc inscriptions are defined as multisets of terms respecting the type of their input and/or output places— the associated union operation is denoted by $\oplus$.

– Conditions may be associated with transitions. They involve attribute and/or message parameter variables.

Example 2. By applying these translating ideas to the account signature, we obtain the CO-NET depicted in Figure 1. In this net, the four message places correspond to the four message declaration, and the object place allows to capture the **Account** object instances. Four transitions reflecting the behaviour of these messages are conceived.

Remark 1. It is worth mentioning that in each transition, the input as well as the output arcs are inscribed just by the **relevant part** of the invoked object state(s). For instance, in the DEP(OSIT) transition only the attribute *balance* is invoked (i.e. $\langle C|bal : B \rangle$ in the input arc and $\langle C|bal : B + D \rangle$ in the output arcs). This constitutes the key ideas for a fully exhibition of the intra- (and inter-) object concurrency. As example, the interest increase and the deposit messages may be performed in parallel for a same account by appropriately splitting its state.

2.2 CO-NETS: Semantical Aspects

After highlighting how CO-NETS templates are constructed, we now focus on the behavioural aspects of such classes. That is, how to construct a *coherent* object society as a community of object states and message instances, and how such a society evolves correctly. For this aim, we present the state evolution schema to be respected and its corresponding semantics.

Evolution of Object States in Classes. For the evolution of object states in a given class, we propose a general pattern that has to be respected in order to ensure the encapsulation property—in the sense that no object states or messages of other classes participate in this communication — as well as the preservation of the object identity uniqueness. Following such guidelines and

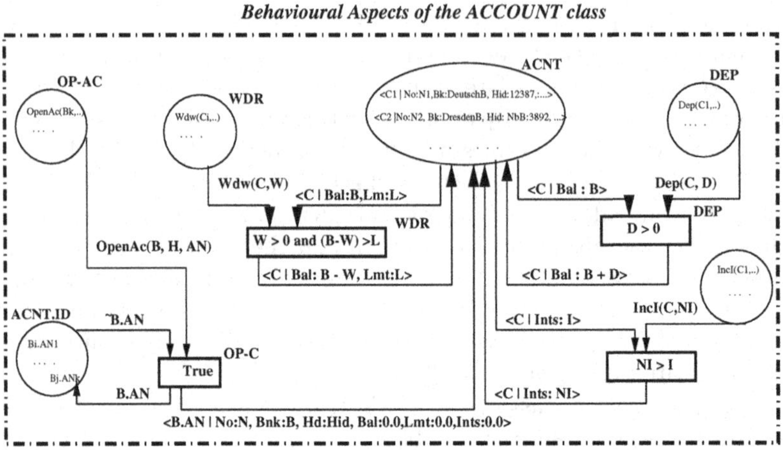

Behavioural Aspects of the ACCOUNT class

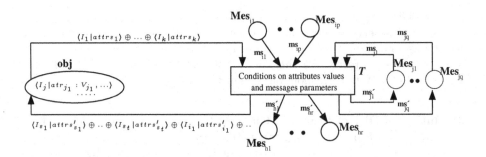

(figure at top — Fig. 1 diagram)

Fig. 1. The CO-NETS Account Specification

in order to exhibit a maximal concurrency, this evolution schema is depicted in Figure 2, and it can intuitively be explained as follows: The contact of just the relevant parts of some object states of a given Cl, —namely $\langle I_1|attrs_1\rangle$;..; $\langle I_k|attrs_k\rangle$— with some messages $ms_{i1}, .., ms_{ip}, ms_{j1}, .., ms_{jq}$—declared as *local or imported* in this class— and under some conditions on the invoked attributes and message parameters results in the following effects:

- The messages $ms_{i1}, .., ms_{ip}, ms_{j1}, .., ms_{iq}$ vanish;
- The state change of some (parts of) object states participating in the communication, namely $I_{s1}, .., I_{st}$. Such change is symbolized by $attrs'_{s1}, .., attrs'_{st}$ instead of $attrs_{s1}, .., attrs_{st}$.
- Deletion of some objects by explicitly sending delete messages for such objects.
- New messages are sent to objects of Cl namely $ms'_{h1}, .., ms'_{hr}, ms'_{j1}, .., ms'_{jq}$.

Fig. 2. The Intra-Component Evolution Pattern

Rewriting Rules Governing the Co-nets **Behaviour.** We propose that each Co-net transition is captured by an appropriate rewriting rule interpreted in rewrite logic. Following the intra-component evolution pattern depicted in Figure 2, the rewrite rules that we associate with it takes the following form:

$$T : (Ms_{i_1}, ms_{i_1}) \otimes .. \otimes (Ms_{i_p}, ms_{i_p}) \otimes (Ms_{j_1}, ms_{j_1}) \otimes .. \otimes (Ms_{j_q}, ms_{j_q}) \otimes$$
$$(obj, \langle I_1 | attrs_1 \rangle \oplus .. \oplus \langle I_k | attrs_k \rangle)$$

$$\Rightarrow$$

$$(Ms_{h_1}, ms'_{h_1}) \otimes ... \otimes (Ms'_{h_r}, ms'_{h_r}) \otimes$$
$$(Ms_{j_1}, ms'_{j_1}) \otimes .. \otimes (Ms'_{j_q}, ms'_{j_q}) \otimes (obj, \langle I_{s_1} | attrs'_{s_1} \rangle \oplus .. \oplus \langle I_{st} | attrs'_{st} \rangle \oplus$$
$$\langle I_{i_1} | attrs'_{i_1} \rangle \oplus .. \oplus \langle I_{i_r} | attrs'_{i_r} \rangle)$$
$$\text{if Conditions and } M(Ad_{Cl}) = \emptyset \text{ and } M(Dl_{Cl}) = \emptyset$$

Remark 2. The operator $\otimes$ is defined as a multiset union and allows for relating different places identifiers with their current marking. Moreover, we assume that $\otimes$ is distributive over $\oplus$ i.e. $(p, mt_1 \oplus mt_2) = (p, mt_1) \otimes (p, mt_2)$ with mt_1, mt_2 multiset of terms over $\oplus$ and p a place identifier. The condition $M(Ad_{Cl}) = \emptyset$ and $M(Dl_{Cl}) = \emptyset$ means that the creation and the deletion of objects have to be performed at first. In other words, before performing the above rewrite rule, the markings in the Ad_{Cl} as well as in the Dl_{Cl} places have to be empty. Finally, please note that the selection of just the *invoked parts* of object states, in this evolution pattern, is quite possible because of the splitting /recombination axiom. This axiom has to be performed before and in accordance with each invoked state evolution.

Example 3. By applying this general form of rewrite rules, it is not difficult to generate the rules governing the **Account** class.

OPENC: $(OP\_AC, OpenAc(B, Hid, AN)) \otimes (ACNT.ID, SetAC)$
$\Rightarrow (ACNT, \langle B.AN | No : AN, Bnk : B, Hd : H, Bal : 0, Lmt : 0, Ints : 0 \rangle)$
$\otimes (ACNT.ID, SetAC \oplus B.AN) \text{ if } Not(B.AN \in SetAC)$

WDR: $(WDR, Wdr(C, W)) \otimes (ACNT, \langle C | Bal : B, Lmt : L \rangle)$
$\Rightarrow (ACNT, \langle Ac | Bal : B - W, Lmt : L \rangle) \text{ if } (W > 0) \wedge (B - W) \geq L$

DEP: $(DEP, Dep(C, D)) \otimes (ACNT, \langle C | Bal : B \rangle)$
$\Rightarrow (ACNT, \langle C | Bal : B + D \rangle) \text{ if } (D > 0)$
INTR: $(INTR, IncI(C, NI)) \otimes (ACNT, \langle C | Ints : I \rangle)$
$\Rightarrow (ACNT, \langle C | Int : NI \rangle) \text{ if } (NI > I)$

2.3 Co-nets: **More Advanced Constructions**

So far, we have only presented how the Co-nets approach allows to conceive independent classes. In what follows, we show how more complex systems can be constructed using advanced abstraction mechanisms, especially inheritance and interaction between classes. However, due to the focus of this paper only general ideas about simple inheritance and interaction are given.

Simple Inheritance. Giving a (super) class Cl modeled as a CO-Net, for constructing a subclass that inherits the structure as well as the behaviour of the superclass Cl and exhibits new behaviour involving additional attributes, we propose the following straightforward conceptualization:

- Define the structure of the new subclass by introducing the new attributes and messages. Structurally, the new attribute identifiers and message generators are described using the *extending* primitive in the OBJ notation.
- As *object place* for the subclass, we use the *same* object place of the superclass. This means that such place should now contain now the object states of the superclass as well as the object states of the subclass. This is semantically sound because the sort of this object place is a supersort for objects including more attributes.
- As previously described, the proper behaviour of the subclass is constructed by associating with each new message a corresponding place and constructing its behaviour (i.e. transitions) with respect to the communication model of Figure 3 under the condition that at least one of the additional attributes has to be involved in such transitions.

Remark 3. Such conceptualization is only possible because of the splitting / recombination operation. Indeed this axiom permits to consider an object state of a subclass, denoted, for instance, as $\langle Id|attrs, attrs' \rangle$ with $attrs'$ the additional attributes (i.e. those proper to the subclass), to be also an object state of the superclass (i.e. $\langle Id|attrs \rangle$). Obviously, this allows a systematic inheritance of the structure as well as the behaviour. The dynamic binding with polymorphism are systematically taken into account in this modeling. Indeed, when a message is sent to a hierarchy of classes we can only know after the firing of the associated transition to which class in the hierarchy the concerned object have been sent.

Interaction between classes. To conceive such interaction, on the one hand, we have to take into account the fact that object states evolution within classes is ensured by the intra-component pattern as depicted in Figure 2. On the other side, we have to respect the encapsulation property which stipulates that internal features of objects have to be hidden from the outside. Following these guidelines, the inter-component interaction we propose is depicted in Figure 3. It may be made explicit as follows: The contact of some external parts of some object states namely $\langle I_1|attrs\_ob_1 \rangle, ..., \langle I_k|attrs\_ob_k \rangle$, which may belong to different classes namely $C_1, ..., C_m$, with some external messages $ms_{i1}, .., ms_{ip}$, $ms_{j1}, .., ms_{jq}$ defined in such classes and under some conditions on attribute values and parameter messages results in the following:

- The messages $ms_{i1}, .., ms_{ip}, ms_{j1}, .., ms_{iq}$ vanish.
- The state change of some (external parts of) object states participating in the communication, namely $I_{s1}, .., I_{st}$. Such a change is symbolized by $attrs'_{s1}, .., attrs'_{st}$ instead of $attrs_{s1}, .., attrs_{st}$. The other participating parts of object states remain unchanged (i.e. deletion or creation of part of states is not allowed).

– New external messages (that may involve deletion/creation ones) are sent to objects of different classes, namely $ms'_{h1}, .., ms'_{hr}, ms'_{j1}, .., ms'_{jq}$.

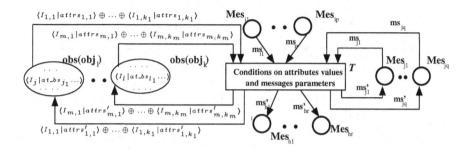

Fig. 3. The Inter-Component Interaction pattern.

3 CO-NETS Object Evolution

As pointed out in the introduction, for dealing with the behaviour runtime modification we propose to introduce new syntactical constructions, namely meta-places and meta-transitions and endowed them with a sound semantics expressed by a new inference rule. For achieving this goal, we first introduce the main characteristics of these syntactical constructions. Second, we present the semantics counterpart of these constructions. Third, we illustrate this new way of handling behaviour modification using a running example.

3.1 Meta-Places and Transitions in CO-NETS

For capturing the dynamic modification, we propose to associate with each component which is subject to future modification a meta-object level[3]. As depicted in Figure 4, the meta-object level associated with a given component is composed of a meta-place and three transitions with corresponding messages for adding, removing, or updating existing behaviour, respectively. Moreover, at the object level there is now two forms of transitions: usual transitions capturing the rigid behaviour— respecting the afore described intra-component evolution pattern— as represented in the left hand-side and non-instantiated or meta-transitions that are directly *related* to the meta-place through an appropriate *read-only*[4] arc.

---

[3] However, although it is also possible to associate another meta-object level for dealing with modification during the cooperation of such components, for sake of understandability of this first step towards runtime modification in CO-NETS we will restrict ourselves to the level of components.

[4] Note that in read-only arc usually represented by arrows there is only enabled conditions reflecting the presence of such tokens in the corresponding place (i.e. there is no deletion or creation of tokens).

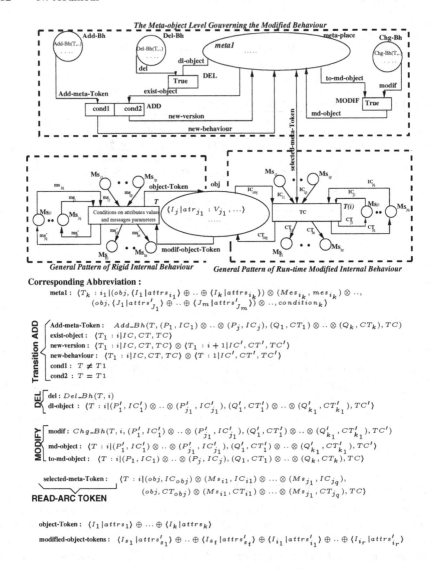

Fig. 4. The Meta General Forms

In contrast to the intra-component evolution pattern for usual transitions, all tokens annotating input as well as output arcs in this meta-component evolution pattern (as depicted in the right hand) are just specific *variables*. In other words, all arc inscriptions, namely $IC_{obj}, CT_{obj}, IC_{i_1}, .., IC_{i_p}, IC_{j_1}, .. IC_{i_q}, CT_{i_1}, .. CT_{i_p}, CT_{j_1}, .. CT_{i_q}$ should be declared as variables with compatible sorts according to their corresponding input / output places. The meta-place is the main component in this meta-construction. It has to contain, as tokens, the different behaviour of meta-transitions. Following the form depicted in Figure 4, each token in the meta-place respects the following form:

$$\langle T : i | (obj, IC_{obj}) \otimes (Ms_{i1}, IC_{i1}) \otimes ... \otimes (Ms_{j_1}, IC_{j_q}), (obj, CT_{obj}) \otimes$$
$$(Ms_{i1}, CT_{i1}) \otimes ... \otimes (Ms_{j_1}, CT_{j_q}), TC\rangle$$

where:

- T stands for the name or the label of the transition which has to exist in the object level as a non instantiated transition. i stands for a particular *version* of the behaviour associated with this transition T. This particularly allows to associate more than one behaviour with a given transition and thereby to keep *trace* of the different change evolution and its strategy.
- The component $(obj, IC_{obj}) \otimes (Ms_{i1}, IC_{i1}) \otimes ... \otimes (Ms_{j_1}, IC_{j_q})$ obviously defines the different input places with their corresponding (multiset of terms as) arc inscriptions. In contrast to the terms in object places, the terms above are not ground terms; rather they contain variables exactly like inscriptions associated with usual transitions.
- The second component $(obj, CT_{obj}) \otimes (Ms_{i1}, CT_{i1}) \otimes ... \otimes (Ms_{j_1}, CT_{j_q})$ captures the different output places and associated arc inscriptions.
- Finally, the component TC reflects the condition that may be associated with a given transition.

For precisely defining this form of meta-tokens using an OBJ notation, first we present a correponding OBJ notation of the notion of CO-NETS state so far used more informally. The two constraint sorts ensure that the marking (terms) sort is compatible with its corresponding place.

```
obj CO-NETS-State is
 extending class-description .
 subsort obj   Mes_{l1}  ...  Mes_{ee} < Place.
 subsort Place < Place_Marking .
 sort Place_Identifier .
 op obj   Mes_{l1}  ...  Mes_{ee} :  → Place_Identifier .
 op _⊕_: Place Place-Marking → Place-Marking. [assoc. comm. id:]
 op (_,_): Place-Identifier Place-Marking → Marking.
 op _⊗_: Marking Marking → Marking.
 vars p : Place_Identifier
 vars T, T1, T2 : Place_Marking
 scr (p,T) : Undefined if p=obj ∧ T:{ Ms_{l1},..,Ms_{ee}} .
 scr (p,T) : Undefined if p ∈ {Ms_{l1},..,Ms_{ee}} ∧ T:obj .
 eq (p,T_1 ⊕ T_2) = (p,T_1) ⊗ (p,T_2) .
endo .
```

```
obj meta-CO-NETS-State is
 extending CO-NETS-State .
 sort meta-place.Id Transition.Id Meta-Marking.
 subsort Input-Tokens Created-Tokens < Component .
 subsort Meta-Token < Meta-Tokens .
```

subsort Condition < Boolean .
op [_] : Marking → Component .
op ⟨_ : _|_, _, _⟩ : Transition.Id Nat Input-Tokens Created-Tokens
  Condition → meta-Token .
op _ ⊕ _: Meta-Token Meta-Tokens → Meta-Tokens [assoc. comm. id:]
op (_, _): Meta-place.Id Meta-Tokens → Meta-Marking.
op _ ⊗ _: Meta-Marking Meta-Marking → Meta-Marking.
vars $T1$, $T2$: Meta-Tokens.
vars p : Meta-place.Id.
eq $(p, T_1 \oplus T_2) = (p, T_1) \otimes (p, T_2)$.
endo .

Finally, the three transitions at the meta-level, namely *Add_beh*, *Del_beh*, and *Chg_beh*, allow to introduce an additional behaviour (i.e., a new version for an already existing transition behaviour), to delete an existing behaviour, or to modify an exisiting behaviour (i.e. replace the input tokens and/or the output tokens and/or the transition condition). The associated rewrite rules for these three transitions can straightforwardly be generated in a same way as at the object level.

3.2   The CO-NETS-meta level semantics

For propagating a given behaviour from the meta-object level to the object level using non instantiated transitions, we have to fully exploit the read-only arc relating the two-levels. For that, we propose a two-steps approach. First, we instantiate the selected transition by the appropriate selected behaviour (as tokens from the meta-place). Second, we use this instantiated rewrite rule as a usual rewrite rule. Henceforth, the crucial step is how to achieve the instantiation in such way that we generate nothing but a usual rewrite rule that respects the intra-component evolution pattern depicted in Figure 2.

Before going into technical detail and its complex notations, let us explain the main ideas of this process of (meta-rule) instantiation and the meta-inference rule that we associate with in a more abstract but yet simplified way. Due to the presence of the read-only arc relating the two levels, the rewrite rule that may be associated with non-instantiated (or meta-) transition can be abstracted away as $T : l \otimes m \Rightarrow r \otimes m$[5]. The terms l and r represent input tokens (as variables) with their associated places and the output tokens (as variables) with their places. The term m stands for the general form of tokens which can be selected from the meta-place. Remark that for appropriately reflecting he read-arc semantics, m must appear in the left as well as in the right without any change. Now assume that in the place *meta-place* there is (at least) a meta-token of the form $\langle T : \_|..\rangle$ representing one behaviour of the transition T. Obviously, it is quite possible to denote this selected meta-token rather by $\sigma(m)$; where σ denote different substitutions of the variables IC_{i_j}, CT_{i_j} in m by their corresponding terms selected from this particular meta-token

---

[5] For sake of simplicity we omit the condition part.

$\langle T : \_|..\rangle$. Altogether, we have now the following (two-components) premise of the inference rule to be proposed : $\sigma(m)$ and $T : l \otimes m \Rightarrow r \otimes m$. As conclusion from this premise, we propose the following (instantiated) rewrite rule: $T : \sigma(l) \Rightarrow \sigma(r)$. Thus, our abstract-meta-inference rule has the form:

$$\frac{\sigma(m) \quad l \otimes m \Rightarrow r \otimes m}{\sigma(l) \Rightarrow \sigma(r)} \qquad (**)$$

After introducing this abstract view, it is not difficult to be more concrete and replace the corresponding abstract terms, namely l, r, and m by their concrete instantiation. Following the general schema represented in Figure 4, the corresponding (multiset of) terms associated with l, r, and m are as follows:

- l stands for the input tokens in the meta-transition $T(i)$ and then have to be instantiated by:
  $(obj, IC_{obj}) \otimes (Ms_{i_1}, IC_{i_1}) \otimes ... \otimes (Ms_{i_p}, IC_{i_p})$
  $\otimes (Ms_{j_1}, IC_{j_1}) \otimes ... \otimes (Ms_{j_q}, IC_{j_q})$.
- r stands for the output tokens in the meta-transition $T(i)$ and hence have to instantiated by:
  $(obj, CT_{obj}) \otimes (Ms_{h_1}, CT_{h_1}) \otimes ... \otimes$
  $(Ms_{h_r}, CT_{h_r}) \otimes (Ms_{j_1}, CT_{j_1}) \otimes ... \otimes (Ms_{j_q}, CT_{j_q})$.
- Also we have to add the condition part as $TC(t)$.
- m stands for the term associated with the read-arc denoted as *selected-meta-Token* and then corresponds to :
  $\langle T : i|(obj, IC_{obj}) \otimes (Ms_{i1}, IC_{i1}) \otimes ... \otimes (Ms_{j_1}, IC_{j_q}),$
  $(obj, CT_{obj}) \otimes (Ms_{i_1}, CT_{i_1}) \otimes ... \otimes (Ms_{j_1}, CT_{j_q}), TC\rangle$.
- σ stands for any substitution of the variables IC_{i_j}, CT_{l_k} and TC by concrete terms of a given selected token from the meta-place. For that, we assume that the *meta-place* contains (at least) the following token :
  $\langle T : i|(obj, \langle I_1|attrs_{i_1}\rangle \oplus .. \oplus \langle I_k|attrs_{i_k}\rangle) \otimes$
  $(Mes_{i_k}, mes_{i_k}) \otimes .., (obj, \langle J_1|attrs'_{J_1}\rangle \oplus .. \oplus$
  $\langle J_m|attrs'_{J_m}\rangle) \otimes .. \otimes (Mes'_{J_k}, mes'_{J_k}), Condition\rangle$.
  In this case, the substitution σ should be defined as a union of the following elementary (variable-terms) replacements:

Variable	Corresponding Substitution
IC_{obj}	$\langle I_1|attrs_{i_1}\rangle \oplus .. \oplus \langle I_k|attrs_{i_k}\rangle$
IC_{l_k}	mes_{l_k} with $l_k \in \{i_1, ..i_p, j_1, ..., j_p\}$
CT_{obj}	$\langle J_1|attrs'_{i_1}\rangle \oplus .. \oplus \langle J_k|attrs'_{J_k}\rangle$
$CT_{l'_{k'}}$	$mes'_{l'_{k'}}$

These tedious (abstract) instantiations become more simple when applied to concrete examples.

3.3   The Account Evolving Specification

The purpose of this subsection is a concrete illustration of the proposed ideas for coping with the dynamic evolution in distributed information systems specified as Co-nets components. Using the already specified **Account** specification, we now assume that only the *Deposit* operation is rigid. This means that the *Withdraw* as well as *Interest-Increase* are conceived (initially) to be logically subject to change during the life cycle of an account.

Following our conceptualization, while the *Deposit* behaviour (i.e., its corresponding transition) remains unchanged as usual transition, transitions associated with *Withdraw* and *IncIntst* have to be conceived as *non-instantiated* transitions. This fact is reflected in Figure 5, where a new meta-object level is introduced. The meta-place *meta-account* is directly related to the two non-instantiated transitions using read-only arcs. The terms associated with these two arcs are

$$\langle WDR : i | (ACNT, ICw1) \otimes (WDR, ICw2), (ACNT, CTw), TCw \rangle$$

for *Withdraw* and

$$\langle INTR : i | (ACNT, ICi1) \otimes (INTR, ICi2), (ACNT, CTi), TCi \rangle$$

for *Deposit*. The non-instantiated transitions have been derived from the two usual transitions associated with *Withdraw* and *Deposit* in two phases. First, we have replaced the instantiated input arcs as well as output arcs associated with these transitions by corresponding variables, namely $ICw1$, $ICw2$, CTw, and TCw for the WDR transition and $ICi1$, $ICi2$, CTi, and TCi for the $INTR$ transition. Second, the corresponding initial behaviour of these two operations is reported as tokens in the meta-place *meta-account*. More precisely, the token reflecting the behaviour of *Withdraw* is:

$$\langle WDR : 1 | (ACNT, \langle C | Bal : B, Lmt : L \rangle) \otimes (WDR, Wdr(C, W)),$$
$$(ACNT, \langle C | Bal : B - W, Lmt : L \rangle), (W > 0 \wedge (B - W) > L \rangle.$$

And the token reflecting the behaviour of *Deposit* is:

$$\langle INTR : 1 | (ACNT, \langle C | Ints : I \rangle) \otimes (INTR, IncI(AN, NI)),$$
$$(ACNT, \langle C | Ints : NI \rangle), (NI > I \rangle.$$

Besides this behaviour, we now assume that managers of this application decide to add new version of withdraw, and to completely change the current behaviour of the Increase-of-interest. For the supplement withdraw behviour they propose, for instance, that only a sum that is less than 2 percent of the current balance may be withdrawn, and there is some tax (as a natural constant tax) to be deduced from the balance (in addition the to withdrawn sum). In the modified form of interest-increase, they require that only accounts with balance more than 3000 are authorized to increase their interest with no more than 1 percent.

This runtime introduction of a new withdraw behaviour as well as the modification of the interest-increase method are are reflected in the corresponding places *Add_Beh* and *Chg_Bh*, in Figure 5, by the presence of the following terms:

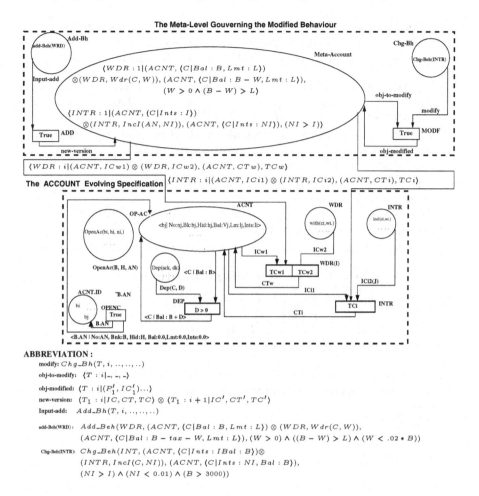

Fig. 5. A Dynamically Evolving Account Specification

$$Add\_Beh(WDR, (ACNT, \langle C|Bal : B, \ Lmt : L \rangle) \otimes (WDR, Wdr(C, W)),$$
$$(ACNT, \langle C|Bal : B - tax - W, Lmt : L \rangle), (W > 0) \wedge ((B - W) > L) \wedge (W < .02 * B))$$

$$Chg\_Beh(INT, (ACNT, \langle C|Ints : I, Bal : B \rangle) \otimes (INTR, IncI(C, NI)),$$
$$(ACNT, \langle C|Ints : NI, Bal : B \rangle), (NI > I) \wedge (NI < 0.01) \wedge (B > 3000))$$

The firing of the meta-transitions ADD and $MODIF$ result in the CO-NET depicted in Figure 6; where the new version of the *withdraw* behaviour is added and the *increase-of-interest* behaviour is modified.

Let us, for instance, explain how the *meta-infernce-rule* is applied for generating this new (additional) behaviour for $Withdraw$.[6] First, we have to apply the (abstract) meta inference-rule (**) with the following replacements:

- l stands for the terms (as variable) with their respective place annotating *input arcs* in the meta-transition $WDR(i)$; hence it is equal to $(ACNT, ICw1) \otimes (WDR, ICw2)$;
- r stands for the terms (as variable) with their respective place annotating *output arcs* in the meta-transition $WDR(i)$; hence it is equal to $(ACNT, CTw1) \otimes (WDR, CTw2)$;
- m stands for the read-arc relating this transition with the meta place *meta-account*, i.e., it is equal to:
  $\langle WDR : i | (ACNT, ICw1) \otimes (WDR, ICw2), (ACNT, CTw), TCw \rangle$;
- the condition C stands for TCw;
- the substitution σ is the union of the following elementary substitution:

Variable	Corresponding Substitution
$ICw1$	$\langle C | Bal : B, Lmt : L \rangle$
$ICw2$	$Wdr(C, W)$
Ctw	$\langle C | Bal : B - tax - W, Lmt : L \rangle$
TCw	$(W > 0 \wedge ((B - W) > L) \wedge (W < .02 * B))$

- The conclusion corresponds to the following (usual) CO-NETS rewrite rule that can be applied exactly in the same way as done for rules of the object level:
  WRD(2^7): $(ACNT, \langle C | Bal : B, Lmt : L \rangle) \otimes (WDR, Wdr(C, W))$
  $\Rightarrow (ACNT, \langle C | Bal : B - tax - W, Lmt : L \rangle)$ *if*
  $(W > 0 \wedge ((B - W) > L) \wedge (W < .02 * B)$

4 Conclusion

The CO-NETS approach is an adequate conceptual model that conceive infomation systems as fully distributed, autonomous yet cooperative components. It is based on a complete integration of OO concepts and constructions into a variant of algebraic Petri nets, and it has the following features. First, CO-NETS allow for modeling components as hierarchy of classes through different forms of inheritance, object composition and aggregation. Second, interaction of such components is achieved using explicit interfaces. Third, CO-NETS semantics is expressed in rewriting logic allowing rapid-prototyping using rewriting techniques

In this paper we have proposed an appropriate extension of the approach for dynamically evolving different system components in a formal way. The main

---

[6] Note the choice of a given withdraw method is completely let to the user.
[7] To say that we now have two *withdraw* behaviours.

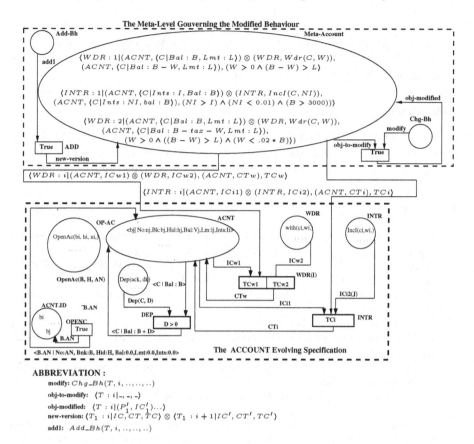

Fig. 6. The Meta-Account Objects after firing the meta-level transitions

ideas under this CO-NETS extension are the use of new forms of places and transitions named respectively meta-places and meta-transitions and the introduction of an adequate inference rule that propagate the behaviour to usual CO-NET rewrite rules. This new form of evolving specification have been illustrated using a simplified account specification.

However, after this crucial first step towards specifying and rapid-prototyping advanced information systems are distributed, dynamically evolving, autonomous yet cooperating components using our CO-NETS approach, we are conscious that much work remain ahead. Thus, our future investigation will focus on the consolidation of this dynamic evolving by drawing up more complex case studies. Furthermore, as a result of this formalization of dynamic evolution, two interesting directions are to be investigated. On the one hand, we plan to extend the meta-place content to deal not only with behaviour but also with object and message instances. This will particularly allow us to include and enforce dynamic as well as static constraints integrity (on the whole component instances).

On the other hand, we also plan to include in these meta-place proof-algebras [7] which keep trace of all fired transitions in the object level using an adequate partial ordering. This will permit us to incorporate a past temporal reasoning as a formal verification in our approach.

Acknowledgments

Sincere thanks are due to Gunter Saake and Can Türker for their careful reading of various versions of this paper and for suggesting significant improvements. This presentation has also benefited from the remarks of the anonymous referees.

References

1. R. Allen and D. Garlan. A Formal Basis for Architectural Connection. Technical report, School of Computer Science, Carnegie Mellon University, 1997.
2. N. Aoumeur and G. Saake. Towards a New Semantics for Mondel Specifications Based on the CO-Net Approach. In J. Desel, K. Pohl, and P. Schuerr, editors, *Proc. Modellierung'99, Karlruhe, Germany, March 1999*, pages 107–122, B. G. Teubner-Verlag, 1999.
3. N. Aoumeur and G. Saake. Towards an Object Petri Nets Model for Specifying and Validating Distributed Information Systems. In M. Jarke and A. Oberweis, editors, *Proc. of the 11th Int. Conf. on Advanced Information Systems Engineering, CAiSE'99, Heidelberg, Germany*, Lecture Notes in Computer Science, Vol. 1626, pages 381–395, Springer-Verlag, 1999.
4. F. Chabot and J. Raskin. The Formal Semantics of ALBERT II. Technical report, Namur University, Computer Science Institute, 1998.
5. M. Clavel, F. Duran, S. Eker, J. Meseguer, and M. Stehr. Maude : Specification and Programming in Rewriting Logic. Technical report, SRI, Computer Science Laboratory, March 1999. URL: http://maude.csl.sri.com.
6. S. Conrad, J. Ramos, G. Saake, and C. Sernadas. Evolving Logical Specification in Information Systems. In J. Chomicki and G. Saake, editors, *Logics for Databases and Information Systems*, chapter 6, pages 167–198, Kluwer Academic Publishers, 1998.
7. G. Denker. From Rewrite Theories to Temporal Logic Theories. In H. Kirchner and C. Kirchner, editors, *Proc. of Second International Workshop on Rewriting Logic*, Electronic Notes in Theoretical Computer Science, Vol. 15, 1998.
8. N. Dershowitz and J.-P. Jouannaud. Rewrite systems. In J. van Leeuwen, editor, *Handbook of Theoretical Computer Science*, chapter 6, pages 243–320, Vol. B: Formal Methods and Semantics, North-Holland, 1990.
9. P. Du Bois. *The Albert II Language: On the Design and the Use of a Formal Specification Language for Requirements Analysis.* PhD thesis, Computer Department, University of Namur, Belgium, September 1995.
10. H.-D. Ehrich, C. Caleiro, A. Sernadas, and G. Denker. Logics for Specifying Concurrent Information Systems. In J. Chomicki and G. Saake, editors, *Logics for Databases and Information Systems*, chapter 6, pages 167–198, Kluwer Academic Publishers, 1998.
11. H.-D. Ehrich, M Gogolla, and A. Sernadas. Objects and Their Specification. In M. Bidoit and C. Choppy, editors, *Proc. of 8th Workshop on Abstract Data*, Lecture Notes in Computer Science, Vol. 655, pages 40–66, Springer-Verlag, 1992.

12. H. Ehrig and B. Mahr. *Fundamentals of Algebraic Specification 2: Module Specification and Constraints.* Springer-Verlag, 1990.

13. Goguen, J. and Winkler, T. and Meseguer, J. and Futatsugi, K. and Jouannaud, J.P. Introducing OBJ. Technical Report SRI-CSL-92-03, Computer Science Laboratory, SRI International, 1992.

14. K. Jensen and G. Rozenberg. *High-level Petri Nets.* Springer-Verlag, 1991.

15. R. Jungclaus, G. Saake, T. Hartmann, and C. Sernadas. TROLL – A Language for Object-Oriented Specification of Information Systems. *ACM Transactions on Information Systems*, 14(2):175–211, April 1996.

16. S. Matsuoka and A. Yonezawa. Analysis of Inheritance Anomaly in Concurrent Object-Oriented Languages. *Research Directions in Object-Based Concurrency*, pages 107–150, 1993.

17. J. Meseguer. Conditional Rewriting Logic as a Unified Model for Concurrency. *Theoretical Computer Science*, 96:73–155, 1992.

18. J. Meseguer. A Logical Theory of Concurrent Objects and its Realization in the Maude Language. *Research Directions in Object-Based Concurrency*, pages 314–390, 1993.

19. M. P. Papazoglou and G. Schlageter, editors. *Cooperative Information Systems: Trends and Directions.* Academic Press, 1998.

20. G. Saake, A. Sernadas, and C. Sernadas. Evolving Object Specifications. In R. Wieringa and R. Feenstra, editors, *Information Systems — Correctness and Reusability. Selected Papers from the IS-CORE Workshop*, pages 84–99, World Scientific Publishing, Singapore, 1995.

21. P. Wegner. Concepts and Paradigms of Object-Oriented Programming. *ACM SIGPLAN OOPS Messenger*, 1(1):7–87, August 1990.

Specifying Active Rules for Database Maintenance*

Leopoldo Bertossi and Javier Pinto

Departamento de Ciencia de la Computación
Escuela de Ingeniería
Pontificia Universidad Católica de Chile
Casilla 306, Santiago, Chile
{bertossi, jpinto}@ing.puc.cl

Abstract In this article we extend previous work on the development of logical foundations for the specification of the dynamics of databases. In particular, we deal with two problems. Firstly, the derivation of *active rules* that maintain the consistency of the database by triggering repairing actions. Secondly, we deal with the correct integration of the specification of the derived rules into the original specification of the database dynamics. In particular, we show that the expected results are achieved. For instance, the derived axiomatization includes, at the object level, the specification that repairing action executions must be enforced whenever necessary.

1   Introduction

In this article we propose a logic based approach to automatically derive active rules [30] for the maintenance of the integrity of a database [5]. This research follows the tradition of specifying the semantics of a database using mathematical logic [20,7]. In particular, we deal with a logical framework in which transactions are treated as objects within the logical language, allowing one to reason about the dynamics of change in a database as transactions are executed.

As shown in [26], it is possible to specify the dynamics of a relational database with a special formalism written in the situation calculus (SC) [17], a language of many-sorted predicate logic for representing knowledge and reasoning about actions and change. Apart from providing a natural and well studied semantics, the formalism can be used to solve different reasoning tasks. For instance, reason about the evolution of a database [3], reason about the hypothetical evolutions of a database [1], reason about the dynamics of views [2], etc.

In the SC formalism, each relational table is represented by a table predicate. Each table predicate has one *situation* argument which is used to denote the state of the database. In order to specify the dynamics of the relations in a database, one derives the so-called *successor state axioms* (SSAs); one SSA per base relation or table.

---

* This research has been partially financed by FONDECYT (Grants 1990089 and 1980945), and ECOS/CONICYT (Grant C97E05).

G. Saake, K. Schwarz, and C. Türker (Eds.): TDD '99, LNCS 1773, pp. 112–129, 2000.

Each SSA describes the exact conditions under which the presence of an arbitrary tuple in the table holds after executing an arbitrary legal primitive transaction[1]. SSAs state necessary and sufficient conditions for any tuple to belong to a relation after a transaction is performed. These conditions refer only to the state[2] in which the transaction is executed and does not make reference to further constraints on the resulting state. Thus, there are no explicit integrity constraints (IC) in the specification.

Given the exhaustive descriptions of the successor states (those obtained after executing primitive transactions) provided by the the SSAs, it is very easy to get into inconsistencies if integrity constraints are introduced in the specification. For example, this is true when *ramification constraints* are introduced. These are constraints that force the database to make indirect changes in tables due to changes in other tables.

There are several options to deal with this problem:

1. One can assume that the ICs are somehow embedded in the SSAs. This is the approach in [26]. They should be logical consequences of the DB specification.
2. Some ICs can be considered as *qualification constraints*, that is, they are considered as constraints on the executability of the database actions. In [14] a methodology for translating these constraints into axioms on the executability of actions, or better, on the legality of actions is presented. In this approach, the so-called *Action Precondition Axioms* are generated.
3. For some interesting syntactical classes of ramification ICs, there are mechanisms for compiling them into *Effect Axioms*, from which the SSAs can be re-computed. Then, the explicit ICs disappear and they turn out to be logical consequences of the new specification [18,23] (see also [3] for implementation issues).
4. It is also possible to think of a database maintenance approach, consisting of adding active rules to a modification of the original specification. These rules enforce the satisfaction of the ICs by triggering appropriate auxiliary actions. Preliminary work on this, in a general framework for knowledge representation of action and change, is shown in [22].

The last alternative is the subject of this paper. There are several issues to be considered. First, a computational mechanism should be provided for deriving active rules and repairing actions from the ICs. Second, the active rules should be consistent with the rest of the specification and produce the expected effects. Third, since the active rules will have the usual *Event-Condition-Action* (ECA) form [30,31], which does not have a direct predicate logic semantics, they should be specifiable in (a suitable extension of) the language of the situation calculus, and integrated smoothly with the rest of the specification. Some work in this direction, on the assumption that general ECA rules are given, is presented in [4].

---

[1] These are the simplest, non-decomposable transactions; they are domain dependent. In the KR literature they are called "actions". We consider the notions *primitive transaction* and *action* as synonyms.

[2] In this paper we do not make any distinction between situations and states.

2   Specification of the Database Dynamics

Characteristic ingredients of a particular language $\mathcal{L}$ of the situation calculus, besides the usual symbols of predicate logic, are:

(a) Among others, the sorts *action, situation*.
(b) Predicate symbols whose last argument is of the sort *situation*. These predicates depend on the state of the world and can be thought of as the tables in a relational database.
(c) Operation symbols which applied to individuals produce actions (or primitive transactions), for example, *enroll*($\cdot$) may be an operation, and *enroll*(*john*) becomes an action term.
(d) A constant, S_0, to denote the initial state of the database.
(e) An operation symbol *do* that takes an action and a situation as arguments, producing a new situation, a successor situation resulting from the execution of the action at the given situation.

In these languages there are first-order variables for individuals of each sort, so it is possible to quantify over individuals, actions, and situations. They are usually denoted by $\forall \bar{x}$, $\forall a$, $\forall s$, respectively.

The specification of a dynamically changing world, by means of an appropriate language of the situation calculus, consists of a specification of the laws of evolution of the world. This is typically done by specifying:

1. Fixed, state independent, but domain dependent knowledge about the individuals of the world.
2. Knowledge about the state of the world at the initial situation given in terms of formulas that do not mention any state besides S_0.
3. Preconditions for performing the different actions (or making their execution possible). The predicate *Poss* is introduced in $\mathcal{L}$. The predicate has one action and one situation as arguments. Thus, $Poss(a, s)$ says that the execution of action a is possible in state s.
4. The immediate (positive or negative) effects of actions in terms of the tables whose truth values we know are changed by their execution.

In Reiter's formalism, the knowledge contained in items 1. and 2. above is considered the initial database Σ_0. The information given in item 3. is formalized by means of action precondition axioms (*APAs*) of the form:

$$Poss(A(\bar{x}), s) \equiv \pi_A(\bar{x}, s),$$

for each action name A, where $\pi_A(\bar{x}, s)$ is a SC formula that is *simple in s*. A situation is said to be *simple* in a situation term s if it contains no state term other than s (e.g., no *do* symbol); no quantifications on states; and no occurrences of the *Poss* predicate [15]. Finally, item 4. is expressed by effect axioms for pairs (primitive transaction, table):

Positive Effects Axioms: For some pairs formed by a table R and an action name A, an axiom of the form:

$$\forall(\bar{x}, \bar{y}, s)[Poss(A(\bar{y}), s) \wedge \varphi_R^+(\bar{y}, \bar{x}, s) \supset R(\bar{x}, do(A(\bar{y}), s))]. \tag{1}$$

Intuitively, if the named primitive transaction A is possible, and the preconditions on the database are true at state s (in particular, on the table R, represented by the meta-formula $\varphi_R^+(\bar{y}, \bar{x}, s)$) then the statement R becomes true of $\bar{x}$ at the successor state $do(A(\bar{y}), s)$ obtained after execution of A at state s. Here, $\bar{x}, \bar{y}$ are parameters for the table and action. Notice that in general we have two kinds of conditions: (a) Preconditions for action executions, independently from any table they might affect. These are axiomatized by the *Poss* predicate. (b) Preconditions on the database for pairs table/action which make the changes possible (given that the action is already possible). These preconditions are represented by $\varphi_R^+(\bar{y}, \bar{x}, s)$.

Negative Effects Axioms: For some pairs formed by a table R and an action name A, an axiom of the form:

$$\forall(\bar{x}, \bar{y}, s)[Poss(A(\bar{y}), s) \wedge \varphi_R^-(\bar{y}, \bar{x}, s) \supset \neg R(\bar{x}, do(A(\bar{y}), s))]. \tag{2}$$

This is the case where action A makes table R to become false of $\bar{x}$ in the successor state.

Example 1. Consider an educational database as in [26], with the following ingredients. Tables: 1. *Enrolled*(stu, c, s), student stu is enrolled in course c in the state s. 2. *Grade*(stu, c, g, s), the grade of student stu in course c is g in the state s. Primitive Transactions: 1. *register*(stu, c), register student stu in course c. 2. *change*(stu, c, g), change the grade of student stu in course c to g. 3. *drop*(stu, c), eliminate student stu from the course c.

Action Precondition Axioms:

$$\forall(stu, c, s)[Poss(register(stu, c), s) \equiv \neg Enrolled(stu, c, s)].$$
$$\forall(stu, c, g, s)[Poss(change(stu, c, g), s) \equiv \exists g'\, Grade(stu, c, g', s)].$$
$$\forall(stu, c, s)[Poss(drop(stu, c), s) \equiv Enrolled(stu, c, s)].$$

Effect Axioms:

$$\forall(stu, c, s)[Poss(register(stu, c), s) \supset Enrolled(stu, c, do(register(stu, c), s))]$$
$$\forall(stu, c, s)[Poss(drop(stu, c), s) \supset \neg Enrolled(stu, c, do(drop(stu, c), s))]$$
$$\forall(stu, c, g, s)[Poss(change(stu, c, g), s) \supset$$
$$Grade(stu, c, g, do(change(stu, c, g), s))].$$

$$\forall(stu, c, g, g', s)[Poss(change(stu, c, g'), s) \wedge g \neq g' \supset$$
$$\neg Grade(stu, c, g, do(change(stu, c, g'), s))]$$

$\square$

A problem with a specification like the one we have so far is that it does not mention the usually many things (entries in tables) that do not change when a specific action is executed. We face the so-called *frame problem*, consisting of providing a short, succinct, specification of the properties that persist after actions are performed. Reiter [25] discovered a simple solution to the frame problem as it appears in the situation calculus. It allows to construct a first-order specification, that accounts both for effects and non–effects, from a specification that contains descriptions of effects only, as in the example above. We sketch this solution in the rest of this section.

For illustration, assume that we have no negative effects, and two positive effect laws for table R: (1) and

$$\forall(\bar{x}, \bar{z}, s)[Poss(A'(\bar{z}), s) \wedge \psi_R^+(\bar{z}, \bar{x}, s) \supset R(\bar{x}, do(A'(\bar{z}), s))]. \tag{3}$$

We may combine them into one general positive effect axiom for table R:

$$\forall(a, \bar{x}, s)[Poss(a, s) \wedge [\exists\bar{y}(a = A(\bar{y}) \wedge \varphi_R^+(\bar{y}, \bar{x}, s)) \vee$$
$$\exists\bar{z}(a = A'(\bar{z}) \wedge \psi_R^+(\bar{z}, \bar{x}, s))] \supset R(\bar{x}, do(a, s))].$$

In this form we obtain, for each table R, a general positive effect law of the form:

$$\forall(a, \bar{x}, s)[Poss(a, s) \wedge \gamma_R^+(a, \bar{x}, s) \supset R(\bar{x}, do(a, s))].$$

Analogously, we obtain, for each table R, a general negative effect axiom:

$$\forall(a, \bar{x}, s)[Poss(a, s) \wedge \gamma_R^-(a, \bar{x}, s) \supset \neg R(\bar{x}, do(a, s))].$$

For each table R we have represented, in one single axiom, all the actions and the corresponding conditions on the database that can make $R(\bar{x})$ true at an arbitrary successor state obtained by executing a legal action. In the same way we can describe when $R(\bar{x})$ becomes false.

Example 2. (cont'd) In the educational example we obtain the following general effect axioms for the table *Grade*:

$$\forall(a, stu, c, g, s)[Poss(a, s) \wedge a = change(stu, c, g) \supset Grade(stu, c, g, do(a, s))]$$
$$\forall(a, stu, c, g, s)[Poss(a, s) \wedge \exists g'(a = change(stu, c, g') \wedge g \neq g')$$
$$\supset \neg Grade(stu, c, g, do(a, s))].$$

□

The basic assumption underlying Reiter's solution to the frame problem is that the general effect axioms, both positive and negative, for a given table R, contain all the possibilities for table R to change its truth value from a state to a successor state. Actually, for each table R we generate its Successor State Axiom:

$$\forall(a, s)Poss(a, s) \supset \forall\bar{x}[R(\bar{x}, do(a, s)) \equiv (\gamma_R^+(a, \bar{x}, s) \vee (R(\bar{x}, s) \wedge \neg\gamma_R^-(a, \bar{x}, s)))]. \tag{4}$$

Here, γ^+ and γ^- are of the form $\bigvee_{some\ A's} \exists \bar{u}(a = A(\bar{u}) \wedge \varphi(\bar{u}, \bar{x}, s))$, meaning that action A, under condition φ, makes $R(\bar{x}, do(A, s))$ true, in the case of γ^+, and false, in the case of γ^-. Thus, the SSA says that if action a is possible, then R becomes true at the successor state that results from the execution of action a if and only if a is one of the actions causing R to be true (and for which the corresponding preconditions, φ, are true), or R was already true before executing a and this action is not one of the actions that falsify R.

Example 3. (cont'd) In our running example, we obtain the following SSAs for the tables in the database:

$$\forall(a, s)Poss(a, s) \supset \quad \forall(stu, c)[Enrolled(stu, c, do(a, s)) \equiv a = register(stu, c) \vee$$
$$Enrolled(stu, c, s) \wedge a \neq drop(stu, c)]$$
$$\forall(a, s)Poss(a, s) \supset \forall(stu, c, g)[Grade(stu, c, g, do(a, s)) \equiv a = change(stu, c, g) \vee$$
$$Grade(stu, c, g, s) \wedge \neg \exists g'(a = change(stu, c, g') \wedge g' \neq g)].$$

□

Notice that, provided there is complete knowledge about the contents of the tables at the initial state, the SSAs completely describe the contents of the tables at every state that can be reached by executing a finite sequence of legal primitive transactions (that is for which the corresponding *Poss* conditions are satisfied). The SSAs have a nice inductive structure that makes some reasoning tasks easy, at least in principle.

In order for the specification to have the right logical consequences, we will assume that the following *Foundational Axioms of the Situation Calculus (FAs)* underlie any database specification [14]:

1. Unique Names Axioms for Actions (*UNAA*): $A_i(\bar{x}) \neq A_j(\bar{y})$, for all different action names A_i, A_j; and $\forall(\bar{x}, \bar{y})[A(\bar{x}) = A(\bar{y}) \supset \bar{x} = \bar{y}]$, for every action name A.
2. Unique Names Axioms for States:

$$S_0 \neq do(a, s),$$
$$do(a_1, s_1) = do(a_2, s_2) \supset a_1 = a_2 \wedge s_1 = s_2.$$

3. For some reasoning tasks we need an Induction Axiom on States:

$$\forall P\ [P(S_0) \wedge \forall s \forall a\ (P(s) \supset P(do(a, s))) \quad \supset \quad \forall s\ P(s)],$$

   that has the effect of restricting the domain of situations to the one containing the initial situation and the situations that can be obtained by executing a finite number of actions. In this way, no *non-standard* situations may appear. The axiom is second order, but for some reasoning tasks, like proving integrity constraints, reasoning can be done at the first-order level [14,3].
4. Finally, we will be usually interested in reasoning about states that are accessible from the initial situation by executing a finite sequence of legal actions.

This *accessibility relation* on states, $\leq$, can be defined from the induction axiom plus the conditions:

$$\neg s < S_0$$

$$s < do(a, s') \equiv Poss(a, s') \wedge s \leq s'.$$

Summarizing, a specification Σ, in the SC, of transaction based database updates consists of the sets: $\Sigma_0 \cup APAs \cup SSAs \cup FAs$.

Example 4. (cont'd) A static IC we would like to see satisfied at every accessible state of the database is the functional dependency for table $Grade^3$. The IC can be expressed by:

$$\forall s(S_0 \leq s \supset \forall stu, c, g_1, g_2 \ (Grade(stu, c, g_1, s) \wedge Grade(stu, c, g_2, s) \supset g_1 = g_2)). \tag{5}$$

According to Reiter [26], this formula should be a logical consequence of a correct specification of the form described above; actually in our example this is the case. Otherwise, we should have to embed the IC into a modified specification of the same form as before or we should have to generate active rules for making the IC hold.   □

3   Integrity Constraints and Internal Actions

In the following, we distinguish between agent or user actions and *internal actions*[4]. We have already considered the first class; they are user defined primitive transactions, and appear explicitly in a possibly more complex user transaction[5]. Instead, the internal actions are executed by the database management system as a response to the state of the database. They will be executed immediately when they are expected to be executed with the purpose of restoring the integrity of the database.

In the rest of this paper, with the purpose of illustrating our approach, we will consider only ICs of the form

$$\forall s(S_0 \leq s \supset \forall \bar{x} \ (R_1(\bar{x}, s) \wedge R_2(\bar{x}, s) \supset R(\bar{x}, s)), \tag{6}$$

where R_1, R_2, R are table names, or negations of them; and the variables in each of them in (6) are among the variables in $\bar{x}$. The Rs could also be built-in predicates, like the equality predicate. In particular, as described in a later example, functional dependencies, fall in this class.

A basic assumption here is that an IC like (6) is not just a logical formula that has to be made true in every state of the database, but it also has a *causal*

---

[3] In this paper we consider only static integrity constraints. A methodology for treating dynamic integrity constraints as static integrity constraints is presented in [1].

[4] In [22] they are called *natural actions*.

[5] Complex database transactions have been treated in [4]. In this paper we restrict ourselves to primitive transactions only.

intention, in the sense that every time the antecedent becomes true, necessarily the consequent has to become true as well, whereas from a pure logical point of view, just making the antecedent false would work (see [13,28] for a discussion about the logical representation of causal rules.).

Example 5. (cont'd) The functional dependency (5) has the form (6). Nevertheless, it is not written in a "causal" form. That is, the intention behind the axiom is not to state that if two grades g_1 and g_2 are recorded for the same student in a course at a given situation, then both grades are caused to be the same. Actually, it would make no sense to try to enforce this. A more appropriate way to write (5) is

$$\forall s(S_0 \leq s \supset \forall stu, c, g_1, g_2 \ (Grade(stu, c, g_1, s) \wedge g_1 \neq g_2 \supset \neg Grade(stu, c, g_2, s), \tag{7}$$

that is, a student having a certain grade is the cause for the same student not having any other different grade.   □

For each IC of this form, we introduce an internal action name A_R with as many arguments as non situational arguments appear in R. We introduce a new predicate, *Internal* on actions; then, for A_R, we specify

$$Internal(A_R(\bar{x})), \tag{8}$$

$$Poss(A_R(\bar{x}), s) \supset R_1(\bar{x}, s) \wedge R_2(\bar{x}, s) \wedge \neg R(\bar{x}, s), \tag{9}$$

$$Poss(A_R(\bar{x}), s) \supset R(\bar{x}, do(A_R(\bar{x}, s)). \tag{10}$$

This says that: (a) the new action is internal; (b) a necessary condition for the internal action to be possible is that the corresponding IC is violated; and (c) if it possible, then, after the internal action is executed, the R, mentioned in the head of (6), becomes true of the tuple $\bar{x}$ at the successor state.

Notice that the right-hand side of (9) should be an evaluable or domain independent formula [29,10]. In addition, as mentioned in Example 5, and according with the causal view of ICs, the literal R there should not be associated to a built-in predicate, because its satisfaction is enforced through formula (10).

As discussed later on, there may be extra necessary conditions at a state s to specify for the execution of A_R at s. Once all these necessary conditions have been collected, they can be placed in a single axiom of the form

$$Poss(A_R(\bar{x}, s)) \supset \varphi_{A_R}(\bar{x}, s). \tag{11}$$

Later, we appeal to Clark's completion [9] for the possibility predicate for the internal action. Thus, transforming necessary conditions into necessary and sufficient conditions. Thus, replacing $\supset$ by $\equiv$ in (11).

In our example, $\varphi_{A_R}(\bar{x}, s)$ would contain the right-hand side of (9) among other things, but not the right-hand side of (10) that corresponds to a new effect axiom.

The need for extra necessary conditions for the repairing action A_R in (9), is related to specific repair policies to be adopted. In our running example, we might decide that when a new grade is inserted for a student in a course, then the old grade has to be eliminated in favor of the new one. Therefore, adding the new grade will be equivalent to performing an update. This should be the effect of the internal, repairing action. Therefore, the extra necessary condition for this action is that the grade to be eliminated was in the database before the new one was introduced. This sort of historical conditions can be handled in our formalism by means of virtual tables that record the changes in the tables [4] (in our example, the old grade would not be recorded as a change, but the new one would; see example 6 below); or by means of a methodology, presented in [1] and based on [6], for specifying the dynamics of auxiliary, virtual, and history encoding views defined from formulas written in past temporal logic.

Once the internal action is introduced, in order to produce the effects described in (10), the action A_R has to be inserted in the SSA of the corresponding table: if the right-hand side of (6) is a table R, with SSA like (4), then $a = A_R$ must now appear in $\gamma_R^+(a, \bar{x}, s)$ in (4) to make R true. If the right-hand side is $\neg R$, then $a = A_{\neg R}$ must be appear in $\gamma_R^-(a, \bar{x}, s)$, to make R false.

Action A_R is specified to make R true. The fact that R is different from R_1 and R_2, or even when R is the same as, say, R_1, the fact that the arguments to which the literals apply are different, will cause that A_R will not affect the truth of $R_1(\bar{x}, s) \wedge R_2(\bar{x}, s)$; it will persist from s to $do(A_R(\bar{x}), s)$, making the IC true at $do(A_R(\bar{x}), s)$, that is, A_R has a repairing effect. Notice also that the IC is not satisfied at the state s, where the internal action A_R will be forced to occur. In this sense, s will be an "unstable" situation.

Since, later on, we will force internal actions to occur at corresponding unstable situations, we define a *stable situation* as every situation where no internal actions are possible:

$$stable(s) \equiv \neg\exists a \,(Internal(a) \wedge Poss(a, s)). \tag{12}$$

Intuitively, the stable situations are those where the integrity constraints are to be satisfied. Instead, unstable situations are a part of a sequence of situations leading to a stable situation; in those unstable, intermediate situations, ICs do not need to hold. The transition to a stable situation is obtained by the execution of auxiliary, repairing actions.

The specification in (11) suggests the introduction of the following *active rule*:

$$E_{A_R}(\bar{x}); \; \{\varphi_{A_R}(\bar{x})\} \;\Rightarrow\; A_R(\bar{x}); \tag{13}$$

where $E_{A_R}(\bar{x})$ is an *Event* associated to the IC that corresponds to changes produced in the database, for example, the insertion of $\bar{x}$ in the tables appearing in (9). This event causes the rule to be considered. Then, *Condition* $\{\varphi_{A_R}(\bar{x})\}$ is evaluated. It includes the fact that R_1, R_2 became true and $\neg R$ became false. If this *Condition* is satisfied, then the *Action* A_R is executed.

An alternative to rule (13) would be to skip E_{A_R}, and always check *Condition* $\{\varphi_{A_R}(\bar{x})\}$ after any transaction, but including in the *Condition* the information about the changes produced in the database by keeping them in an auxiliary view, so that they can be taken into account for the *Action* to be executed. This approach is illustrated in the next example.

Example 6. (cont'd) Given the functional dependency (7), we introduce the internal action $A_{Grade}(stu, c, g)$. Assume that we already have a view

$$Changes_{Grade}(stu, c, g, s)$$

that records the changes in *Grade*. That is, $Changes_{Grade}(stu, c, g, s)$ means that $Grade(stu, c, g, s) \land \neg Grade(stu, c, g, s')$, where s' is the situation that precedes s. Then, the precondition axiom for the new action is

$$Poss(A_{Grade}(stu, c, g), s) \equiv Grade(stu, c, g_1, s) \land g_1 \neq g \land Grade(stu, c, g, s)$$
$$\land Changes_{Grade}(stu, c, g_1, s).$$
(14)

The new action should have the effect of deleting tuple (stu, c, g) from *Grade*. This is specified with the effect axiom:

$$Poss(A_{Grade}(stu, c, g), s) \supset \neg Grade(stu, c, g, do(A_R(stu, c, g), s)), \quad (15)$$

that corresponds to (10).

Thus, when the IC is violated (this violation is expressed by the first three conjuncts on the right side of (14)), the action A_{Grade} is possible. When the internal action becomes possible, it must be executed. As a result of the execution, the repair is carried out, by eliminating the old grade.

Notice that predicate *Changes* could be pushed to the *Event* part of the rule, as discussed before, because it keeps record of the changes in the database. The dynamics of an auxiliary view like *Changes* could be specified, and in this way, integrating everything we need into the same specification, by means of a corresponding SSA. This can be achieved by means of a general methodology developed in [2] and [1] for deriving SSAs for views and history encoding relations, resp.

4   Specifying Executions

The approach presented in the previous section is still incomplete. Indeed, for this approach to work, we need to address two independent but important problems. First, we need to specify that executions should be enforced, since, up to now, the formalism presented deals with hypothetical executions. Second, we need to deal with the problem of executions of *repairing* actions arising from several ICs violated in the same situation. We deal with these issues below.

Notice that there is nothing in our SC specification that forces the action A_R to be executed. The whole specification is hypothetical in the sense that *if the actions ... were executed, then the effects ... would be observed.*. Thus, from the logical specification of the dynamics of change of a traditional database, it is possible to reason about all its possible legal evolutions. However, these specifications do not consider transactions that *must be executed* given certain environmental conditions (i.e., the database state). In order to include active rules in this style of specifications, it is necessary to extend the situation calculus with *executions*. This is necessary, given that the actions specified by active rules must be *forced to be executed* when the associated *Event* happens and the corresponding *Condition* is satisfied. That is, the future is not open to all possible evolutions, but constrained by the necessary execution of actions mentioned in the rules that fire, given that their related conditions hold.

The notion of execution in SC was first introduced in [24][6]. This problem has subsequently been treated in [19,22]. Our discussion is based upon [22]. The starting point is the observation that every situation s identifies a unique sequence of actions. That is, situations can be identified with the history of actions that lead to them (starting in S_0): $s = do(a_n, \ldots (do(a_2, do(a_1, S_0)) \ldots))$. We say that the actions $a_1, a_2, \ldots, a_n$ belong to the history of s. The predicate *executed*, that takes an action and a situation as arguments, is introduced in order to specify constraints in valid or *legal* histories. For illustration purposes, let us assume that we have situations S, S', such that $S < S'$. Further, assume that we specify that $executed(A, S)$. The fact that A has to have been executed in S, from the perspective of S', should entail that action A must appear in the history of S' (unless S' were not legal), immediately after S. To specify such a constraint we use the predicate *legal* for situations. This predicate characterizes the situations that conform to the executions that should arise in their histories; the specification of *legal* is as follows:

$$legal(s_h) \equiv S_0 \leq s_h \wedge \forall a, s \; (s < s_h \wedge executed(a, s) \supset do(a, s) \leq s_h). \quad (16)$$

The notion of legality, defined with the *legal* predicate, introduces a more restrictive form of legality for situations than the notion strictly based upon the *Poss* predicate. A situation is considered *legal*, in this more restrictive sense, if the executions that must arise in its history appear in it, and if all the situations in the history are reached by performing possible transactions starting in S_0. When modeling active databases, we consider that situations are legal when their histories are consistent with the intended semantics of the rule executions.

Whenever the condition of an active rule in consideration is satisfied, the action mentioned in the rule must be executed. Therefore, the specification of an active rule must include the presence of the predicate *executed* associated to its *Action*, actually, an internal action in our context. In a database whose situations are all *legal* will be such that active rules, when triggered, are properly dealt with. Thus, in a situation calculus tree we only consider branches in which actions that must be executed by rule triggerings are actually executed.

Now we can force internal actions to be executed. This is specified as follows:

$$\forall a, s \; Poss(a, s) \wedge Internal(a) \supset executed(a, s). \quad (17)$$

That is, if an internal action is possible, it must be executed. In this way the repairing internal actions are executed immediately. Nevertheless, it should not

---

[6] It was called *occurrence* there.

be difficult to specify in our SC formalism delayed executions. In [4], these issues are considered along with other issues dealing with execution priority of rules, and execution of complex transactions.

The active rule (13) is not written in the SC object language of the specification, and in that sense its semantics is not integrated with the rest of the first-order semantics. Nevertheless, it can now be eliminated from the specification in favor of axioms (8), (9), (10), and (17). Recall that, in addition to the introduction of these new axioms, the SSA (4) for table R has to be modified by introducing $a = A_R$ in the formula $\gamma_R^+(a, \bar{x}, s)$, since new positive effects have been specified for table R. This possible re-computation of the SSAs is a very simple task. Only one action for IC with its condition has to be plugged into an SSA. If the active rules for database maintenance are given in advance, then the SSAs for the tables can be computed incorporating the corresponding actions from the very beginning.

Now, it can be proved that the following formula is a logical consequence of the new specification:

$$\forall s(S_0 \leq s \wedge stable(s) \supset \forall \bar{x} \ (R_1(\bar{x}, s) \wedge R_2(\bar{x}, s) \supset R(\bar{x}, s)). \tag{18}$$

It says that the IC is satisfied at all stable situations of the database.

There is, however, a problem with the above axiomatization in the context of our specification. The specification of executions in [22] is given in a situation calculus with concurrent (simultaneous) actions. In our specification, primitive actions are executed non concurrently. This may be a problem if two separate IC repairing actions are possible in the same situation. In fact, assume that two separate ICs are violated in a given situation S. Assume further that there are two internal repairing actions A_1 and A_2, that are defined for each of these two ICs. Since both ICs are violated in S, then we need both A_1 and A_2 to be executable in S.

The situation calculus that we have been using is *non-concurrent*, in the sense that given a situation s, any successor situation is obtained by the execution of a single primitive action. one way out of this problem is to ensure that the views that record changes to the databases (*Changes* in the running example) are updated only after *non-internal* actions are executed. In the example, we can non-deterministically execute a_1, and reevaluate the applicability of a_2 once the first repairing action has been executed. In this case, it would be possible to have a_1 repair both ICs without having to execute a_2. It would also be possible to have situations where one repair introduces other violations to ICs, forcing yet other repairs. Chaining of repairs and further details related to this problem are still to be worked out. In order for this approach to work, we need to drop axiom (17) in favor of:

$$\forall a, s \ Poss(a, s) \wedge Internal(a) \supset pexecuted(a, s), \tag{19}$$

$$(\forall s)[(\exists a)pexecuted(a, s) \supset (\exists b)executed(b, s) \wedge pexecuted(b, s)]. \tag{20}$$

Here, we introduce the predicate *pexecuted* to represent the notion of *possibly executed*. Thus, if some action is possibly executed in a situation s, then some possibly executed action *must* be executed in *s*. Notice that this has a non-deterministic flavor. Thus, if several internal actions are possible, then the specification is satisfied if either of them is executed.

5   A Causal Approach to Integrity Constraints

In this paper we have not considered the problem of determining all possible repairs of a database in detail. From a logical point of view, there are many possible minimal repairs for an inconsistent database [11,8]. In principle, we could choose any of them and specify corresponding maintenance rules for enforcing that particular kind of repair. This could be accommodated in our formalism. Nevertheless, we might have some preference for some repairs instead of others. For example, we may want to keep the changes produced by a sequence of primitive transactions even in the case they take the database to a state that does not satisfy the ICs. In this case, we would generate new, additional changes which restore the consistency of the database, pruning out some of the logically possible repairs (like the ones that undo some of the new primitive transactions). This kind of repairs are possible only if the updated database is consistent with the ICs [27].

In our approach, there is implicit a notion of causality behind the ICs (see example 5). There are cases where the ICs have an implicit causal contents, and making them explicit may help us restrict ourselves, as specifiers, to some preferred forms of database repairs, like in our running example. Introducing explicit causality relations into the ICs can be seen as form of user intervention [5], that turns out to be a way of predetermining preferred forms of database repairs.

It is possible to make explicit the causal relation behind a given integrity constraint by means of a new causality predicate, as introduced by Lin in [13]. This avoids considering a causal relation as a classical implicative relation.

Lin's approach is also based upon the situation calculus, albeit in a different dialect. The main difference is that the tables are not predicates but functions. For instance, in order to express that a property p is true of an object x in a situation s, we write $p(x, s)$. In the dialect used by Lin, this same statement is written as $Holds(p(x), s)$. The advantage of treating tables at the object level, is that one can use properties as arguments in a first-order setting. In particular, Lin's approach to causality is based upon the introduction of a special predicate $Caused$, which takes a table, a truth value[7], and a situation as arguments. Thus, one can write $Caused(p(x), True, s)$ with the intent of stating that table p has been caused to be $True$ of x in situation s. In our framework, we will use the alternative syntax $Caused(p(x, s), True)$, as a meta-formula, and will eliminate the $Caused$ predicate, as discussed below.

In Lin's approach, the $Caused$ predicate is treated in a special manner. First, there is an assumption, formalized using circumscription [16], that $Caused$ has

---

[7] In Lin's framework, a special sort for truth values is introduced. The sort is fixed, with two elements denoted with the constants $True$ and $False$ respectively.

minimal extent. That is, *Caused* is assumed to be false, unless it must be *True*. Furthermore, if a table is caused to be true (false) in a situation, then it must be true (false) in that situation. If there is no cause for the table to take a truth value, then the table does not change.

It turns out that it is possible, in many interesting cases, to translate Lin's handling of the *Caused* predicate into a specification in the style proposed in this article (making use of *Internal* actions) [21]. We illustrate this approach by interpreting *Caused* as syntactic sugar and by providing a translation of a *causal* formula to our language.

The IC (7) of our example, can be expressed in *causal* terms as follows:

$$Changes_{Grade}(stu, c, g, s) \supset (\forall g')[g \neq g' \supset Caused(Grade(stu, c, g', s), False)].$$
$$(21)$$

Keeping in mind that *Changes*$_{Grade}$ records the addition of a grade for a student in a course, the formula above should be interpreted as *if the grade g has been provided for student stu in course c, then there is a cause for the student not to have any other grade.*

To eliminate Lin's causality predicate, taking the specification back to the formalism based on table names, actions and situations only, we pursue the following idea. We admit the existence of unstable situations in which the causal rules (ICs) can be violated. In these unstable situations some internal actions become possible which repair the ICs. The approach introduces a new action function per causal rule. Let A_I denote the new action function for rule (21). The rule is replaced by the following axioms:

$$Internal(A_I(stu, c, g)).$$
$$(22)$$

$$Poss(A_I(stu, c, g), s) \equiv Changes_{Grade}(stu, c, g, s) \wedge$$
$$\neg(\forall g')[g \neq g' \supset \neg Grade(stu, c, g', do(A_I(stu, c, g), s))]$$
$$(23)$$

$$Poss(A_I(stu, c, g), s) \supset (\forall g')[g \neq g' \supset \neg Grade(stu, c, g', s)]$$
$$(24)$$

Notice that the elimination of the causal relation follows a mechanical procedure which can be applied to a set of *stratified causal rules*, as defined by Lin. The stratification simply ensures that there are no circular causalities. In this setting, it can be proved that both approaches, using explicit *causal* rules, and the translation, lead to the same results [21].

It is illustrative to compare axioms (22)-(24) with the axioms obtained for the integrity constraint (7) in the approach described in Section 3, which results in an axiomatization (see example 5) that yields equivalent results. Therefore, from a methodological point of view, one can use a logical language extended with a *causality* relation that would enhance the expressive capabilities of the language. This extra expressive power gives the modeler a more natural way to express preferences regarding database repairs. Furthermore, the semantics for the new causal relations can be understood in terms of a more conventional logical language.

6   Determining Events for the Maintenance Rules

So far, we have not said much about the events in the active rules (see last part of section 3). In [5], Ceri and Widom handle this problem in detail, although without saying much about deriving *Actions* for the maintenance rules. They provide a mechanism which, from the syntactic form of an IC, derives the transition predicate. This transition predicate determines the *Event* part of the active rule that will maintain the constraint. This predicate is defined in terms of the primitive transactions that might lead to a violation of the IC. Ceri and Widom present a methodology for determining those transactions. The primitive transactions considered are insertions, deletions, and updates in tables.

In our case, we have user defined primitive transactions that may affect several tables simultaneously. In addition, by the presence of the SSAs, we know how each base table evolves as legal actions are executed, and which actions may affect them. Now, it is possible to associate a view to an IC. Namely, the view that stores the tuples that violate the IC (hopefully this view remains empty). This is what we have in the RHS of condition (9). Since this view is a derived predicate and not one of the base tables in the database, we may not have an SSA for it. Nevertheless, as shown in [2], it is always possible to automatically derive an SSA for a view. Then, we may easily compute an SSA for the violation predicate (or view) associated to an IC.

Having an SSA of the form (4) for the violation predicate, it can be easily detected which are the primitive transactions that can make it change. In particular, which primitive transactions can make it change from empty to not empty. This change entails a violation of the corresponding IC (this can be detected from the γ^+ part of the SSA). In this way, we are in position to obtain a mechanism for determining events leading to violations of ICs, as in [5]. However, our approach can be used for more general primitive transactions. In addition, it also allows to identify repairing actions from the derived SSAs[8]. This possibility is not addressed in [5], and that part is left to the application designer; this approach can be complemented or replaced by an approach, such as ours, which allows the automatic identification of repairing policies. Even in this scenario, the application designer could specify his/her repairing preferences by using causality predicates, as described before.

7   Conclusions

In this paper we have considered the problem of specifying policies for database maintenance in a framework given by the specification of the dynamics of a relational database. The specification is given in the situation calculus, a language that includes both primitive actions and database states at the same level as the objects in the database domain. Among others, we find the following advantages in using the SC as a specification language: (1) It has a clear and well understood semantics. (2) Everything already done in the literature with respect to

---

[8] In [2] other applications of derived SSAs for views storing violating tuples of ICs are presented.

applications of predicate logic to DBs can be done here. In particular, all static and extensional aspects of databases and query languages are included. (3) Dynamic aspects at the same object level can be considered, in particular, it is possible to specify how the database evolves as transactions are executed. (4) It is possible to reason in an automated manner from the specification and to extract algorithms for different computational tasks from it. (5) In particular, it is possible to reason explicitly about DB transactions and their effects. (6) In this form it is possible to extend functionalities of usual commercial DBMSs.

Repairing actions are introduced for the integrity constraints that are expected to be satisfied. They are integrated into the original specification by providing their effects and preconditions. Then simple active rules are created for repairing the ICs. Since these active rules do not have a predicate logic semantics, there are alternatively specified in the same formalism as the database dynamics.

The ICs are expected to be logical consequences of the modified specification, which must be true at every legal state of the database. Nevertheless, IC violations may give rise to a transition of the database along a sequence of executions of repairing actions, during which the ICs are not necessarily satisfied. Since we may not exclude those intermediate states from the database dynamics, we distinguish in our formalism between stable and unstable states. It is only at stable states where the ICs have to be satisfied, and this can be proved from the new specification. Instead, the unstable states are related to executions of the repairing actions.

The original specification has a hypothetical nature, in the sense of describing what the database would be like if the actions were executed. Therefore, no executions can be said to necessarily occur. To overcome this limitation, we extended the formalism with the notion of executed action. In this way, we can deal with the imperative nature of active rules, thus forcing executions of repairing actions.

We have considered the derivation of repairing actions for a simple case of actions (primitive actions) and ICs. Reparations policies for more complex cases of ICs based on sequences of atomic transactions [12] could be integrated in our specification formalism. For doing this, a treatment of more complex active rules would be necessary. In [4], we developed in an extended formalism for specifying a database dynamics, the whole framework needed for specifying this kind of active rules, including complex user transactions and the *Actions* in the rules, priorities among rules, database transitions and rollbacks.

By using the derived specification of the dynamic of views storing the tuples that violate an IC, it is possible to determine the right events for the maintenance rules. For restoring the consistency new, internal, primitive actions are introduced. Which repairing actions will be introduced and with which effects may depend on the causal contents that the user attributes to the ICs.

The final result of the whole process of new axiom derivation will be a new specification, extending the original one. The resulting specification has a clear standard Tarskian semantics, and includes an implicit imperative declaration of active rules for IC maintenance. From the resulting specifications, direct first-order automated reasoning is possible; e.g., about the behavior of active rules. The causal content of an IC, that the application designer might have in mind, can be easily specified in the resulting specification, without leaving its classical semantics. In this way, preferences for particular maintenance policies can be captured.

References

1. M. Arenas and L. Bertossi. Hypothetical Temporal Queries in Databases. In A. Borgida, V. Chaudhuri, and M. Staudt, editors, *Proc. "ACM SIGMOD/PODS 5th Int. Workshop on Knowledge Representation meets Databases (KRDB'98): Innovative Application Programming and Query Interfaces*, pages 4.1–4.8, 1998. http://sunsite.informatik.rwth-aachen.de/Publications/CEUR-WS/Vol-10/.
2. M. Arenas and L. Bertossi. The Dynamics of Database Views. In B. Freitag, H. Decker, M. Kifer, and A. Voronkov, editors, *Transactions and Change in Logic Databases*, Lecture Notes in Computer Science, Vol. 1472, pages 197–226, Springer-Verlag, 1998.
3. L. Bertossi, M. Arenas, and C. Ferretti. SCDBR: An Automated Reasoner for Specifications of Database Updates. *Journal of Intelligent Information Systems*, 10(3):253–280, 1998.
4. L. Bertossi, J. Pinto, and R. Valdivia. Specifying Database Transactions and Active Rules in the Situation Calculus. In *Logical Foundations for Cognitive Agents. Contributions in Honor of Ray Reiter*, pages 41–56, Springer, 1999.
5. S. Ceri and J. Widom. Deriving Production Rules for Constraint Maintenance. In D. McLeod, R. Sacks-Davis, and H.-J. Schek, editors, *Proc. of the 16th Int. Conf. on Very Large Data Bases, VLDB'90, Brisbane, Australia, August 13–16, 1990*, pages 566–577, Morgan Kaufmann Publishers, 1990.
6. J. Chomicki. Efficient Checking of Temporal Integrity Constraints Using Bounded History Encoding. *ACM Transactions on Database Systems*, 20(2):149–186, June 1995.
7. J. Chomicki and G. Saake, editors. *Logics for Databases and Information Systems*. Kluwer Academic Publishers, 1998.
8. T. Chou and M. Winslett. A Model-Based Belief Revision System. *J. Automated Reasoning*, 12:157–208, 1994.
9. K. L. Clark. Negation as Failure. In H. Gallaire and J. Minker, editors, *Logic and Databases*, pages 293–322, Plenum Press, 1978.
10. A. Van Gelder and R. Topor. Safety and Correct Translation of Relational Calculus Formulas. In *Proc. ACM Symposium on Principles of Database Systems, PODS'87, San Diego, CA*, pages 313–327, ACM Press, 1987.
11. M. Gertz. An Extensible Framework for Repairing Constraint Violations. In S. Conrad, H.-J. Klein, and K.-D. Schewe, editors, *Integrity in Databases – Proc. of the 7th Int. Workshop on Foundations of Models and Languages for Data and Object, Schloss Dagstuhl, Sept. 16-20, 1996*, Preprint No. 4, pages 41–56, Institut für Technische Informationssysteme, Universität Magdeburg, 1996.
12. M. Gertz. *Diagnosis and Repair of Constraint Violations in Database Systems*, Dissertationen zu Datenbanken und Informationssystemen, Vol. 19. infix-Verlag, Sankt Augustin, 1996.
13. F. Lin. Embracing Causality in Specifying the Indirect Effects of Actions. In *Proc. International Joint Conference on Artificial Intelligence, Montreal*, pages 1985–1991, Morgan Kaufmann Publishers, 1995.

14. F. Lin and R. Reiter. State Constraints Revisited. *Journal of Logic and Computation. Special Issue on Actions and Processes*, 4(5):655–678, 1994.
15. F. Lin and R. Reiter. How to Progress a Database. *Artificial Intelligence*, 92(1–2):131–167, 1997.
16. J. McCarthy. Circumscription a form of Non-Monotonic Reasoning. *Artificial Intelligence*, 13:27–39, 1980.
17. J. McCarthy and P. Hayes. Some Philosophical Problems from the Standpoint of Artificial Intelligence. In B. Meltzer and D. Michie, editors, *Machine Intelligence*, Vol. 4, pages 463–502. Edinburgh University Press, Edinburgh, Scotland, 1969.
18. S. McIlraith. Representing Actions and State Constraints in Model-Based Diagnosis. In *Proc. of the National Conference on Artificial Intelligence (AAAI-97)*, pages 43–49, 1997.
19. R. Miller and M. Shanahan. Narratives in the Situation Calculus. *The Journal of Logic and Computation*, 4(5):513–530, 1994.
20. J. Minker. Logic and Databases. Past, Present and Future. *AI Magazine*, pages 21–47, 1997.
21. J. Pinto. Causality, Indirect Effects and Triggers (Preliminary Report). In *Seventh International Workshop on Non-monotonic Reasoning, Trento, Italy*, 1998. URL=http://www.cs.utexas.edu/users/vl/nmr98.html.
22. J. Pinto. Occurrences and Narratives as Constraints in the Branching Structure of the Situation Calculus. *Journal of Logic and Computation*, 8:777–808, 1998.
23. J. Pinto. Compiling Ramification Constraints into Effect Axioms. *Computational Intelligence*, 13(3), 1999.
24. J. Pinto and R. Reiter. Adding a Time Line to the Situation Calculus. In *Working Notes: The Second Symposium on Logical Formalizations of Commonsense Reasoning, Austin, Texas, USA*, pages 172–177, 1993.
25. R. Reiter. The Frame Problem in the Situation Calculus: a Simple Solution (sometimes) and a Completeness Result for Goal Regression. In V. Lifschitz, editor, *Artificial Intelligence and Mathematical Theory of Computation: Papers in Honor of John McCarthy*, pages 359–380, Academic Press, 1991.
26. R. Reiter. On Specifying Database Updates. *Journal of Logic Programming*, 25(1):53–91, 1995.
27. K.-D. Schewe and B. Thalheim. Limitations of the Rule Triggering Systems for Integrity Maintenance in the Context of Transition Specifications. *Acta Cybernetica*, 13:277–304, 1998.
28. M. Thielscher. Ramification and Causality. *Artificial Intelligence*, 89:317–364, 1997.
29. J. Ullman. *Principles of Database and Knowledge-Base Systems, Vol. I*. Computer Science Press, 1988.
30. J. Widom and S. Ceri. *Active Database Systems: Triggers and Rules for Advanced Database Processing*. Morgan Kaufmann Publishers, 1996.
31. C. Zaniolo, S. Ceri, Ch. Faloutsos, R. T. Snodgrass, V.S. Subrahmanian, and R. Zicari. *Advanced Database Systems*. Morgan Kaufmann Publishers, 1997.

Nested Transactions with Integrity Constraints[*]

Anne Doucet[1], Stephane Gançarski[1], Claudia León[12], and Marta Rukoz[2]

[1] LIP6, Case 169, Université P&M Curie, 4, place Jussieu,
75252 Paris cedex 5. France.
{Anne.Doucet, Stephane.Gancarski, Claudia.Leon}@lip6.fr
[2] CCPD, U.C.V. Apdo. 47002, Los Chaguaramos,
1041A. Caracas. Venezuela.
mrukoz@flynn.ciens.ucv.ve

Abstract. This paper presents a solution to check integrity constraints in database systems supporting nested transactions. Using nested transactions allows to introduce parallelism inside a transaction and to partially recover failing transactions by defining a hierarchy of sub-transactions. If a constraint is violated by some sub-transactions, it is possible to reach the validation of the nested transaction, even if some part of it had to be aborted. In our solution, (i) only constraints that might be violated are checked, (ii) constraints are checked as soon as possible during the execution of the nested transaction and (iii) as few sub-transactions as possible are aborted. We do not interfere with the execution control of nested transactions and users do not have to add any control code in the definition of constraints or of transactions. The main idea of our solution is to attach the checking of a constraint to the smallest common ancestor of the sub-transactions which could violate the constraint.

Keywords: integrity constraints, nested transactions, partial abort.

1 Introduction

It is clear now that the classic model of flat transactions [19] is not suitable to express the complexity of nowadays applications. Many works have been devoted to extend the flat transaction model in order to allow modeling complex long duration transactions and distributed applications in cooperative environments. In order to fulfill this need for more flexibility, other transaction models have arisen such as nested transactions [34], multi-level transactions [43], Sagas [18], ConTracts [38], transactional activity model [11] among others. A detailed revision about advanced models of transactions can be seen in [20]. However, none of the extended models defined up to now has turned out to be general enough to accommodate all types of applications. ACTA [9,10] is a first-order logic-based formalism intended to unify the existing models. It can be used as a common framework within one can specify and reason about the nature of interactions

---

[*] This work was partially financed by CDCH-UCV y CONICIT Venezuela and by CNRS-France.

G. Saake, K. Schwarz, and C. Türker (Eds.): TDD '99, LNCS 1773, pp. 130–149, 2000.
© Springer-Verlag Berlin Heidelberg 2000

between transactions of extended models. [40] extends the ACTA formalism and introduces the notion of transaction closure. It considers general transaction structures and distinguishes different dependencies among transactions.

Using nested transactions allows to decompose a transaction into sub-transactions. This offers the possibility to introduce parallelism inside a transaction, and to partially recover failing transactions. Since they were introduced by Moss [34], nested transactions have been an object of vast studies. Different variations on this model can be found in [14]. Correct and reliable algorithms to manage concurrency control, including detection of deadlock and failure recovery have been proposed [35,39,24,32]. Some systems providing nested transactions have been developed, such as Argus [30], Camelot [16], SIMA [29], and the work described in [6] proposes an architecture at three levels to support nested transactions on top of standard commercial DBMS's. Recently, with the commercialisation of Encina [4,1] a system that provides nested transaction facilities, many critical applications in the industry and bank [2] areas have been developed based on this transaction model.

On the other hand, the growing complexity of present database applications necessitates the development of efficient consistency management systems. Consistency means that the database must be semantically correct. It is classically ensured by the definition of integrity constraints, which are assertions defined on the database, which must be satisfied at the end of each transaction. Much work has been devoted to this problem [36,8,23,7,22] and many DBMS provide now this functionality [26,42,15]. Good surveys describing the various approaches are given in [21,17].

In the great majority of cases, consistency management systems are designed for simple and classical flat transaction models and very few solutions have been proposed for the management of integrity constraints in the context of nested transactions. Although it seems natural that the nested transactions model allows checking the constraints in each sub-transaction, this it is not necessarily the best solution. Indeed, this could cause that a constraint is checked many times, if it is touched by more of one sub-transaction of the nested transaction. Surprisingly, very few approaches have treated this problem. [28] presents a transaction model, named NT/PV –nested transactions with predicates and versions– which allows correctness without serializability for long-duration transactions. In the NT/PV model, each transaction has a pre-condition and a post-condition. The pre-condition of every transaction describes the database state which is required for the transaction to execute correctly. The post-condition describes the database state which would exist after a transaction is executed in isolation on a database state which satisfies its pre-condition. In this approach, integrity constraints are integrated only in the post-condition of the top-level transaction. This allows checking the integrity constraints only in the top-level transaction. [12] proposes a mechanism to express and check integrity constraints for object-oriented database allowing nested transactions. In this approach, integrity constraints are defined at method level, using pre- and post-conditions, associated with an exception handling mechanism. An exception is raised whenever a pre- (post-) condition is violated. The main drawback of this proposal is that the programmer is in charge of describing, in a procedural way, the actions to perform in case of violation of a constraint. Moreover, he must also decide at which level inside the nested transactions these actions are described and performed.

In this paper, we propose a mechanism to manage integrity constraints for database systems using nested transactions. This mechanism integrates a conventional nested transaction execution control with the ability to check global integrity constraints as soon as possible during the execution of a transaction. We do not interfere with the execution control of nested transactions, which renders our approach very flexible. Transparency is provided since users do not have to add any control code in the definitions of constraints or of transactions. Integrity constraints are defined in a global way, at the database schema level and are checked by the system. A syntactic analysis allows to know, at transaction compile time, the structures manipulated by both the leaf transactions and the constraints, and thus to determine the set of constraints that might be violated by the nested transaction. The checking code of the constraint is automatically inserted into the transaction.

This paper is organised as follows. Section 2 presents the nested transaction model, while Section 3 describes the main principles of Thémis, an object database language allowing to define and automatically check integrity constraints. Section 4 presents our solution to integrity checking in the context of nested transactions. We first detail our solution in a simple case, where all sub-transactions must commit in order to commit the whole nested transaction. Then we describe our solution in a more general case, where sub-transactions might be optional. Section 5 concludes and proposes some directions of future works.

2   Nested Transactions

Nested transactions, as presented by Moss [34], are an appropriate solution in systems where transactions are "huge" tasks [4,1,6,29,2]. In these cases, a complex task can be divided into logical functions, which can be performed under certain independence and which can as well be divided into other logical tasks and so on. In the context of nested transactions, the complex task corresponds to the root transaction and each logical function corresponds to one of its sub-transactions. We remind in the following the concept of nested transactions and their properties.

A nested transaction (NT) is a transaction formed by

- operations on database objects, and/or
- other transactions (called sub-transactions) that can also be nested.

An NT can be represented as a tree where the nodes are transactions and the arcs reflect the nesting relationship that relates a (parent) transaction and its child transactions. Each sub-transaction of an NT is executed independently, and possibly in parallel; this means that it can decide either to commit or to abort at any time. This decision may depend on the results of the execution of its sub-transactions. If a sub-transaction aborts, it does not mean that its parent must be aborted, but on the contrary that its sub-transactions must abort. If a sub-transaction decides to commit, this is not definitive, since the update of the system will only happen when all the transactions that contain it decide to commit, i.e. when the root transaction completes.

This consequently leads to a redefinition of the idea of atomicity of a transaction ("all or nothing") for NT. In this context, when a root transaction commits, it must guarantee that the updates of all sub-transactions which decided to commit and having no aborting ancestor, will be taken into account. An NT may complete, while preserving consistency, although some of its sub-transactions have aborted, which is called in this context *"partial abortion"*. The behaviour of nested transactions with respect to the well known ACID properties can be summed up as follows: all the transactions in an NT (including the root) must follow this new definition of atomicity as well as the classic property of isolation. However, only the root of the NT has to preserve consistency and to be durable.

Since many transactions can be executed concurrently, the transactions management system must ensure that operations of one transaction do not interfere with other transactions. The classic two phases locking mechanism has been adapted to nested transactions in [34] and proved by [31]. It states the following: when a sub-transaction commits, its locks are not released but are inherited by its parent. A transaction can thus have a lock either by request or by inheritance. A transaction can only use an object if it requests and obtains a lock on this object. Rules for handling read and write locks are described below:

1. A transaction may obtain a lock in *write* mode if all other transactions holding the lock (in any mode) are ancestors of the requesting transaction.
2. A transaction may obtain a lock in *read* mode if all other transactions holding the lock, in write mode, are ancestors of the requesting transaction.
3. When a transaction aborts, all its locks, both *read* and *write* are simply discarded. If any other transaction among its ancestors holds the same locks, it continues to do so, in the same mode as before the abort.
4. When a non-root transaction commits, all its locks, both *read* and *write*, are inherited by its parent. This means the parent holds each of those locks, in the same mode as the child held them.
5. When a transaction cannot obtain a lock, it must wait until it is granted.
6. Once a transaction obtains a lock, it cannot release it before its termination (abort or commit).

The preceding rules guarantee the serializability of nested transactions [31]. An object can be updated by only one transaction at the same time. When a transaction aborts, only its descendants will be affected by this abortion since the modifications of the objects used by that transaction are known only by the sub-transactions belonging to its sub-tree.

3   Integrity Constraints

Databases are supposed to be consistent. Consistency is generally assured by integrity constraints (IC), which are logical assertions that must always hold in the database. A database state is consistent if and only if all constraints are satisfied. Much work concerning the checking of integrity constraints has already been done [36,8,23,7,22]. Good surveys describing the various approaches are given in [21,17]. Some approaches are adapted for on-line transactions, such as active rules and triggers [45] where the user is in charge of determining the events raising the checking of a given constraint. Other solutions use compilation techniques to reduce the constraint checking process at execution time [5,25,41,27]. Our work is related to this second approach. We choose to use Thémis to illustrate our proposal. However, it can be adapted to any constraint management mechanism using the same principles.

Thémis [3,37,13,33] is an object database programming language that supports the specification of integrity constraints. In this language, IC are defined in a global and declarative way. A syntactic analysis of both constraints and transactions allows to automatically determine a set of constraints which could be violated by a transaction, and checking code is automatically generated. We present in this section the main features of Thémis. For more details about Thémis the reader may refer to [3].

3.1   Basic Concepts of Thémis

Thémis is a strongly and statically typed object-oriented database language. A schema in Thémis is defined in a classic way using concrete and abstract types, classes and integrity constraints. Concrete types are recursively built using atomic types (integer, string and boolean) and constructors (tuple, set and list). Abstract types are composed of a structural part, which is similar to concrete types, and a behavioural part. Instances of concrete types are non-shared values, while instances of abstract types are objects, having an identity independent of their values. Objects may be shared. Classes in Thémis are the persistent roots of the database.

Integrity constraints are boolean expressions built using the classes of the schema, and general operators. First, terms are defined as follows:

- Constants are terms.
- Each variable x is a term.
- Let t be a term, let a be an attribute, $t.a$ is a term. (t is a tuple structured attribute, and a is an attribute).
- Let t be a term, let $x_1 \cdots x_n$ be variables, let m be a method, $t.m(x_1 \cdots x_n)$ is a term.
- Let t_1 and t_2 be two terms, let θ be an arithmetic operator $(+, -, *, \div)$, $t_1 \theta t_2$ is a term.

An integrity constraint C is an expression of the form:

$$C = Q x_1 \in S_1, \cdots Q x_k \in S_k M(x_1, \cdots, x_k)$$

where $Q \in \{\forall, \exists\}$, S_i is a set-valued expression (e.g. a class name), and $M(x_1, \cdots, x_k)$ is a quantifier free formula.

Formulas are defined as follows:

- Let θ be a comparison predicate $(=, \neq, <, >, \leq, \geq)$, let x and y be two terms, then x θ y is an atomic formula.
- Each atomic formula is a formula.
- Let M and M' be two formulas, $M \wedge M'$, $M \vee M'$, $\neg M$ and (M) are formulas.
- Nothing else is a formula.

Updates are performed through transactions. In [3], only flat transactions are considered. A flat transaction FT has the following syntactic form:

$$FT = (t_1 \cdots, t_n)\{\Gamma\}$$

where the t_i are parameters and Γ represents the body of the transaction, built using elementary statements: *assignment, method call, composition, conditional test, iteration loop, insertion* of an element in a set and **deletion** of an element from a set.

3.2   Nested Transactions in Thémis

In order to consider nested transactions, we extend the syntax of Thémis with the following instructions:

- '{' and '}' are used as sub-transactions delimiters.
- '||' and ';' which indicate the execution mode (**EM**) of sub-transactions (respectively concurrent and sequential execution).
- 'op' and 'ob' (denoted **O**) indicate whether a sub-transaction is optional (**op**) or obligatory (**ob**). A sub-transaction is obligatory if its abort implies the abort of its parent, otherwise it is optional [1].
- Sub-transactions (ST_i) are defined in the same way as transactions.

A nested transaction NT, is syntactically defined in the following way:

$$
\begin{aligned}
NT &= FT \mid (t_1 \cdots, t_n) \ \mathbf{EM} \ \{\mathbf{O}ST_1 \cdots \mathbf{O}ST_n\} \\
ST_i &= NT \\
FT &= (t_1 \cdots, t_n)\{\Gamma\}
\end{aligned}
$$

In this way, Thémis allows to define nested transactions where only leaf transactions manipulate the data. This does not affect the expressive power of the transaction model, since every general nested transaction can be transformed into an equivalent nested transaction where only leaf transactions can update objects, i.e., as shown in [34], the two models are equivalent. These leaf transactions are structured in the same way that flat transactions in Thémis.

---

[1] They are respectively called *vital* and *not-vital* in [9,10,40], *critical* and *not-critical* in [6]

3.3   Principles of Checking Integrity Constraints in Thémis

The checking process of integrity constraints in Thémis consists of two steps:

1. reduce the number of constraints to be checked by a transaction at compile time, and
2. automatically generate an efficient run-time checker.

For the first step, a syntactic analysis of both constraints and transactions is used to determine which constraints might be violated by a given transaction. Intuitively, a transaction T might violate a constraint C if they manipulate the same data structures. The basic principle of this purely syntactic analysis consists of detecting, for each constraint and each transaction, the set of structures it involves. The result of the analysis is a set of paths in the database, which gathers the various structures. When the intersection of the analysis of T and the analysis of C is not empty, T might violate C. For the sake of simplicity, we say that transaction T touches constraint C. The syntactic analysis process for flat transactions and constraints that do not include methods is described in [3]. In [37] the syntactic analysis is extended to constraints that can include methods. In the nested transaction model, we consider that only leaf transactions can modify the database and these ones are flat transactions. Thus, it is possible to apply the same syntactic analysis defined in [37] to each leaf transaction and to determine, at compile time, the set of constraints that it touches. Therefore the constraints set touched by a parent transaction is the union of the constraints touched by its sub-transactions.

Given a transaction and a constraint touched by this transaction, the second step consists of generating a checking algorithm. This algorithm will operate on the smallest set of objects involved in the checking process. This set is determined at run-time. It is composed of objects whose attributes which have been modified by the transaction are relevant to the constraint. [3] details how to automatically generate optimised algorithms for constraint checking. Those algorithms are generated, at the end of flat transactions, for a sub-class of formulae: universally quantified formulae. In this work, we keep the same principle of generation of checking algorithms, as proposed in [3].

3.4   Example

In this section, we give an example to illustrate the concepts of Thémis presented above. Figure 1 shows the schema of a Restaurant database. '[...]' denotes a tuple, '{...}' denotes a set.

This schema has six persistent roots (classes). They are sets of abstract type instances. The abstract type Item represents the dishes offered in the restaurant. Dishes are classified in four categories: first courses, main courses, desserts and drinks. They are respectively modeled by classes First_Courses, Main_Courses, Desserts and Drinks. Dishes are characterised by a name, a price, and the quantity available in the restaurant. This quantity is automatically updated each time a dish is ordered. The abstract type Order models a client order. The attributes

```
type Item is abstract     [          name: string,
                                     price:real,
                                     quantity:integer ]
end;
type Order is abstract     [         num-client: integer,
                                     date: string,
                                     description: list(Item) ]
method     orderfirstcourse();
           ordermaincourse();
           orderdessert();
           orderdrink();
           nb_orders():integer;
end;
class      Orders:Order;
class      First_Courses:{Item};
class      Main_Courses:{Item};
class      Desserts:{Item;}
class      Drinks:{Item};
class      Items: First_Courses  ∪ Main_Courses ∪ Desserts ∪ Drinks;
```

Fig. 1. Schema of the Restaurant Database

are self-understandable. The methods orderfirstcourse(), ordermaincourse(), order-dessert(), and orderdrink() are used to perform an order, one per category of dish: an item is chosen by the client in the corresponding category. The item is added to the order description list and its available quantity is decreased by one. The last method, nb_orders(), gives the number of dishes ordered by a client.

For this schema, we define four integrity constraints, presented in Figure 2. Constraint C_{10} expresses that each item must have a unique name. Constraints C_{20} and C_{30} are needed for the management of the item stocks. They specify that the quantity of an item must be positive (otherwise it cannot be served!). We only give here two of these constraints (for First_Courses and Main_Courses), but obviously the same kind of constraint exists for the other categories of dishes. Finally, constraint C_{40} states that an order must contain at least two items.

Figure 3 gives an example of a nested transaction representing the order of a client. Transaction T_5 is a sequence (specified by ';') of three sub-transactions, T_{51}, T_{52}, and T_{53}. T_{52} is composed of three sub-transactions (T_{521}, T_{522}, and T_{523}) executed concurrently (specified by '∥'). T_{51} is obligatory (specified by 'ob'), as well as T_{52} and T_{523}. The other sub-transactions are optional.

$$
\begin{array}{l}
(C_{10}) \ \forall \, e_1, e_2 \in Items, \ e_1 = e_2 \vee e_1.name \neq e_2.name \\
(C_{20}) \ \forall \, f \in First\_Courses, \ f.quantity > 0 \\
(C_{30}) \ \forall \, m \in Main\_Courses, \ m.quantity > 0 \\
(C_{40}) \ \forall \, c \in Orders, \ c.nb\_orders() \geq 2
\end{array}
$$

Fig. 2. Integrity Constraints

```
T₅ ()        ; {
/ * T₅₁ * /   ob () {    o = new(Order) }
/ * T₅₂ * /   ob () ‖ { op () {o → orderdrink()}           / * T₅₂₁ * /
                        op () {o → orderfirstcourse()}     / * T₅₂₂ * /
                        ob () {o → ordermaincourse()} } / * T₅₂₃ * /
/ * T₅₃ * /   op () {    o → orderdessert()}               }
```

Fig. 3. Nested Transaction in Thémis

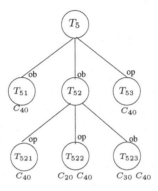

Fig. 4. Nested Transaction Tree

Figure 4 represents nested transaction T_5 as a tree, and the constraints touched by the leaves (sub-transactions which perform updates). C_{40} is a general constraint, concerning every order, thus each sub-transaction. C_{20} only concerns First_Courses, it must be satisfied after T_{522}. The same holds for C_{30} and T_{523}. C_{10} is not concerned by this transaction which does not modify the name of Items. Constraint C_{40} must obviously be verified at the end of the root transaction. This is not the case for the other constraints, which can be verified earlier, at a lower level in the tree. Indeed the set of objects which should be used for the checking of a constraint can be obtained immediately after the last sub-transaction that touches it has finished. In absence of failures, the state of the database with regard to this constraint will no more change. Our goal is to determine the level at which a constraint must be verified. Our solution is presented in the following.

4   Checking Integrity Constraints in Nested Transactions

Checking integrity constraints may be very costly when long-duration transactions are performed using a conventional flat transaction model. Nested transactions have been proved to be much more adapted to cope with the problems of long-duration transactions. As systems supporting nested transactions have been implemented, including execution control, concurrency control, and recovery control, they may be used to develop a mechanism allowing to check integrity constraints integrated with the execution of nested transactions. The main idea of our solution is to choose for each constraint a sub-transaction which will be responsible of its checking: the smallest common ancestor of the sub-transactions touching it. The communication between the leaf transactions touching the constraint and the sub-transaction responsible for its checking allows to launch the checking of a constraint as soon as all the sub-transactions touching it have terminated and, in case of violation, to abort as few operations as possible. We also take into account the possible re-checking of a constraint if a sub-transaction touching it aborts because of another constraint. We first describe the hypothesis about the execution environment we address. Then we develop the different steps of our solution.

4.1   Description of the Environment

We sum up here the features of the nested transaction system and of the integrity constraint manager, which we take into account :

- Only leaf transactions can update objects, being thus the only ones likely to violate the consistency of the database (cf. 3.2). This restriction allows a simplified definition of the consistency control in nested transactions.
- At transaction compile time, we assume that we can get information about its structure. We particularly need to know which node is the smallest common ancestor of a set of leaf transactions. This does not raise any problem when defining nested transactions as shown in 3.2.
- Integrity constraints are expressed using the Thémis language. When a transaction is created and compiled, it is possible to determine -through a syntactic analysis- which constraints are *touched*, i.e., nearly to be violated by the transaction. Applying this analysis to the components of a nested transaction, we determine:
  - For each leaf transaction Tl_j of the nested transaction T, the set $C(Tl_j)$ of all the constraints touched by Tl_j.
  - In the same way we can determine the set $T(C_i)$ of all the leaf transactions touching a given constraint C_i. We note $SCA(C_i)$ the smallest common ancestor of all the leaf transactions included in $T(C_i)$. $SCA(C_i)$ is responsible for the maintenance of constraint C_i.

In the remainder of this article, we use the example shown in Figure 5. The whole tree of the nested transaction T is represented, each transaction being represented by a node in the tree. Below each leaf transaction Tl_j, the set of constraints touched by Tl_j, i.e. $C(Tl_j)$ is shown. For instance, $C(Tl_{211}) = \{C_2\}$. We can see that $T(C_1) = \{Tl_{212}, Tl_{222}\}$, i.e. constraint C_1 is touched by leaves Tl_{212} and Tl_{222}. T_2 is the smallest common ancestor of Tl_{212} and Tl_{222}, T_2 is thus the node responsible for the checking of C_1. The checking procedure of each constraint C_i is represented by a rectangle and associated with the node sub-transaction responsible to perform it. For instance, T_2 is associated with the checking procedure of C_1.

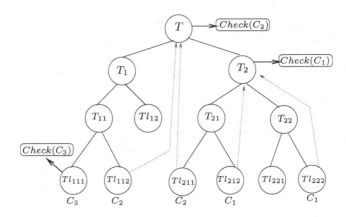

Fig. 5. Example of Nested Transaction

4.2   The Proposed Solution

Taking into account the behaviour rules of a nested transaction described in Section 2, together with the principles of Thémis described in Section 3, it is possible to integrate a consistency checking mechanism into the nested transaction execution control. Our main goal is twofold:

1. To check a constraint as soon as possible, i.e. as soon as all the operations touching it are performed, and in case of a violation, to abort as few sub-transactions as possible, and
2. to interfere as few as possible with the underlying execution control and concurrency control mechanisms.

Our solution ensures that if the root transaction commits, then the database is in a consistent state. The key point is to designate for each constraint C_i, a node sub-transaction to be responsible of its checking. For this purpose, we determine, at transaction compile-time, the smallest common ancestor of all the leaf transactions touching the constraint C_i , i.e. $SCA(C_i)$ as defined above. As this node controls the execution of its sub-tree, it is possible to ensure, in case of violation of C_i, that not only the sub-transactions which violated C_i , but also the ones which used their results, will be aborted. On the other hand, as opposed to conventional integrity mechanisms for flat transactions, we let other sub-transactions not concerned with C_i continue their execution.

Transaction $SCA(C_i)$, responsible for checking constraint C_i, knows the identification of all its leaf transactions touching C_i. Each of those leaf transactions knows the identification of $SCA(C_i)$. When all of them have terminated, $SCA(C_i)$ can launch the checking procedure $Check(C_i)$. If C_i is satisfied, $SCA(C_i)$ has no action to perform. Otherwise, if C_i is violated, then $SCA(C_i)$ performs a set of actions in order to restore consistency.

In the remainder of the paper, we present how we detect a constraint violation and which actions are performed to restore consistency of the database.

To clarify this article, we distinguish two cases. In the first case, which we call "all mandatory", all the children of a sub-transaction have to commit to enable the sub-transaction to commit. Thus the root of the nested transaction can only commit when all nodes of the tree representing the nested transaction have decided to commit. In the second -general- case, called "with options", a node transaction can commit even if some of its child transactions have decided to abort (according to predefined users decisions). We first treat the case "all mandatory" since it is much simpler, and then extend the solution to cope with the general case "with options".

The Simple Case "All Mandatory". If all the children of a transaction have to commit to enable their parent to commit, it is clear that, as soon as a constraint violation is detected, the whole nested transaction (included its root node) has to abort. As a consequence, in this simple case, our problem can be expressed as follows:

1. to detect as soon as possible if a constraint is violated and
2. to abort the whole transaction as fast as possible in case of any constraint violation.

This solution can be implemented in a very straightforward way. When a leaf transaction has terminated its actions, it sends (for each constraint C_i it touches) an additional message to notify $SCA(C_i)$ of its decision (commit or abort). When $SCA(C_i)$ has received decision messages from all the leaf transactions touching C_i and at least one of those decision messages is "commit", it launches the checking procedure of C_i. This clearly solves the issue 1. In case of violation of C_i, $SCA(C_i)$ sends an abort message to the root of the nested transaction which will at its turn send abort messages to all its children and recursively to all the nested transaction, solving the issue 2. This recursive way of aborting the nested transaction is already implemented in the execution and recovery control mechanism of nested transaction systems. Of course, as in this case the nested transaction model does not allow optional sub-transactions, the only solution to restore consistency is to abort the whole transaction, as in the case of conventional flat transactions. But the advantage of the solution is that any long duration transaction written in a flat transaction model can be translated in a rather simple way to a nested transaction with all sub-transactions mandatory. Thus our solution allows, with few effort for the programmers, to detect inconsistencies and abort the transaction as soon as possible, which is already a substantial gain in case of long duration transaction.

Of course, in case of a nested transaction having optional sub-transactions, the abort of the whole transaction if one constraint is violated is not satisfying. Indeed there may be a possibility to abort only optional sub-transactions and then to commit as many as possible sub-transactions. The new definition of atomicity induced by the possibility of optional sub-transactions allows a refined treatment of consistency management explained in the following subsection.

The General Case with Optional Sub-transactions. In the general case, we use the feature of *"partial abortion"* included in the nested transaction model to refine our solution and obtain a database consistent state without having to abort the whole transaction. As explained in Section 2, each sub-transaction can commit even if some of its children declared as optional decide to abort. As there is a possibility to maintain consistency in the database without aborting the whole transaction, the problem is more complicated. While the issue (1) remains the same, the issue (2) is turned into the more complex (2'), which consists of "abort as few sub-transactions as possible from the nested transaction".

In this context, each time a constraint C_i is violated, we must abort the leaf transactions that touche C_i, and recursively the sub-transactions which already used their results.

All the sub-transactions to be aborted because of the violation of constraint C_i are inside the sub-tree of $SCA(C_i)$. During the abort process inside this sub-tree, the sub-transactions not belonging to this sub-tree may continue their execution until reaching the eventual commit of the nested transaction. Of course, the abort of some sub-transaction within the sub-tree may raise the abort of $SCA(C_i)$ itself, but this decision of $SCA(C_i)$ will be handled by the nested transaction execution control.

To abort as few sub-transactions as possible in case of the violation of C_i, we process as follows: $SCA(C_i)$ sends a special abort message through the branches of its sub-tree which contain leaf transactions involved in the violation of C_i. The message is propagated top-down until reaching the smallest ancestor still active (i.e. not having yet decided) of each of those involved leaf transactions. This smallest ancestor will take the decision to abort, consequently ordering its whole sub-tree to abort.

In the remaining of this subsection, we describe the sub-transactions behaviour according to the above mentioned principles. We use the example shown in Figure 5 to represent the different cases.

As mentioned in subsection 4.2, our solution is based on the fact that we can determine the structural information about nested transaction T at compile time. This means that we can get the complete structure $G(T)$ of the tree formed by T: identification of all the sub-transactions and parent-children relationships. As well, we can determine $C(Tl_j)$ which is the set of constraints that a leaf transaction Tl_j could violate. This information allows us to build a table CCT (Constraints Checking Table), with one entry $CCT(C_i)$ per constraint C_i, as follows:

$$CCT(C_i) = (C_i, SCA(C_i), list(Tl_j, Termination(Tl_j)))$$

where

- C_i is the constraint identifier
- $SCA(C_i)$ is the node responsible for checking C_i
- $list(Tl_j, Termination(Tl_j))$ is the list of all the leaf transactions Tl_j that *could violate* C_i together with the status of Tl_j:
  - 'S' if Tl_j is still in progress,
  - 'A' if Tl_j has aborted, and
  - 'V' if Tl_j decided to commit.

For instance, the *CCT* table corresponding to the example of Figure 5 would be initialised as follows:

Table 1. Constraints Checking Table

C_i	$SCA(C_i)$	$list(Tl_j, Termination(Tl_j))$
C_1	T_2	$((Tl_{212}, S), (Tl_{222}, S))$
C_2	T	$((Tl_{112}, S), (Tl_{211}, S))$
C_3	Tl_{111}	$((Tl_{111}, S))$

The following four points describe the sub-transactions behaviour:

1. When a leaf transaction Tl_j terminates its execution, it sends its decision (commit or abort) and its own identifier to each node sub-transaction responsible for the checking of a constraint it touches:

   Tl_j: on terminating execution,
       sends the termination message (Tl_j, $'A'$ or $'V'$)
       to each $SCA(C_i)$, such as $C_i \in C(Tl_j)$.

   In the example of Figure 5,
   - Tl_{111} will send its decision message to Tl_{111}, for the checking of C_3,
   - Tl_{112} and Tl_{211} will send their decision message to T, for the checking of C_2 and
   - Tl_{212} and Tl_{222} will send their decision message to T_2 for the checking of C_1.

2. When a sub-transaction $SCA(C_i)$ receives a decision message from a leaf transaction Tl_j touching C_i, it updates the C_i entry of the *CCT* table with the decision sent by Tl_j, 'A' or 'V':

   $SCA(C_i)$: on receiving message (Tl_j, $'A'$ or $'V'$),
       switches $Termination(Tl_j)$ to $'A'$ or $'V'$ in $CCT(C_i)$

   For instance, if T receives a decision message from Tl_{112} willing to commit, it will switch the $Termination(Tl_{112})$ from $(Tl_{112},'S')$ to $(Tl_{112},'V')$ in the entry corresponding to C_2.

3. When $SCA(C_i)$ has received decision messages from all the leaf transactions touching C_i, i.e. when no more $(Tl_j,'S')$ remains in the C_i entry of *CCT*, it launches $Check(C_i)$. If the constraint is satisfied, no other action is performed by $SCA(C_i)$. If the constraint is violated, for each Tl_j in $CCT(C_i)$, $SCA(C_i)$ sends a message (R^*, C_i) to its child which is an ancestor of Tl_j (which can be determined by looking at $G(T)$). This message means "rollback Tl_j and everything that used the results of Tl_j". Of course, if one child of $SCA(C_i)$ already decided to commit, or if $SCA(C_i)$ is the parent of Tl_j, or $SCA(C_i)$ is Tl_j, $SCA(C_i)$ itself must abort. If not, the message is propagated. We can sum up the behaviour of $SCA(C_i)$ by the following algorithm:

```
If (∀ (Tl_j, Termination(Tl_j)) ∈ CCT(C_i)) Termination(Tl_j) ≠' S' then
    If (Check(C_i) then perform Propagate(SCA(C_i), C_i)
    Endif
Endif
```

where $Propagate(trans, constr)$ is the procedure which performs the propagation of the message R^*.

```
Propagate(trans,constr):
    Set := {T_k | T_k child of trans and T_k ancestor of Tl_j,
           Tl_j ∈ T(constr)}
    If (∀ T_k ∈ Set, T_k is active) and
       ¬(trans parent of Tl_j, Tl_j ∈ T(constr)) then
       For each T_k ∈ Set, Send(R*, constr) to T_k
    Else
       Replace each (Tl_j,' V') ∈ CCT with (Tl_j,' A')
       Abort sub-tree of trans
       Abort trans
    Endif
```

If, in our example, Tl_{112} and Tl_{211} both decide to commit and send the corresponding message to T, then the entry corresponding to C_2 contains the list $((Tl_{112},' V'), (Tl_{211},' V'))$ and T checks C_2. We suppose C_2 satisfied, thus no other action is performed. Assume that both Tl_{212} and Tl_{222} decide to commit, raising the execution of checking C_1 by T_2, and that C_1 is violated. If both T_{21} and T_{22} are still active, then T_2 sends (R^*, C_1) to its children T_{21} and T_{22}. Otherwise, T_2 decides to abort.

4. In order to abort each leaf transaction Tl_j which touched C_i, the message (R^*, C_i) is propagated from generation to generation, until reaching the smallest active ancestor of Tl_j, which we denote $SAA(Tl_j)$. It is easy to prove that the abort of $SAA(Tl_j)$, provoking the abort of its sub-tree, corresponds to our goal. Indeed, we abort Tl_j and all the transactions that, directly or indirectly, may have used the results of Tl_j. Of course, $SAA(Tl_j)$ cannot be statically determined, since it depends on the progress state of the nested transaction execution. To determine it and perform the adequate rollback, each sub-transaction T_k has the following behaviour:

```
T_k: on receiving message (R*, C_i)
     Perform Propagate (T_k, C_i)
```

With points 1 to 4, we ensure that, whenever a constraint is violated, the leaf transactions who caused this violation will be aborted, together with the sub-transactions which used their results, as few as possible. Thus we ensure that the corresponding constraint will be satisfied by the state of the database after an eventual commit of the nested transaction. However, this cascading abort may cause side effects on the other constraints, forcing us to check them again.

For instance, consider that in our example Tl_{112}, Tl_{211}, and Tl_{212} have terminated and T has checked C_2 and no violation is detected. After that Tl_{222}

terminates, T_2 launches the checking of C_1, since both Tl_{212} and Tl_{222} have terminated. If C_1 is violated, then the smallest active ancestor of Tl_{212} may be either T_{21} or T_2. In both cases, the rollback process includes Tl_{211}. As a side effect, the checking of C_2 performed by T is no more valid, since it was done considering the effects of both Tl_{112} and Tl_{211}. Thus, T has to check again C_2 with only the effects of Tl_{112}. To warn T that it has to check C_2 again, the sub-transaction responsible for the abort of Tl_{211}, i.e. T_{21} or T_2, sends a message to T. It is worth to notice that this new checking of C_2 is performed as soon as possible. In fact, the first checking performed while the transaction was still in progress induced no delay in the process. Even if C_2 is checked several times, the actual checking (the last one) is always started as soon as the final state of the database concerning C_2 is produced.

Another important point is that it is always possible to check again a constraint if the previous checking has been invalidated by the abort of a sub-tree. A situation where a constraint C_i has to be checked again by an already committed sub-transaction is impossible. Indeed, assume a sub-transaction T_k and its sub-tree abort because of a constraint violation. Each constraint C_i touched by leaf transactions in this sub-tree has to be checked by $SCA(C_i)$ which is an ancestor of these leaf transactions, therefore either an ancestor of T_k or a descendant of T_k. In the first case, it is sure that $SCA(C_i)$ has not committed yet. In the second case, all the sub-transactions touching C_i are included in the sub-tree of T_k. As all of them will be aborted, C_i cannot be violated and there is no need to check it again. To take into account eventual re-checking of constraints, we change the Propagate procedure so that whenever a sub-transaction aborts, it sends a warning message to each sub-transaction responsible for a constraint that has to be checked again because of aborting the sub-tree.

But the abortion of a sub-transaction may occur because of other reasons (e.g. deadlock detection), implying constraints to be checked again. This situation is out of the control of the Propagate procedure. Two solutions allow taking into account aborts due to causes external to the integrity mechanism. The first solution is to include the sending of warning messages into the abort process of a leaf transaction. This is clearly the most efficient solution but leads to alter the nested transaction execution control, which is contradictory with our goal to modify as few as possible the underlying transaction system. The second solution is that each $SCA(C_i)$, after having received the decision of all its children, checks whether C_i has to be checked again or not. This solution can be implemented in the behaviour of each node sub-transaction without changing the nested transaction execution control, but defers the eventual new checking of C_i until the whole sub-tree of $SCA(C_i)$ has finished.

Efficiency of the Checking Process. In our solution, we do not block the execution of the nested transaction because of the checking of a constraint. The checking process of a constraint is launched by the smallest common ancestor of the sub-transactions touching it and performed in parallel with the nested transaction. Each time it is possible, the checking process is performed on copies of the involved objects, thus the locks on involved objects can be released by the concerned sub-transaction to allow the continuation of the nested transaction. This is always the case for universally quantified constraints, were all the objects involved by a constraint are collected during the execution of a sub-transaction touching it. For existentially quantified constraints, the checking process may require to access other objects in the database, thus it may be executed in concurrency with some sub-transaction of the nested transaction. The main advantage of our approach is that, at least for universally quantified constraints, when no constraint is violated, the nested transaction is not disrupted by the constraint checking. In other words, our approach is optimistic : when no constraint is violated, the concurrency level of a nested transaction is the same as it would be if there were no constraints.

5   Conclusion

This article presents a mechanism to maintain integrity constraints in databases supporting nested transactions. Constraints and nested transactions are defined using the general features of Thémis enriched with nested transaction features. By analysing constraints and transactions, we check constraints as soon as possible and, in case of violation, abort as few as possible sub-transactions until reaching, whenever possible, the commit of the nested transaction. The key point to reach this goal is to attach the control and the checking of a constraint to the smallest common ancestor of all the sub-transactions touching the constraint. Our solution does not require any significant change in the execution control mechanism of nested transactions and does not impose users to add any additional code into transactions and/or constraints.

In our approach, constraints are maintained by a mechanism integrated with the nested transaction execution control. In contrast to the approach of [12], where the programmer not only has to define when a constraint has to be checked within the execution of the nested transaction, but also must define the behaviour to follow whenever a constraint is violated, our approach offers a fully automatic consistency management. Moreover, our solution does not require significant modifications of the nested transaction manager, thus rendering it adaptable to any nested transaction manager. In [28] the checking of integrity constraints are attached to the top-level transaction, as opposed to our approach where we attach the control and the checking of a constraint to the smallest common ancestor of all the sub-transactions touching it.

Works are in progress to develop and improve our mechanism. A first prototype, which will implement the ideas presented in this paper, is being designed. It will not only help us to test the efficiency and the relevance of our approach, but also serve as a support for further theoretical developments.

We currently investigate different points to improve our approach. The first point is to adapt our approach to other NT models, such as Open Nested Transaction [44] and the Transaction Closures [40] which generalises most of the existing NT models. The second point consists of using information from the concurrency controller to abort fewer sub-transactions. Indeed, in the present version of the mechanism, we abort a node whenever one of its children concerned by a violated constraint has already committed (cf. the Propagate procedure of section 4.2.2). If we can determine that this child has not influenced other children of the node, then it is sufficient to abort this child instead of the node to ensure that consistency is preserved. The third point concerns distributed databases. We must take into account more carefully the cost of additional messages, the possibility of loosing messages, and the way in which the checking of a constraint can be performed efficiently, depending on the location of the involved objects in the network.

Acknowledgments

We would like to thank E. Kindler and all the participants of TDD'99, as well as the anonymous referees for their suggestions and comments.

References

1. Transarc Encina Product Information.
   http://www.transarc.com/Product/Txseries/Encina/.
2. Transarc Solutions. http://www.transarc.com/Solutions/index.html.
3. V. Benzaken and A. Doucet. Thémis: A Database Programming Language Handling Integrity Constraints. *The VLDB Journal*, 4(3):493–517, July 1995.
4. P. A. Bernstein and E. Newcomer. *Transaction Processing for the Systems Professional*. Morgan Kaufmann Publishers, 1996.
5. B. T. Blaustein. *Esforcing Database Assertions*. PhD thesis, Harvard University, Cambridge, MA, 1981.
6. E. Boertjes, P. W. P. J. Grefen, J. Vonk, and P. M. G. Apers. An Architecture for Nested Transactions Support on Standard Database Systems. In G. Quirchmayr, E. Schweighofer, and T. J. M. Bench-Capon, editors, *Proc. 9th Int. Conf. Database and Expert Systems Applications, DEXA'98, Vienna, Austria, August 1998*, LNCS, Vol. 1460, pages 448–459, Springer-Verlag, 1998.
7. S. Ceri, P. Fraternali, S. Paraboschi, and L. Tanca. Automatic Generation of Production Rules for Integrity Maintenance. *ACM Transactions on Database Systems*, 19(3):367–422, September 1994.
8. S. Ceri and J. Widom. Deriving Production Rules for Constraint Management. In D. McLeod, R. Sacks-Davis, and H.-J. Schek, editors, *Proc. of the 16th Int. Conf. on Very Large Data Bases, VLDB'90, Brisbane, Australia, August 1990*, pages 566–577, Morgan Kaufmann Publishers, 1990.
9. P. K. Chrysanthis and K. Ramamritham. ACTA: A Framework for Specifying and Reasoning about Transaction Structure and Behavior. In H. Garcia-Molina and H. V. Jagadish, editors, *Proc. of the 1990 ACM SIGMOD Int. Conf. on Management of Data, Atlantic City, NJ, USA*, ACM SIGMOD Record, Vol. 19, No. 2, pages 194–203, ACM Press, 1990.
10. P. K. Chrysanthis and K. Ramamritham. Synthesis of Extended Transaction Models Using ACTA. *ACM Transactions on Database Systems*, 19(3):450–491, September 1994.

11. U. Dayal, M. Hsu, and R. Ladin. A Transaction Model for Long-Running Activities. In G. M. Lohmann, A. Sernadas, and R. Camps, editors, *Proc. of the 17th Int. Conf. on Very Large Data Bases, VLDB'91, Barcelona, Spain, September 1991*, pages 113–122, Morgan Kaufmann Publishers, 1991.

12. B. Defude and H. Martin. Integrity checking for Nested Transactions. In R. Wagner and H. Thoma, editors, *Database and Expert System Applications, Proc. of the 7th Int. Workshop., DEXA'96, Zurich, Switzerland, September 1996*, pages 147–152, IEEE Computer Society Press, 1996.

13. A. Doucet, S. Gançarski, G. Jomier, and S. Monties. Integrity Constraints in Multiversion Databases. In R. Morrison and J. B. Keane, editors, *Advances in Databases: 14th British National Conf. on Databases, BNCOD 14, Edinburgh, UK, July 1996*, LNCS, Vol. 1094, pages 56–73, Springer-Verlag, 1996.

14. A. K. Elmagarmid, editor. *Database Transaction Models For Advanced Applications*. Morgan Kaufmann Publishers, 1992.

15. D. Enser and I. Stevenson. *Oracle8 Design Tips*. O'Reilly & Associates, 1997.

16. J. L. Eppinger, L. B. Mummert, and A.Z. Spector, editors. *Camelon and Avalon — A Distributed Transaction Facility*. Morgan Kaufmann Publishers, 1991.

17. C. Fahrner, T. Marx, and S. Philippi. DICE: Declarative Integrity Constraint Embedding into the Object Database Standard ODMG-93. *Data & Knowledge Engineering*, 23(2):119–145, August 1997.

18. H. Garcia-Molina and K. Salem. Sagas. In U. Dayal and I. L. Traiger, editors, *Proc. of the 1987 ACM SIGMOD Int. Conf. on Management of Data, San Franscisco, CA, USA*, ACM SIGMOD Record, Vol. 16, No. 3, pages 249–259, ACM Press, 1987.

19. J. Gray. The Transaction Concept: Virtues and Limitations. In C. Zaniolo and C. Delobel, editors, *Proc. of the 7th Int. Conf. on Very Large Data Bases, VLDB'81, Cannes, France, September 1981*, pages 144–154, IEEE Computer Society Press, 1981.

20. J. Gray and A. Reuter. *Transaction Processing: Concepts and Techniques*. Morgan Kaufmann Publishers, 1993.

21. P. W. P. J. Grefen and P. M. G. Apers. Integrity Control in Relational Database Systems — An Overview. *Data & Knowledge Engineering*, 10:187–223, 1993.

22. P. W. P. J. Grefen and J. Widom. Protocols for Integrity Constraint Checking in Federated Databases. *Distributed and Parallel Databases*, 5(4):327–355, October 1997.

23. A. Gupta and J. Widom. Local Verification of Global Integrity Constraints in Distributed Databases. In P. Buneman and S. Jajodia, editors, *Proc. of the 1993 ACM SIGMOD Int. Conf. on Management of Data, Washington, D.C., USA*, ACM SIGMOD Record, Vol. 22, No. 2, pages 49–58, ACM Press, 1993.

24. T. Härder and K. Rothermel. Concurrency Control Issues in Nested Transactions. *The VLDB Journal*, 2(1):39–74, January 1993.

25. A. Hsu and T. Imielinski. Integrity Checking for Multiple Updates. In S. Navathe, editor, *Proc. of the 1985 ACM SIGMOD Int. Conf. on Management of Data, May 1985, Austin, Texas, USA*, ACM SIGMOD Record, Vol. 14, No. 4, pages 152–168, ACM Press, 1985.

26. IBM Corporation. *IBM Database Referencial Integrity Usage Guide*, 1989.

27. H. V. Jagadish and X. Qian. Integrity Maintenance in an OODB. In L.-Y. Yuan, editor, *Proc. of the 18th Int. Conf. on Very Large Data Bases, VLDB'92, Vancouver, Canada*, pages 469–480, Morgan Kaufmann Publishers, 1992.

28. H. F. Korth and G. D. Speegle. Formal Aspects of Concurrency Control in Long-Duration Transactions Systems Using the NT/PV Model. *ACM Transactions on Database Systems*, 19(3):492–535, September 1994.

29. C. León, M. Rukoz, and M. Rivas. Una Herramienta Java para Aplicacionnes Distribuidas de Tratamiento de Imágenes Biomémedicas. In *Proc. XXIV Conferencia Latinoamericana de Informática, PANEL'98, October 1998, Quito, Ecuador*, pages 855–866, Centro de Estudios Latinoamericanos de Informática, 1998.

30. B. Liskov. Distributed Computing in Argus. *Communications of the ACM*, 31(3):300–312, March 1988.

31. N. A. Lynch. Concurrency Control for Resilient Nested Transactions. *Advances in Computing Research*, 3:335–373, 1986.

32. S. K. Madria. A study of Concurrency Control and Recovery Algorithms in Nested Transaction Environment. *The Computer Journal*, 40(10):630–639, 1997.

33. S. Monties. *Cohérence des Bases d'Objets Multiversion*. PhD thesis, Université de Paris I, Paris, France, 1997.

34. J. E. B. Moss. *Nested Transactions: An Approach to Reliable Distributed Computing*. MIT Press, Cambridge, MA, 1985.

35. J. E. B. Moss. Log-Based Recovery for Nested Transactions. In P. M. Stocker and W. Kent, editors, *Proc. of the 13th Int. Conf. on Very Large Data Bases, VLDB'87, Brighton, England, September 1–4, 1987*, pages 427–432, Morgan Kaufmann Publishers, 1987.

36. J.-M. Nicolas. Logic for Improving Integrity Checking in Relational Data Bases. *Acta Informatica*, 18(3):227–253, 1982.

37. P.-Y. Policella. *Cohérence dans les Bases de Données Orientées Objet*. PhD thesis, Université de Paris XI, Paris, France, 1996.

38. A. Reuter and H. Wächter. The ConTract Model. *Bulletin of the IEEE Technical Committee on Data Engineering*, 14(1):39–44, 1991.

39. M. Rukoz. Hierarchical Deadlock Detection for Nested Transactions. *Distributed Computing*, 4:123–129, 1991.

40. K. Schwarz, C. Türker, and G. Saake. Analyzing and Formalizing Dependencies in Generalized Transaction Structures. In M. Tamer Özsu, A. Dogac, and Ö. Ulusoy, editors, *Proc. of the Third Int. Conf. on Integrated Design and Process Technology, IDPT - Volume 2, Int. Workshop on Issues and Applications of Database Technology, IADT'98, July 1998, Berlin, Germany*, pages 55–62, Society for Design and Process Science, 1998.

41. T. Sheard and D. Stemple. Automatic Verification on Database Transaction Safety. *ACM Transactions on Database Systems*, 14(3):322–368, September 1989.

42. Sybase Inc. Press, Emeryville,CA (USA). *Sybase SQL Server*, 1989.

43. G. Weikum. A Theoretical Foundation of Multi-Level Concurrency Control. In *Proc. of the 5th ACM SIGACT-SIGMOD-SIGART Symposium on Principles of Database Systems, PODS'86, March 1986, Cambridge, MA, USA*, pages 31–42, ACM Press, 1986.

44. G. Weikum and H.-J. Schek. Concepts and Applications of Multilevel Transactions and Open Nested Transactions. In A. K. Elmagarmid, editor, *Database Transaction Models for Advanced Applications*, pages 515–553, Morgan Kaufmann Publishers, 1992.

45. J. Widom and S. Ceri, editors. *Active Database Systems — Triggers and Rules for Advanced Database Processing*. Morgan Kaufmann Publishers, 1996.

Declarative Specifications of Complex Transactions
with an Application to Cascading Deletes

Bert De Brock

University of Groningen
Faculty of Management and Organization
P.O.Box 800, NL–9700 AV Groningen, The Netherlands
e.o.de.brock@bkd.rug.nl

Abstract. While specifications of queries usually are of a declarative nature (since the work of Codd in the early seventies), specifications of transactions mainly are of an operational and descriptive nature. Especially descriptions of complex transactions (such as cascading deletes) tend to be very operational. Declarative specifications of transactions usually suffer from the so-called frame problem or do not have a clear semantics. Often these descriptions turn out to be nondeterministic as well. A problematic consequence is that the semantics of transactions and of several related notions is often unclear or even ambiguous. For a database designer this surely is not a good starting point for building applications. Another tendency we recognize is that the current literature on transactions is mainly driven by technical solutions offered by research prototypes and commercial systems and not so much by advanced specification requirements from a user's or database designer's point of view. In our opinion, the research questions should (also) include what kind of complex transactions (advanced) users would like to specify (and not only what e.g. the expressive power of a given technical solution is), and how these specifications can be translated to implementations in the currently available (advanced) database management systems. And, moreover, was it not our purpose (with the introduction of 4GL's and the like) to become declarative instead of operational, concentrating on the "what" instead of the "how"? This paper offers a general framework for declarative specifications of transactions, including complex ones. Transactions on a state space $\mathcal{U}$ are considered as functions from $\mathcal{U}$ into $\mathcal{U}$. We also take the influence of static and dynamic constraints on the alleged transactions into account. This leads to the notion of the adaptation of a transaction. Applications of our theory included in this paper are the declarative specification of cascading deletes and the distinction between allowable and available transitions. Basic set theory is our main vehicle.

Keywords: Transactions, semantics, transaction models, transaction design, database dynamics, declarative specifications of database behavior, (static and dynamic) integrity constraints, adaptations, (allowable versus available) transitions, cascading deletes.

G. Saake, K. Schwarz, and C. Türker (Eds.): TDD '99, LNCS 1773, pp. 150–166, 2000.
© Springer-Verlag Berlin Heidelberg 2000

1   Introduction

While specifications of queries usually have a declarative form ([3,4,9,1]), specifications of transactions mainly are of an operational/imperative and descriptive
nature (see [9,1,5]), as still recalled by, e.g., [1]. Especially descriptions of complex transactions (for instance cascading deletes) tend to be very operational,
using some kind of execution model. Declarative specifications of transactions
usually suffer from the so-called frame problem or do not have a clear semantics.
In the survey [2], Bonner and Kifer discuss various proposals, including their
strong and weak points. Often these descriptions turn out to be nondeterministic. This holds in particular for the area of active databases (e.g., [19,12,15]);
see for instance [1, Section 22.5] for a discussion. A problematic consequence is
that the semantics of transactions and of several related notions is often unclear
or even ambiguous. This surely is not a good starting point for building applications. Another tendency we recognize is that the current literature on transactions is mainly driven by technical solutions offered by research prototypes and
commercial systems (e.g., [16,20]) and not so much by advanced specification
requirements from a user's or database designer's point of view. In our opinion,
the research questions should (also) include what kind of complex transactions
(advanced) users such as database designers would like to specify (and not only
what e.g. the expressive power of a given technical solution is), and how these
specifications can be translated to implementations in the currently available
(advanced) database management systems. Moreover, with the introduction of
4GL's and the like it was our purpose to become declarative instead of operational, concentrating on the "what" instead of the "how". This intention has to
apply for transactions as well! This paper contributes to the theory of databases
by offering a general framework for declarative specifications of transactions. In
our treatment we take a semantic approach. We also take the influence of static
and dynamic constraints on the alleged transactions into account, by introducing the notion of the adaptation of a transaction. Moreover, we can also put
the distinction between allowable and available transitions in place. An advanced application of our theory concerns the declarative specification of cascading
deletes. In our treatment of cascading deletes, the start set of tuples to be deleted is not restricted to only one table, the "cascading reference graph" may also
contain cycles, and rollback is incorporated (in case of a violation of any integrity constraint). The paper is organized as follows. Section 2 introduces a quite
general definition of transactions, on arbitrary state spaces and within arbitrary
transition relations. The adaptation of a transaction (determined by the given
static and dynamic constraints) is also defined in this section. Theorem 1 shows
that this operation has indeed the nice properties we want it to have. Section 3
introduces a formal declarative definition of cascading deletes. Finally, we draw
our conclusions and sketch our plans for further research in this area. The paper
also contains an appendix explaining the basic notions and notations we used.

2   Transactions and Adaptations

2.1   Transactions

The state of an organization is usually liable to change: employees, customers, and products come and go, orders and invoices are received and handled, and salaries, stocks, and prices go up and down in the meantime. The administrative repercussions of such changes — in the field of databases referred to as modification or manipulation or maintenance — can be specified formally by means of functions that assign to each possible (database) state the (database) state reflecting the new situation. We call such functions from a state space $\mathcal{U}$ into $\mathcal{U}$ itself transactions on $\mathcal{U}$. The general definition, for arbitrary state spaces, reads as follows:

Definition 1. *If $\mathcal{U}$ is a set, then:*

$$f \text{ is a } \textbf{transaction on } \mathcal{U} \Leftrightarrow f \in \mathcal{U} \to \mathcal{U}.$$

Example 1. We will use a simple employees-and-departments database as an example to illustrate our points. The database keeps track of the employee number, department number, salary, and bonus of each employee, and of the department number, manager number, and budget of each department. Our example is based on the following database schema g_1, which enumerates each table symbol and its corresponding set of attributes:

$$g_1 = \{(EMP; ENO, DNO, SAL, BON),$$
$$(DEP; DNO, MNO, BUD)\}$$

We now define a database universe EXU over the database schema g_1. First, the set-valued functions FE and FD introduce the (employee and department) attributes and their corresponding value sets. Then the sets WE and WD determine the set of allowed employee tables and department tables, respectively. The function HF introduces the relation symbols (or table names) EMP and DEP and associates them with their corresponding sets of allowed tables. Finally, the DB universe EXU determines the set of allowed database states. For referential purposes we numbered our key constraints and referential constraints; for instance, the key constraint (KC1) expresses that employee numbers must be uniquely identifying in the employee table, and the inclusion dependency (RC2) expresses that each department manager must also be mentioned in the employee table. Our notations are defined in the appendix.

$FE = \{$		
$(ENO; \mathbb{N})$,		employee number
$(DNO; \mathbb{N})$,		department number
$(SAL \; ; \mathbb{N})$,		salary
$(BON; \mathbb{N})\}$;		bonus

$FD = \{$		
$(DNO; \mathbb{N})$,		department number
$(MNO; \mathbb{N})$,		manager number
$(BUD; \mathbb{N})\}$;		budget

$WE = \{T \mid T \subseteq \prod(FE) \text{ and} \qquad\qquad \text{| the set of allowed employee tables}$
$\qquad\qquad \{ENO\} \text{ is u.i. in } T\}; \qquad\qquad \text{| (KC1)}$

$WD = \{T \mid T \subseteq \prod(FD) \text{ and} \qquad\qquad \text{| the set of allowed department tables}$
$\qquad\qquad \{DNO\} \text{ is u.i. in } T\}; \qquad\qquad \text{| (KC2)}$

$HF = \{ (EMP; WE), \qquad\qquad\qquad \text{| employees}$
$\qquad\qquad (DEP ; WD)\}; \qquad\qquad\qquad \text{| departments}$

$EXU = \{v \mid v \in \prod(HF) \quad \text{and}$
$\qquad\qquad \{t(DNO) \mid t \in v(EMP)\} \subseteq \{t(DNO) \mid t \in v(DEP)\} \text{ and } \text{| (RC1)}$
$\qquad\qquad \{t(MNO) \mid t \in v(DEP)\} \subseteq \{t(ENO) \mid t \in v(EMP)\}\} \qquad \text{| (RC2)}$

We now illustrate the notion of a transaction by means of the DB universe EXU and the tuple

$$t_0 = \{(DNO; 3), (MNO; 7), (BUD; 1000000)\}$$

We might well be tempted, at first sight, to describe the addition of the department tuple t_0 by means of the following function f_1, which assigns to each DB state v in EXU the new DB state with t_0 added to the DEP-table:

$$f_1 = \lambda v \in EXU : \{(EMP; v(EMP)),$$
$$(DEP; v(DEP) \cup \{t_0\})\}$$

Yet, the function f_1 turns out not to be a transaction on EXU! Indeed, f_1 is a function over EXU, but not into EXU: for some v in EXU, $f_1(v)$ is not an element of EXU. This holds in particular if $t_0 \notin v(DEP)$ while the department number 3 does already occur in the table $v(DEP)$ or the employee number 7 does not occur in the table $v(EMP)$, due to the requirements (KC2) and (RC2), respectively. Should we want to leave the state unaltered in those special cases, then the description of such an insertion attempt or request (see [2, Page 25]) could look like this:

$$f_2 = \lambda v \in EXU : \begin{cases} f_1(v) & : \quad \text{if } f_1(v) \in EXU \\ v & : \quad \text{otherwise} \end{cases}$$

It is clear from this description that the function f_2 is indeed a transaction on EXU.

If, in addition, dynamic constraints have been established on EXU, then it must also be the case that $(v; f_1(v))$, the transition from state v to state $f_1(v)$, is an admissible transition. Suppose for instance that new departments can only be added in certain situations, e.g., if the number of employees is a fourfold or, shortly after, a fourfold plus one. So, more formally, if the number of employees is not a fourfold or a fourfold plus one, then the projection of the new DEP-table $v'(DEP)$ on $\{DNO\}$ must be a subset of the projection of the old DEP-table $v(DEP)$ on $\{DNO\}$. Let us denote this example of a dynamic constraint by (DC1). This dynamic constraint determines our transition relation (see the appendix). So, we want to have the following transition relation R_0 (telling us which direct state transitions are allowed):

$$R_0 = \{(v; v') \mid (v; v') \in EXU \times EXU \text{ and }$$
$$\text{if } |v(EMP)| \bmod 4 \notin \{0, 1\}$$
$$\text{then } \pi_{\{DNO\}}(v'(DEP)) \subseteq \pi_{\{DNO\}}(v(DEP))\} \quad \mid (DC1)$$

Note that this is an example of a conditional inclusion dependency "in time". Again if we want to leave the state unaltered in the event of a non-allowed transition, then the intended transaction is f_3:

$$f_3 = \lambda v \in EXU : \begin{cases} f_1(v) & : \text{ if } (v; f_1(v)) \in R_0 \\ v & : \text{ otherwise} \end{cases}$$

We want to note that $(v; f1(v)) \in f1$, since $f1$ is a function (and hence a set of ordered pairs), and that $v \in dom(f1)$. So the function $f3$ can be rewritten in a closed formula as follows (by using the θ-operation as defined in the appendix):

$$f3 = \{(v; f_1(v)) \mid v \in EXU \text{ and } (v; f_1(v)) \in R_0\} \cup$$
$$\{(v; v) \mid v \in EXU \text{ and } (v; f_1(v)) \notin R_0\}$$
$$= id(EXU)\,\theta\,(R_0 \cap f_1) \qquad \qquad \square$$

In Example 1 we put forward that a transaction should also satisfy all dynamic constraints and should therefore "fit" in the transition relation R_0. In that case we speak of a transaction within R_0. In general we define:

Definition 2. *If R is a relation, then:*

f is a **transaction within** $R \Leftrightarrow f$ is a function and $f \subseteq R$.

We can now summarize the results of Example 1 as follows:

- f_1 is not a transaction on EXU,
- f_2 is a transaction on EXU, yet not a transaction within R_0, and
- f_3 is a transaction within R_0.

When we compare Definition 1 with Definition 2 for the special case that $R = \mathcal{U} \times \mathcal{U}$ (i.e., in case there are no dynamic constraints), we observe that each transaction *on* $\mathcal{U}$ is a transaction *within* $\mathcal{U} \times \mathcal{U}$ as well. We note that the reverse does not need to hold, since the domain of a transaction within $\mathcal{U} \times \mathcal{U}$ is not necessarily equal to $\mathcal{U}$ (or, in other words, since the transaction is not necessarily defined in each state).

One popular (but implicit) way of specifying the set of "allowable" transitions is by specifying the (currently) available transactions on a given database universe $\mathcal{U}$. However, we note that we can make a distinction between

1. the set of (user-defined) *allowable* transitions as specified by means of a transition relation R on the database universe $\mathcal{U}$, i.e., $R \subseteq \mathcal{U} \times \mathcal{U}$, and

2. the set of (currently) *available* transitions as determined by a set S of (currently) available transactions on $\mathcal{U}$.

We note that our distinction between allowable and available transitions corresponds to the distinction between the *behaviour layer* and the *action layer* in [14]. We also note that in practice the set S of (currently) available transactions might be subject to change independently from R. Of course each available transition must also be allowed. On the other hand, whether an allowable transition is actually available depends on the set of currently available transactions! So, $\forall f \in S : f \subseteq R$, that is, $\bigcup S \subseteq R$, but not necessarily $\bigcup S = R$.

2.2 Adaptations

The two adjustments made to the function f_1 in Example 1, finally resulting in the transaction f_3 within the transition relation R_0, are of a more general interest. We therefore introduce the following concept (generalizing the closed formula at the end of Example 1):

Definition 3. *If $\mathcal{U}$ is a set and $R \subseteq \mathcal{U} \times \mathcal{U}$ and f is a function, then:*

$$Ad(\mathcal{U}, R, f) = id(\mathcal{U}) \, \theta \, (R \cap f).$$

We call $Ad(\mathcal{U}, R, f)$ the adaptation of f (determined) by $\mathcal{U}$ and R. We speak of *the adaptation of f (determined) by $\mathcal{U}$* if there are no dynamic integrity constraints, in which case we are in fact dealing with the transition relation $\mathcal{U} \times \mathcal{U}$, which is the most "liberal" transition relation on $\mathcal{U}$. We denote this adaptation (solely determined by the static constraints) by $Adap(\mathcal{U}, f)$:

Definition 4. *If $\mathcal{U}$ is a set and f is a function, then:*

$$Adap(\mathcal{U}, f) = Ad(\mathcal{U}, \mathcal{U} \times \mathcal{U}, f).$$

We give the following alternative descriptions of the two concepts just introduced:

$$Adap(\mathcal{U}, f) = \lambda v \in \mathcal{U} : \begin{cases} f(v) & : \quad \text{if } v \in dom(f) \text{ and } f(v) \in \mathcal{U} \\ v & : \quad \text{otherwise} \end{cases}$$

$$Ad(\mathcal{U}, R, f) = \lambda v \in \mathcal{U} : \begin{cases} f(v) & : \quad \text{if } v \in dom(f) \text{ and } (v; f(v)) \in R \\ v & : \quad \text{otherwise} \end{cases}$$

Returning to Example 1, we observe that

$$f_2 = Adap(EXU, f_1) \text{ and}$$

$$f_3 = Ad(EXU, R_0, f_1) \text{ hold.}$$

In the "otherwise" cases, which means that the alteration attempt is cancelled, we speak of a *rollback* of the alteration attempt. The following theorem shows that the adaptations of functions indeed possess the nice properties we would like them to have. The adaptation of a function is indeed a transaction on the state space concerned (a and b) and within the underlying transition relation extended with the identity function on that state space (c), if the underlying transition relation R is reflexive on the state space $\mathcal{U}$ (as is usually the case) then the adaptation is a transaction within that transition relation (d), if the function already was a function on the state space and within that transition relation concerned then the adaptation operation has no effect anymore (e), and (hence) the adaptation operation is "idempotent" for reflexive transition relations, i.e. it has no use to apply the adaptation operation more than once (f). The proof of this theorem can be found in [7].

Theorem 1. *If $\mathcal{U}$ is a set and $R \subseteq \mathcal{U} \times \mathcal{U}$ and f is a function, then:*

(a) *$Adap(\mathcal{U}, f)$ is a transaction on $\mathcal{U}$;*

(b) *$Ad(\mathcal{U}, R, f)$ is a transaction on $\mathcal{U}$;*

(c) *$Ad(\mathcal{U}, R, f)$ is a transaction within $R \cup id(\mathcal{U})$;*

(d) *if R is reflexive on $\mathcal{U}$, then $Ad(\mathcal{U}, R, f)$ is a transaction within R;*

(e) *if f is a transaction on $\mathcal{U}$ and within R, then $Ad(\mathcal{U}, R, f) = f$;*

(f) *if R is reflexive on $\mathcal{U}$, then $Ad(\mathcal{U}, R, Ad(\mathcal{U}, R, f)) = Ad(\mathcal{U}, R, f)$.*

We also introduced the adaptation concepts above because they model so well what the architecture of interactions between a user and a database management system could look like in general: for each "naive" function f, given by the user as a maintenance attempt (hence, as a special sort of "application"), the DBMS could de facto carry out the adaptation of f determined by the DB universe and the transition relation as known to the DBMS. Consequently, this means that every static and dynamic constraint that can be specified in the DBMS under consideration need not be "interwoven" in all those separate applications, but could be dealt with by the DBMS itself. As to the extent to which all sorts of refined constraints can be given as input to existing DBMSs when specifying DB universes and transition relations, we refer the reader to, e.g., "Focal Point 4" in [11] or, as the most actual sources, to the reference manuals of the DBMSs themselves. For systematic translations of formally specified database universes, (static) integrity constraints, and queries into SQL2 we refer to [7, Chapter 9].

We stress that the successive application of the adaptations of two functions f and g need not at all give the same result as the application of the adaptation of the composed function $g \circ f$ as one "atomic unit" (alias one unit of work). In other words, it might be that the transaction $Ad(\mathcal{U}, R, g) \circ Ad(\mathcal{U}, R, f)$ is another function than the transaction $Ad(\mathcal{U}, R, g \circ f)$! [7, Section 7.1] contains a careful case analysis.

In order to position the common sorts of transaction possibilities supported by actual relational DBMS's and by the SQL2-standard (see [10,6]) within our framework, we introduced some special classes of transactions in [7] that together cover the largest part of the actual transaction possibilities in SQL. In a sense, our transactions constitute a formal semantics for those SQL-statements.

3   Cascading Deletes

A well-known transaction phenomenon in databases is that of cascading deletes (see for instance [5,10,13]). As an illustration, consider a database with data on a company's clients and their orders. When we want to delete some clients, we (implicitly) might want to delete their orders as well. And if there is a separate table for the order lines then we (implicitly) want to delete the corresponding order lines too. So, a deletion of clients "triggers" deletions of orders, which in turn trigger deletions of order lines. We call this chain of triggering deletes cascading deletes. However, if such chains of deletes happen to contain cycles, things can become quite complex. The reason for this complexity is that the triggering of additional deletes can go on recursively, as the next section will show.

3.1   An Example of Cascading Deletes

The following example will show how the deletion of one tuple in one table can trigger the deletion of all tuples in almost all tables. The example will also be helpful in illustrating the ideas in the next section.

Example 2. Suppose that we have a database universe with six table names, say A, B, C, D, E, and F, and with six "cascading" referential integrity constraints, say from C to A, from C to B, from D to C, from F to D, from E to D, and from B to E; see Figure 1.

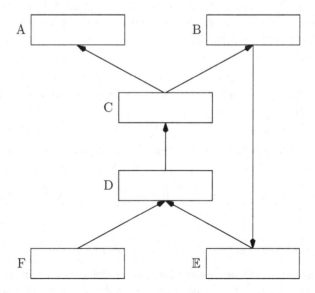

Fig. 1. A diagram with cascading referential integrity constraints

In order to introduce our ideas presented in the following sections with a concrete example, we will consider an actual database state with its referencing tuples as depicted in Figure 2. For simplicity we will call the tuples A1, A2, .., B1, B2, .., and so on.

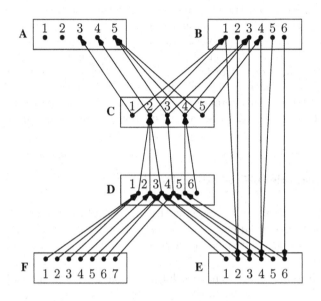

Fig. 2. An actual database state with referencing tuples

Below we will "calculate" the cumulative effect of deleting tuple 1 from the B-table; here "$X \to Y$" stands for the fact that the deletion of the tuples X triggers the deletion of the tuples Y.

B1	$\to$ C1, C2	$\to$ D1, D2, D3	$\to$ E1, E2, E3, F1–F6	$\to$
B2, B3	$\to$ C3, C4	$\to$ D4, D5, D6	$\to$ E4, E5, E6, F7	$\to$
B4, B5, B6	$\to$ C5			+
B1–B6	C1–C5	D1–D6	E1–E6, F1–F7	

Fig. 3. The cumulative effect of the cascading delete of tuple B1

Adding everything up, we see that within a few cycles *all* tuples of *all* tables but the A-table will be deleted!   □

3.2   Informal Sketch of the Basic Ideas

We now turn to the semantics of cascading deletes and want to deduce a general, declarative formal specification of the result of cascading deletes. We will start with an informal sketch of the basic ideas of our solution. The core of our solution is to consider the transitive closure of the "graph of referencing tuples" (such as depicted in Figure 2). In order to specify this graph, we "label" each tuple with the name of its table. Hence, the set of all labelled tuples of a database state v is

$$\{(E;t) \mid E \in dom(v) \text{ and } t \in v(E)\},$$

which can also be denoted as $\biguplus v$, the generalized disjoint union of v (see the appendix for the terminology and notations we used). The "referencing tuple graph" Rtg consisting of all reference pairs of labelled tuples can be described informally as

$$Rtg = \{((E;t);(E';t')) \mid \text{tuple } t \text{ in table } v(E) \text{ refers to tuple } t' \text{ in table } v(E')\}.$$

For the determination of the graph Rtg we have to consider only those referential integrity constraints that are declared as "cascading" by the database designer. We will work this out later by adding the set of those referential integrity constraints as a parameter. Let $Delset$ denote the set of all labelled (!) tuples to be deleted *initially*. We note that $Delset$ need not be restricted to only one table. The set of all labelled tuples to be deleted *eventually* will consist of

– all elements of $Delset$ and
– all labelled tuples that directly or indirectly refer to an element in $Delset$:

$$Delset \cup \{(E;t) \mid \exists y \in Delset : ((E;t);y) \in Tcl(Rtg)\},$$

where $Tcl(Rtg)$ denotes the transitive closure of Rtg, i.e., the set of (begin point; end point)-pairs of all possible non-empty walks in the graphical representation of Rtg (see e.g. [18,7] for a formal definition of transitive closure).

So, for each table name E, the following subset Nt_E of $v(E)$ is the E-table in the intended new state:

$$Nt_E = \{t \in v(E) \mid (E;t) \notin Delset \text{ and } \neg\exists y \in Delset : ((E;t);y) \in Tcl(Rtg)\}.$$

But also with cascading deletes, the intended new state might not be allowed, e.g., due to other static or dynamic constraints. In that case the database should remain completely unchanged. This calls again for our adaptation operation of Section 2. Thus, if f denotes the function assigning to each state v of the database universe $\mathcal{U}$ the intended new state just described, then $Ad(\mathcal{U}, R, f)$ would be the actual transaction on $\mathcal{U}$ (and within the given transition relation R).

3.3   Formal Model of Cascading Deletes Results

We are now ready for the formalization of these ideas. First we define the notions of a foreign key dependency and a reference graph. Informally, a foreign key dependency consists of two table names E and E' and an attribute transformation h such that the inclusion dependency "$E.dom(h) < E'.rng(h)$" holds on $\mathcal{U}$ and that $rng(h)$ is a key of E' in $\mathcal{U}$ (see the appendix for the terminology and notations used):

Definition 5. *If $\mathcal{U}$ is a DB universe over a DB schema g, then:*

$(E; E'; h)$ *is a **foreign key dependency in** $\mathcal{U}$*

$$\Leftrightarrow E \in dom(g) \text{ and } E' \in dom(g) \text{ and}$$
$$h \text{ is a function and } rng(h) \text{ is a key of } E' \text{ in } \mathcal{U} \text{ and}$$
$$\forall v \in U : h \text{ connects } v(E) \text{ with } v(E').$$

If $(E; E'; h)$ is a foreign key dependency in $\mathcal{U}$ then $dom(h)$ is called a *foreign key* in the literature.

Definition 6. *If $\mathcal{U}$ is a DB universe, then:*

G *is a **reference graph on** $U \Leftrightarrow G$ is a set of foreign key dependencies in $\mathcal{U}$.*

Figure 1 augmented with a labelling of each arrow with the proper underlying attribute transformation h would constitute a representation of a reference graph. We note that it is possible that $E = E'$ (for instance, a reference to the manager of an employee) or that there are two different arrows from a given table symbol E to a given table symbol E' (for instance, references to the product as well as to the part in a bill of material). Note that in the latter case the two arrows must have different labels. In Definition 6 we deliberately talk about *a* reference graph on $\mathcal{U}$ and not necessarily about *the* reference graph of *all* foreign key dependencies in $\mathcal{U}$. Our intention (from Definition 7 on) is to concentrate on the set of all foreign key dependencies that have to be *cascading*. For a reference graph G on a database universe $\mathcal{U}$ the following (auxiliary) function $Gt(\mathcal{U}, G)$ assigns to each database state v of $\mathcal{U}$ the graph of referencing tuples according to G:

Definition 7. *If $\mathcal{U}$ is a DB universe and G is a reference graph on U, then:*

$$Gt(\mathcal{U}, G) = \lambda v \in U : \{((E; t); (E'; t')) \mid (E; E'; h) \in G \text{ and } t \in v(E) \text{ and}$$
$$t' \in v(E') \text{ and } t \lceil dom(h) = t' \circ h\}.$$

So, $Gt(\mathcal{U}, G)(v)$ denotes the graph of referencing tuples in *DB* state v (according to G). Hence,

   (a) $Gt(\mathcal{U}, G)(v)$ represents our former Rtg.

During the informal sketch in Section 3.2 we already noted that the originally intended deletes need not be restricted to just one table symbol. In our next definition we will represent the originally intended deletes by means of a function Q over $\mathcal{U}$ such that $Q(v)$ assigns to each relation symbol E the set of E-tuples to be deleted initially. Therefore,

   (b) $\biguplus Q(v)$ represents our former *Delset* and

   (c) $t \in Q(v)(E)$ is equivalent to $(E; t) \in Delset$.

$Casdelint(\mathcal{U}, G, Q)$ will denote the function that assigns to each DB state v the *intended* new state. So, $Casdelint(\mathcal{U}, G, Q)(v)(E)$ has to represent our former subset Nt_E of $v(E)$. Rewriting Nt_E using (c), (b), and (a) above will lead to the following definition of $Casdelint(\mathcal{U}, G, Q)$.

Definition 8. *If $\mathcal{U}$ is a DB universe and G is a reference graph on $\mathcal{U}$ and Q is a function over $\mathcal{U}$ such that $\forall v \in \mathcal{U} : Q(v)$ is a set-valued function over $Head(\mathcal{U})$, then:*

$$Casdelint(\mathcal{U}, G, Q) = \lambda v \in U : \lambda E \in dom(v) :$$
$$\{t \in v(E) - Q(v)(E) \mid \neg \exists y \in \biguplus Q(v) : ((E; t); y) \in Tcl(Gt(\mathcal{U}, G)(v))\}.$$

We can prove that the function $Casdelint(\mathcal{U}, G, Q)$ preserves not only all attribute, tuple, and key constraints (like all deletes do), but also that the function $Casdelint(\mathcal{U}, G, Q)$ preserves all foreign key dependencies that occur in G, by which we mean that if $v' = Casdelint(\mathcal{U}, G, Q)(v)$ with $v \in \mathcal{U}$ and $(E; E'; h) \in G$, then $\pi_{dom(h)}(v'(E)) \subseteq v'(E') \infty h$ and, of course, $rng(h)$ is u.i. in $v'(E')$.

Theorem 2. *If $\mathcal{U}$ is a DB universe and G is a reference graph on $\mathcal{U}$ and Q is a function over $\mathcal{U}$ such that $\forall v \in U : Q(v)$ is a set-valued function over $Head(\mathcal{U})$, then:*

> *$Casdelint(\mathcal{U}, G, Q)$ preserves all attribute, tuple, and key constraints and all foreign key dependencies in G.*

Nevertheless, as we already noted above, the intended new state might not be allowed, e.g., due to other constraints. In that case the database should remain completely unchanged. This calls again for our adaptation operation of Section 2. Thus, with $f = Casdelint(\mathcal{U}, G, Q)$, the adaptation $Ad(\mathcal{U}, R, f)$ of f would be the actual transaction on $\mathcal{U}$ (and within a given transition relation R). We will denote this transaction by $Casdel(\mathcal{U}, R, G, Q)$:

Definition 9. *If $\mathcal{U}$ is a DB universe, $R \subseteq \mathcal{U} \times \mathcal{U}$, G is a reference graph on $\mathcal{U}$, and Q is a function over $\mathcal{U}$ such that $\forall v \in U : Q(v)$ is a set-valued function over $Head(\mathcal{U})$, then:*

$$Casdel(\mathcal{U}, R, G, Q) = Ad(\mathcal{U}, R, Casdelint(\mathcal{U}, G, Q)).$$

This completes our formalization of the result of cascading deletes. We note that the "restricted" (or non-cascading) delete operation $Del(\mathcal{U}, R, E, q)$ in [7] is a special case of the delete operation of Definition 9 above, namely if there are no cascading foreign key dependencies and, moreover, Q only mentions E-tuples: Take $G = \varnothing$, $Q(v)(E) = q(v)$, and $Q(v)(E') = \varnothing$ for each $E' \neq E$.

With Definition 9 we have a new standard form of adaptation which is much more "active" than the first one (in Definition 3). Nevertheless we could give a declarative specification of this complex transaction. This opens the way to give declarative semantics for more generally "active" databases as well.

4   Conclusions and Future Work

While specifications of queries usually are of a declarative nature, specifications of transactions mainly are of an operational and descriptive nature. Especially descriptions of complex transactions (such as cascading deletes) tend to be very operational. Declarative specifications of transactions usually suffer from the so-called frame problem or do not have a clear semantics.

Often these descriptions turn out to be nondeterministic as well. This paper offers a general framework for declarative specifications of transactions, including complex ones. We also take the influence of static and dynamic constraints on the alleged transactions into account. Applications of our theory included in this paper are the declarative specification of cascading deletes and the distinction between allowable and available transitions.

Our plans for further research in the area of declarative transaction specification include the incorporation of the declarative semantics of active databases, the design of trigger generators, and the treatment of databases as algebra's (consisting of a state space, a transition relation, a collection of transactions, a collection of queries, etc.).

Acknowledgments

The author is grateful to Herman Balsters and the referees for their comments on an earlier version of this paper, to the participants of the workshop for their stimulating discussions and remarks, and to Can Türker for the nice conversion of the paper into LaTeX.

References

1. S. Abiteboul, R. Hull, and V. Vianu. *Foundations of Databases*. Addison-Wesley, 1995.
2. A. J. Bonner and M. Kifer. The State of Change: A Survey. In B. Freitag, H. Decker, M. Kifer, and A. Voronkov, editors, *Transactions and Change in Logic Databases*, Lecture Notes in Computer Science, Vol. 1472, pages 1–36, Springer-Verlag, 1998.
3. E. F. Codd. A Relational Model of Data for Large Shared Data Banks. *Communications of the ACM*, 13(6):377–387, 1970.
4. E. F. Codd. Relational Completeness of Data Base Sublanguages. In R. Rustin, editor, *Data Base Systems*, pages 65–98, Vol. 6, Prentice Hall, 1972.
5. C. J. Date. *An Introduction to Database Systems*, Vol. 1. Addison-Wesley, 6 edition, 1995.
6. C. J. Date and H. Darwen. *A Guide to the SQL Standard*. Addison-Wesley, 4 edition, 1997.
7. E. O. de Brock. *Foundations of Semantic Databases*. Prentice Hall, 1995.
8. E. O. de Brock. A General Treatment of Dynamic Integrity Constraints. *Data & Knowledge Engineering*, 2000. *To appear*.
9. R. Elmasri and S. B. Navathe. *Fundamentals of Database Systems*. Benjamin/Cummings, 2 edition, 1994.
10. International Organization for Standardization (ISO). *Database Language SQL, Document ISO/IEC 9075:1992*, 1992.
11. Independent Database Team Holland. *A Functional Evaluation of Relational Systems Using the Functional Benchmark*. IDT/EIT, The Hague, 1990.

12. A. Koschel and P. C. Lockemann. Distributed Events in Active Database Systems: Letting the Genie out of the Bottle. *Data & Knowledge Engineering*, 25(1–2):11–28, 1998.
13. C. Liu, H. Li, and M. E. Orlowska. Supporting Update Propagation in Object-Oriented Databases. *Data & Knowledge Engineering*, 26(1):99–115, 1998.
14. G. Saake. Descriptive Specification of Database Object Behaviour. *Data & Knowledge Engineering*, 6:47–73, 1991.
15. Y. Saygin, Ö. Ulusoy, and S. Chakravarthy. Concurrent Rule Execution in Active Databases. *Information Systems*, 23(1):39–64, 1998.
16. E. Simon, J. Kiernan, and C. de Maindreville. Implementing High-Level Active Rules on Top of Relational Databases. In L.-Y. Yuan, editor, *Proc. of the 18th Int. Conf. on Very Large Data Bases, VLDB'92, Vancouver, Canada, August 23–27, 1992*, pages 315–326, Morgan Kaufmann Publishers, 1992.
17. J. M. Spivey. *The Z Notation: A Reference Manual.* Prentice Hall, 1989.
18. D. F. Stanat and D. F. McAllister. *Discrete Mathematics in Computer Science.* Prentice Hall, 1977.
19. J. Widom and S. Ceri, editors. *Active Database Systems — Triggers and Rules for Advanced Database Processing.* Morgan Kaufmann Publishers, 1996.
20. J. Widom and S. J. Finkelstein. Set-Oriented Production Rules in Relational Database Systems. In H. Garcia-Molina and H. Jagadish, editors, *Proc. of the 1990 ACM SIGMOD Int. Conf. on Management of Data, Atlantic City, NJ*, ACM SIGMOD Record, Vol. 19, No. 2, pages 259–270, ACM Press, 1990.

Appendix: Basic No(ta)tions

In this appendix we establish the basic notions and notations as we use them in this paper (see also [7]). We suppose that the reader is familiar with the notions of sets and functions (which are special sets of ordered pairs), and the fact that functions can be set-valued or even function-valued. Given a set A, we will use the notation "$\lambda x \in A$ and $c_x : u_x$" (where u_x represents some expression in x and c_x some condition for x) as an abbreviation for the function "$\{(x; u_x) \mid x \in A$ and $c_x\}$". Since functions can be function-valued, λ's can be nested. We denote the domain of a function f (i.e., the set of all actual first coordinates of f) by $dom(f)$, the range of a function f (i.e., the set of all second coordinates of f) by $rng(f)$, function composition by $g \circ f$ (g after f), functional overriding, where the function g "modifies" and/or "extends" the function f (see [17]), by $f \theta g$, the identity function on a set A by $id(A)$, and the set of all functions from a set A into a set B by $A \rightarrow B$. Thus:

$$dom(f) = \{x \mid (x; y) \in f\}$$
$$rng(f) = \{y \mid (x; y) \in f\}$$
$$g \circ f = \lambda x \in dom(f) \text{ and } f(x) \in dom(g) : g(f(x))$$
$$f \theta g = \{(x; y) \in f \mid x \notin dom(g)\} \cup g$$
$$id(A) = \lambda x \in A : x$$
$$A \rightarrow B = \{f \mid f \text{ is a function and } dom(f) = A \text{ and } rng(f) \subseteq B\}$$

Note that $g \circ f$ is a function over $\{x \in dom(f) \mid f(x) \in dom(g)\}$ and $f \theta g$ is a function over $dom(f) \cup dom(g)$.

We consider a table over a set A as a set of functions over A, i.e., functions with domain A. If A is a set, then:

T is a **table over** $A \Leftrightarrow T$ is a set and $\forall t \in T : t$ is a function over A.

An element of a table T is called a tuple and an element of A is called an attribute of T. So, tuples are considered as functions assigning values to attributes. Since every table is a (special) set, every concept defined for sets also applies to tables. Thus, for example, the notions of union and intersection of two tables make sense. Similarly, since every tuple is a (special) function, every concept defined for functions also applies to tuples. For example, $dom(t)$, the domain of a tuple t, is the set of attributes of t.

By a *database schema* (or briefly DB schema) we mean a set-valued function, assigning to each table name its set of attributes. As a frame of reference we present Date's well-known example in the database literature concerning suppliers, parts, and shipments (cf. [5]). The suppliers/parts/shipments-example has the following DB schema, which we will call g_0:

$$g_0 = \{ \ (S; \{S\#, SNAME, STATUS, CITY\}), \quad | \text{ suppliers}$$
$$(P; \{P\#, PNAME, COLOR, WEIGHT, CITY\}), \quad | \text{ parts}$$
$$(SP; \{S\#, P\#, QTY\}) \} \quad | \text{ shipments}$$

Here $S\#$ stands for supplier number, $P\#$ for part number, and QTY for quantity. Since every database schema is a function, every concept and notation defined for functions also applies to database schemas. For instance, we can speak about the domain of a database schema, which happens to be the set of table names (also called relation symbols). Note that in our example above, $dom(g_0) = \{S, P, SP\}$ and, e.g., $g_0(SP) = \{S\#, P\#, QTY\}$. We define the concept of a database state (or briefly DB state) over g for any DB schema g:

If g is a database schema, then:

v is a **DB state over** $g \Leftrightarrow v$ is a function over $dom(g)$ and
$$\forall E \in dom(g) : v(E) \text{ is a table over } g(E).$$

Since every database state is a function, every concept defined for functions also applies to database states. The set of admissible states (to be determined by the organization in question) is some set of database states over g_0. We call such a set a database universe (or briefly DB universe) over g_0. In general we define:

If g is a database schema, then:

$\mathcal{U}$ is a **DB universe over** $g \Leftrightarrow \mathcal{U}$ is a set of DB states over g.

Example 1 in Section 2 contains the specification of a DB universe called EXU. Since every DB universe is a (special) set, each concept defined for sets applies to DB universes as well. If $\mathcal{U}$ is a DB universe over g, then we call g *the DB schema of $\mathcal{U}$*, $dom(g)$ *the heading of $\mathcal{U}$*, also denoted by $Head(U)$, an element E of $dom(g)$ a *table symbol* (or "table name", or "relation symbol") *of $\mathcal{U}$*, $g(E)$ *the heading of E in $\mathcal{U}$*, and an element of $g(E)$ an *attribute* (or "attribute name") *of E in $\mathcal{U}$*.

An element of the Cartesian product $\mathcal{U} \times \mathcal{U}$ is called a *transition within* $\mathcal{U}$. Dynamic constraints can be captured by establishing the set of admissible (direct) transitions as a subset R of $\mathcal{U} \times \mathcal{U}$, having the intuitive meaning that $(v; v') \in R$ iff $(v; v')$ is an allowed consecutive state pair, i.e., iff the direct transition from state v to state v' is allowed. (See [8] for an in-depth treatment.)

If $\mathcal{U}$ is a set, then:

$$R \text{ is a } \textbf{transition relation on } \mathcal{U} \Leftrightarrow R \subseteq \mathcal{U} \times \mathcal{U}.$$

Usually, a transition relation R has to be reflexive on $\mathcal{U}$, i.e., $\forall v \in \mathcal{U}: (v; v) \in R$, in order to account for "dummy" transitions, e.g., when we try to delete some non-existing tuple. The *restriction* of a tuple t to an attribute set B is denoted by $t \lceil B$, the *projection* of a table T on B is denoted by $\pi_B(T)$, and the *renaming* of a table T by an attribute transformation h, i.e., a function that assigns to each "new" attribute the "old" attribute it replaces, is denoted by $T \infty h$:

$$t \lceil B = \{(a; w) \,|\, (a; w) \in t \text{ and } a \in B\}$$
$$\pi_B(T) = \{t \lceil B \,|\, t \in T\}$$
$$T \infty h = \{t \circ h \,|\, t \in T\}$$

We define the familiar notion of uniqueness on the "incidental" level of tables (where we will talk about *uniquely identifying*) as well as on the "structural" level of database universes (where we will talk about *keys* or *superkeys*).

If A and B are sets and T is a table over A, then:

$$B \text{ is } \textbf{uniquely identifying (or u.i.) in } T$$
$$\Leftrightarrow \forall t \in T : \forall t' \in T : \text{ if } t \lceil B = t' \lceil B \text{ then } t = t'.$$

If g is a *DB* schema, $\mathcal{U}$ is a *DB* universe over g, and $E \in dom(g)$, then:

$$B \text{ is a } \textbf{(super)key of } E \textbf{ in } \mathcal{U} \Leftrightarrow \forall v \in \mathcal{U} : B \text{ is u.i. in } v(E).$$

The following notion constitutes a generalization of the notions of *referential integrity* and of *inclusion dependency*. Let h be a function which maps a set B of "referencing" attributes of a table T onto a set B' of corresponding "referenced" attributes of a table T'. Thus, the "attribute renaming function" or "attribute transformation" h indicates which attributes in B correspond to which attributes in B'. We say that h connects T with T' iff, informally speaking, all B-values in T also occur as B'-values in T'. Formally:

If T is a table over A, T' is a table over A', and h is a function over A and $rng(h) \subseteq A'$, then:

$$h \textbf{ connects } T \textbf{ with } T' \Leftrightarrow \pi_{dom(h)}(T) \subseteq T' \infty h.$$

For the special case that h connects $v(E)$ with $v(E')$ for each *DB* state v of a *DB* universe $\mathcal{U}$, we have a so-called *inclusion dependency* on $\mathcal{U}$, sometimes written as "$E.dom(h) < E'.rng(h)$" (see [9]). In our more general definition, however, T and T' might also be *subsets* of $v(E)$ and $v(E')$; another important special case is that $T = v(E)$ and $T' = v'(E)$, i.e. considering the same table symbol at two different "points in time". Often, $h = id(B)$ for some attribute set B. The connection requirement then reduces to: $\pi_B(T) \subseteq \pi_B(T')$.

In our examples, we will use $\mathbb{N}$ to denote the set of all natural numbers (including 0). If S is a set of sets then $\bigcup S$ denotes the *generalized union* of S:

$$\bigcup S = \{x \mid \exists A \in S : x \in A\}.$$

For each set-valued function F, $\prod(F)$ denotes the *generalized product* of F and $\biguplus F$ denotes the *generalized disjoint union* of F. Formally:

$$\prod(F) = \{f \mid f \text{ is a function over } dom(F) \text{ and } \forall x \in dom(f) : f(x) \in F(x)\};$$

$$\biguplus F = \{(x; y) \mid x \in dom(F) \text{ and } y \in F(x)\}.$$

Open Nested Transactions: A Support for Increasing Performance and Multi-tier Applications

Malik Saheb, Ramzi Karoui, and Simone Sedillot

Institut National recherche en Informatique et en Automatique
Domaine de Voluceau B.P. 150
F-78158 Le Chesnay Cedex, France
{Malik.Saheb, Ramzi.Karoui, Simone.Sedillot}@infia.fr

Abstract. The two-phase commit protocol is combined with the strict two-phase locking protocol as means for ensuring atomicity and serializability of transactions. The implication of this combination on the length of time a transaction may holding locks on various data items might be severe. There are certain classes of applications where it is known that resources acquired within a transaction can be "released early", rather than having to wait until the transaction terminates. Furthermore, there are applications involving heterogeneous competing business organizations, which do not allow to block their resources; therefore, the preservation of local autonomy of individual systems is crucial. This paper describes an extension of the OMG's Object Transaction Service, by adding the "open nested transaction model", which greatly improves transaction parallelism by releasing the nested transaction locks at the nested transaction commit time. Open nested transactions relax the isolation property by allowing the effects of the committed nested transaction to be visible to concurrent transactions. We also describe how we take benefit of this model using the proposed Asynchronous Nested Transaction model to overcome the limits of the current messaging products and standard specifications when they are confronted with the problem of guaranteeing the atomicity of distributed multi-tier transactional applications.

1 Introduction

The concept of a transaction has been developed to permit management of activities and resources in a reliable computing environment. Indeed, transactions are useful to guarantee consistency of applications even in case of failure and in the case of conflicting concurrent applications. The traditional flat transaction model, proposed by the OMG (Object Management Group) Object Transaction Service (OTS) [20], although suitable for applications using short transactions, may not provide enough flexibility and performance when used for more complex applications, such as CAD applications, connection establishment in telecommunication, or business travel including several servers on different sites and need access to many resources involved within a relatively long-lived transaction. Typically, the two-phase commit (2PC) protocol [7] is combined with the strict

G. Saake, K. Schwarz, and C. Türker (Eds.): TDD '99, LNCS 1773, pp. 167–192, 2000.

two-phase locking protocol [3] to guarantee atomicity and serializability of transactions. The implication of this combination on the length of time a transaction may holding locks on various data items might be severe. At each site, and for each transaction, locks must be held until either a commit or an abort message is received from the coordinator of the 2PC protocol. Since the 2PC protocol is a blocking protocol, the length of time these locks are held can be unbounded. There are certain classes of applications where it is known that resources acquired within a transaction can be "released early", rather than having to wait until the transaction terminates. These applications share a common feature that application-level consistency is maintained, despite any non-ACID behavior they may exhibit. For some applications, failures do not result in application-level inconsistency, and no form of compensation is required. However, for other applications, some form of compensation may be required to restore the system to a consistent state from which it can then continue to operate.

Moreover, the impact of indefinite blocking and long-duration delays is exacerbated in distributed systems where heterogeneous domains or database systems are integrated to enable the processing of multi-site or global transactions. The integrated systems may belong to distinct and possibly competing business organizations (e.g. competing computerized reservation agencies). Therefore, the preservation of local autonomy of individual systems is crucial. It is undesirable, for example, to use a protocol where a site belonging to a competing organization can harmfully block the local resources; a phenomenon that can occur under the 2PC protocol. Although such applications can perhaps be implemented using traditional transaction systems, currently application programmers are required to build application specific mechanisms to do this (such as create mechanisms for saving application state, create ad hoc locking mechanisms, create mechanisms for compensating transactions and so forth). CORBA functionality for supporting flexible ways of composing an application using transactions, with the support for enabling the application to possess some or all ACID properties, will greatly reduce the burden on application builders.

In this paper we describe an extension to the OTS by adding the open nested transaction model, a generalization of Sagas [5], which introduces a two-level hierarchy between saga and its child transactions, and multilevel transactions [24], which impose a strict layered hierarchy of subtransactions capable of preserving serializability.

The open nested transaction (ONT) model greatly improves transaction parallelism by releasing the nested transaction locks at the nested transaction commit time. That is, open nested transactions relax the isolation property by allowing the effects of the committed nested transaction to be visible to concurrent transactions, thus waiving the locks transfer rule of closed nested transactions (CNT). To design this model, all functionalities provided by the current OTS specification are fully used in the sense that the commitment protocol and the nested structuring exist.

The remainder of this paper is organized as follows. Section 2 gives an overview of related works. Section 3 presents our transaction model built on the concept of open and closed nested transactions. Section 4 describes the experimentation of our transaction model in a conformant OTS implementation named MAAO OTS, developed by INRIA. The extension we propose to the interfaces provided by OTS are based on the prototype named eXtended OTS (XTS), which has been prototyped in the scope of the ReTINA project [6]. Section 5 describes how we can guarantee the atomicity of a distributed work unit by integrating the queueing transaction model with the open nested transaction model. Finally, Section 6 concludes the paper.

2   Related Work

Several enhancements to the traditional flat-transaction model have been proposed by relaxing the conventional ACID properties. In the literature, the proposed solutions are described as advanced transaction models [8,18]. Each of these models is well suited for a special class of applications, but none of them seems to be suitable and applicable for all kind of complex and long-lived applications.

By allowing nesting of transactions [17], OTS supports a finer control over recovery and concurrency. In particular, nested transactions (subtransactions) could be executed concurrently. The outermost transaction of such a hierarchy is typically referred to as the top-level transaction. Unlike top-level transactions, the commit of a subtransaction is provisional upon the commit/rollback of the enclosing transaction. Hence, the failure of a subtransaction does not necessarily leads to the failure of its enclosing transaction. *Resource* objects acquired within a subtransaction are inherited (retained) by parent transactions upon the commit of the subtransaction, and (assuming no failures) only released when the top-level transaction completes, i.e., they are retained for the duration of the top-level transaction. Thus, although subtransactions provide increased flexibility in the construction of transactional applications, they do so within the context of the ACID properties of transactions. We refer as a "closed nested transaction model".

Some database vendors provide various kinds of isolation levels (Read Uncommitted, Read Committed, Repeatable Read, Serializable). The concept of isolation level has been specified by the ANSI/SQL-92 [2] and re-used by the JDBC [11] and the Imprise Submission [10] in response to the OMG Persistence Service Request For Proposal. Lower isolation levels increase transaction concurrency at the risk of allowing transactions to observe an incorrect state of data. Although offering better performance at the cost of relaxed isolation, this flexibility does not guarantee atomicity within distributed transaction requiring a higher isolation level.

Another approach to handling long-running activities is to have each step run as a transaction. Thus, an activity consists of multiple transactions. To deal with failures or exceptions across the steps of an activity, several models have been proposed [23,11]. These models support declarative specification of the control flow and an automatic compensation capability that offers some level of failure atomicity for the activity. These models are based on the conventional flat transaction model in which transactions are strictly sequential.

The concept of compensation has also been used in several transactional workflow systems which can be used to provide scripting facilities for expressing the composition of an activity (a business process) out of other activities (which could be transactional), with specific compensation activities [18]. The workflow specification adopted by the OMG [19], based on the Workflow Management Coalition [25], specifies interaction between activities belonging to a same business process or interaction between business processes, and logging (auditLog) of each activity or process execution which can usually be used for compensation, though the specification does not describe how the compensation is triggered. Transactional activities are in fact independent of flat transactions. Their corresponding transactions coordinators are independents from the enclosing coordinator of the enclosing process or activity; that is a final issue of an activity is known by query its corresponding auditLog and a transaction abort of an enclosing activity cannot be propagated to its sub-activities since they are executed in separate transactions. Hence, it seems left to the application to be aware of the transaction outcome (rollback outcome) and decide to eventually propagate the rollback to other activities and compensate those already committed [1].

Although the workflow management systems could be a more appropriate framework to address advanced applications [1] by a set of dependencies between activities, they lead to an overhead of messages in order to keep a workflow context across several participants. In turn this overhead generates a delay which can be detrimental for some applications looking for performance.

Another possibility to deal with competing organizations and long-running transactions is the use of asynchronous communication. Asynchrony exalts time independent processing [16], which in turn favors the parallelism. One way to support asynchrony between applications is to use message queuing systems. The solutions adopted by the major message queuing products vendors rely on the use of the queuing transaction model (also called off-line transaction model [8]). In this model, the message producer sends its message to one transaction; the message queuing mechanism delivers the message in an other transaction only if the first one commits.

IBM MQSeries [9] and BEA Tuxedo/Q [22] are product leaders in the field of messaging. More recently, OMG has adopted a new specification, called CORBA messaging [4]. This specification aims at an asynchronous operation invocation, using message passing. The OMG approach is to place the required changes at the Object Request Broker level, which implies a revision and changes to several parts of its architecture, mainly to the GIOP protocol.

The current products as well as the ongoing CORBA messaging specification do not address the issue of the atomicity of a work expected by a client in its initial transaction involving several servers. Indeed, if a client invokes several different remote servers using message queueing mechanism, each server will execute the message request in a separate transaction. Hence, each server transaction may have an independent outcome and the initial atomicity the client asked for may be lost.

3   Nested Transaction Models

Our transaction model is based on the concept of nested transactions as introduced by Moss [17,14,15]. In this model a transaction may contain any number of nested transactions which may recursively contain other nested transactions giving rise to a tree of nested transactions or transaction family. In addition, we distinguish two nested models: closed nested and open nested transactions.

Closed Nested Features

Closed nested transactions exhibit at least two important advantages over flat transactions. First, they allow the potential internal consistent parallelism to be exploited. Second, they provide finer control over failures by limiting the effects of failures to a small part of the global transaction. These properties are achieved by allowing nested transactions within a given transaction to fail independently of their invoking transaction.

Changes made by a closed nested transaction, when it is "committed", remain contingent upon commitment of all of its ancestors. But, since a committed closed nested transaction may be rolled back later, the nested transaction model achieves serializability by requiring nested transactions to transfer all their acquired resources (e.g., locks) during their execution to their parent when they commit.

The closed nested transaction commit is not a two-phase commit protocol (2PC) but only relevant notifications (e.g., end of work related to the nested transaction and synchronization) are sent to the participants to allow the nested transaction's parent to acquire their locks. We call this protocol as the "finish protocol".

Open Nested Features

The open nested transaction model is different from the closed nested transaction model in the following aspects: The open nested transaction model relaxes isolation by allowing the effects of a committed subtransaction to be visible to other concurrent transactions and thus avoiding the transfer of locks to the parent as done in the closed nested model. On the other hand, a closed nested transaction extends the sphere of control of its parent so that its effects are still isolated against concurrent transactions.

Since the locks acquired during the execution of an open nested transaction are released at commit, the dependency induced by a parent transaction on its open nested transaction cannot rely on traditional rollback as done for closed nested transaction. When an ancestor rolls back, undo of a committed open nested transaction has to be performed by a compensating activity. We note that not all transactions are compensable. Transactions involving some real actions such as firing a missile or dispensing cash, may not be compensable. A formal approach to recovery by compensating transactions can be found in [13].

3.1   Transaction Tree

Each transaction or nested transaction may involve one or several transaction node. A transaction node can be either a root or a subordinate node. Moreover, a transaction node or simply a node may also be a child or a parent node depending on the parent transaction relationship as illustrated in Fig. 1.

3.2   Transaction and Nested Transactions States

At a given time, each node is characterized by a state as illustrated in Fig. 2, which describes significant transaction and subtransaction state transitions. The different paths correspond to the executions of different types of actions.

When a transaction or a subtransaction is started, its node is created in the ACTIVE state. A subordinate node changes from the ACTIVE state into the PREPARED state once it has received the two-phase commit first request, or the prepare request. Then from the PREPARED state it moves either into COMMITTING or ROLLBACKING state depending on the second two-phase commit request, which is either a commit request or a rollback request.

A root node never goes in the PREPARED state. Once it has received a ready reply from all its subordinates, it decides to propagate commit to all its subordinates and then moves into the COMMITTING state. When completely committed a top-level node participant move from the COMMITING state

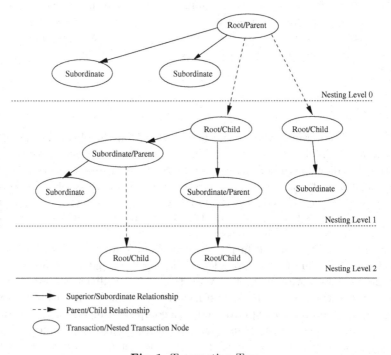

Fig. 1. Transaction Tree

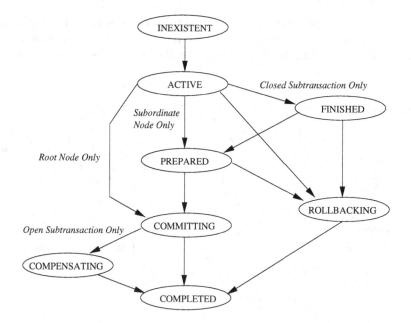

Fig. 2. Transaction and Subtransaction States

the INEXISTENT state. After the rollback, any node moves from the ROLLB-ACKING state into the INEXISTENT state.

In the same way, as for a top-level transaction a root node of nested transaction may move from the ACTIVE state into the COMMITTING State. However if a compensating action has been specified for its nested transaction, this node move, when completed, from the COMMITTING state into the COMPENSA-TING state in order to receive its ancestors outcome. That is any rollback will notify this node that the compensating action needs to be triggered.

When terminated with the closed nested semantic, a node moves from the ACTIVE state into the FINISHED state. Then it becomes a subordinate of its parent's transaction, it can either remain in the FINISHED state, if its parent transaction is a nested transaction terminated with the closed semantic, or it moves into the PREPARED state, if its parent is the top-level transaction or a nested transaction terminated with open nested semantics.

4 Experimenting the ONT Model in a OMG Conformant Implementation

4.1 MaaoOTS Implementation of OTS

The "Moniteur d'Actions Atomiques Ouvertes" (MAAO) OTS developed by INRIA [12] is an implementation of the Object Transaction Service (OTS) as defined by the Object Management Group (OMG) [20].

MAAO OTS supports three distributed transaction models: the flat transaction model, the optional nested model we referred as the closed nested model and the open nested transaction model described in the previous section.

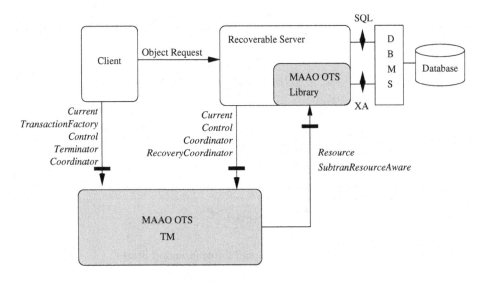

Fig. 3. MAAO OTS Architecture

Globally, MAAO OTS illustrated in Fig. 3 consists of two major parts:

- MAAO OTS Transaction Manager (TM), is a transaction manager which provides OTS interfaces and manages transactions.
- MAAO OTS Library, is a library linked within applications. It provides OTS *Resource* interface to enable application to access legacy database and to enable hidden legacy database to participate in the transaction managed by the MAAO OTS TM.

MAAO OTS provides transaction management services and a transaction propagation protocol by a set of well-defined interfaces. These interfaces, described in the OTS specification, are briefly described below:

- *Current* defines operations that allow a client of the Transaction Service to explicitly manage the association between threads and transactions. The *Current* interface also defines operations that simplify the use of the Transaction Service for most applications. These operations can be used to *begin* and *commit/rollback* transactions or nested transactions and to obtain information about the current transaction.
- *TransactionFactory* is provided to allow the transaction originator to begin a transaction. This interface defines two operations, *create* and *recreate*, which create a new representation of a top-level transaction.

- *Control* allows a program to explicitly manage or propagate a transaction context. An object supporting the *Control* interface is implicitly associated with one specific transaction and provides two operations, *get_terminator* and *get_coordinator*, which respectively a *Terminator* object and a *Coordinator* object.
- *Terminator* supports operations to *terminate* commit and rollback to complete a transaction.
- *Coordinator* provides operations that are used by participants in a transaction to query the transaction about its status and relationship with other transactions, e.g., *get_status*, *is_same_transaction*, *is_related_transaction*, or *is_top_level_transaction*. The register_resource operation allows a recoverable object to register a resource as a participant in the transaction. If the transaction is a nested, the resource is implicitly registered with the top-level transaction. When the top-level commits, the *Resource* objects will participate in the two-phase commit protocol to commit or rollback the updates performed as part of the transaction family. The *register_subtran_aware* operation registers a resource with a subtransaction such that it will be notified when the subtransaction commits or rolls back. The *create_subtransaction* operation creates a child transaction of the current transaction and returns a *Control* object of the new subtransaction. The *Coordinator* object is a key component to expend a transaction and control the transaction completion between distributed participants.
- *RecoveryCoordinator* provides the *replay_completion* operation invoked by a recoverable object to determine the state of the transaction after the associated resource has been prepared. A reference to the *RecoveryCoordinator* object is returned by the *register_resource* operation to recover from failure.
- *Resource* defines operations invoked by the OTS to participate in the two-phase commit protocol. The operations supported by the *Resource* interface are very similar to the ones defined by the X/Open XA interface, namely *prepare*, *rollback*, *commit*, *commit_one_phase*, and *forget*.
- *SubtransactionResourceAware* is a specialization of the *Resource* interface that supports subtransactions. This interface provides two operations, *commit_subtransaction* and *rollback_subtransaction*, invoked by the OTS to notify a *Resource* object about the completion of a subtransaction.
- *TransactionalObject* is a special interface to indicate the transaction quality of service. By supporting this interface an object implicitly requires that the transactional context associated with the current thread be propagated on remote invocations.

The CORBA architecture provides access transparency and location transparency. The interactions between the Transaction Service and application objects are all performed through the ORB. This feature implies that the type of transaction (local or distributed) is transparent to the Transaction Service. All transactions are processed in the same way.

4.2   Interposition

The OTS specification defines a technique, named interposition, which allows multiple Transaction Services to cooperate in order to support a global transaction. When a transaction is spanned onto a new OTS domain, the transaction context is exported and used by the importing Transaction Service implementation to create a new instance of a Transaction Service object.

In the case of interposition, since the interposed Transaction Service registers with the superior as a *Resource* object, the interposition is invisible to the superior Transaction Service. The superior Transaction Service propagates the transaction semantics to its subordinate without being aware of whether it is a real *Resource* or a subordinate Transaction Service.

4.3   Open Nested Transactions Extension: The User's View

MAAO OTS extends the OTS by allowing any combination of open and closed nested transactions. Open nested transactions behave like closed nested transactions while they are active: the behavior of the two models only differ in the commit semantics. MAAO OTS allows the programmer to procrastinate the decision of the nesting semantics until the commit decision. Then, to differentiate the open semantic from the closed semantics, MAAO OTS provides a new operation, named *definite_commit*, which has been added to both interfaces *Current* and *Terminator*.

The *definite_commit* operation informs the Transaction Service to definitely commit a nested transaction thereby implying the open semantics for that nested transaction. In contrast to the *commit* operation, *definite_commit* forces a definitive commit by triggering the two-phase commit protocol for the nested transaction so that its effects are made permanent and visible to others transactions. All locks acquired by the nested transaction and by its possible closed nested descendants transactions are released.

The IDL definition part dealing with the open nested management is described below.

```
module CosTransactions {
  ...
  interface Terminator {
    void commit(in boolean report_heuristics)
        raises(HeuristicMixed, HeuristicHazard);
    void rollback();
    void definite_commit(in boolean report_heuristics,
                      in Compensator c, in any data)
        raises(NoTransaction, HeuristicMixed, HeuristicHazard);
  };
  interface Current : CORBA::Current {
    void begin()
        raises(SubtransactionsUnavailable);
    void commit(in boolean report_heuristics)
        raises(NoTransaction, HeuristicMixed, HeuristicHazard);
```

```
    void definite_commit(in boolean report_heuristics,
                         in Compensator c, in any data)
        raises(NoTransaction, HeuristicMixed, HeuristicHazard);
    void rollback();
    ...
}
...
interface Compensator {
    void compensate(in any data);
};
};
```

Compensation activities are typically for specific applications (and specific operations). If compensation activities are required, it may be more efficient to exploit application-level semantics and allow the application programmer to initiate compensation behavior, rather than rely upon it being system-driven. However, the trigger of a compensation should be done automatically by the Transaction Service. This means that a generic operation should be well known by the Transaction Service which it can use.

A new interface, named *Compensator*, offers the *compensate* operation which is invoked by a Transaction Service to compensate a committed open nested transaction. If the behavior of the compensate operation is application-dependent, then its corresponding method is implemented by the application itself.

In order to inform the Transaction Service of a nested transaction about the existence of a *Compensator* object, this one is given as parameter in the *definite_commit* operation. If a nil *Compensator* object is passed in the *definite_commit* operation, then the nested transaction is invoked to commit with open semantic, but no compensation is required if an ancestor transaction aborts.

The data parameter wrapped in the *CORBA::Any* format is application-dependent. That is, an application can "cast" its own data to this generic format. It is passed to the Transaction Service using the *definite_commit* operation, where it is used to invoke the *Compensator* object, which "recast" it to its original format. In fact, the Transaction Service is not aware of the real nature of this data.

The data parameter can be nil meaning that the compensation action does not need any data. The *Compensator* object in the operation can be nil meaning that a compensating action is not needed if an ancestor aborts.

The following example illustrates how a nested transaction can be terminated with open semantics using the *Current* object:

```
current->begin();      // begin a top level transaction 1
obj->op1();            // the op1 is called within the transaction 1
current->begin();      // begin a nested transaction 1.1 whose
                       // parent is the transaction 1
obj->op2();            // the op2 is called within the nested
                       // transaction 1.1
current->definite_commit(cp, param_cp); // commit transaction 1.1
current->commit();     // commit the top level transaction 1
```

4.4 Implementation Issues

When invoked to initiate a transaction with the create operation, the *TransactionFactory* object creates a Transaction Service node (TS) dedicated for the top-level transaction. This node offers the interfaces *Control*, *Coordinator*, and *Terminator* to the programmer in order to manage the top-level transaction. When a Transaction Service node is invoked through its *Coordinator* interface to create a nested transaction, a new Transaction Service node (nesTS) is created, which in turn provides the same interfaces to the programmer as its parent creator to manage the created nested transactions. Fig. 4 illustrates the creation of a Transaction Service node.

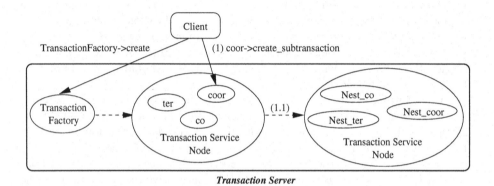

Fig. 4. Transaction Service Node Creation

During a (sub)transaction's lifetime, *Resource* objects may be registered to the Transaction Service associated with this (sub). Fig. 5 describes the transaction tree involving Transaction Service nodes and their associated *Resource* objects. In the remainder, we will simplify the Transaction Service node to the *Coordinator*. The transaction specification requires that certain protocols are used to implement the atomicity property. These protocols affect the implementation of recoverable servers (recoverable objects that register for participation in the two-phase commit process) and of the coordinators that are created by a transaction factory. These responsibilities ensure the execution of the two-phase commit protocol and include maintaining state information in stable storage, so that transactions can be completed in case of failures.

The first coordinator, referred as the root coordinator and created for a top-level transaction, is responsible for executing the two-phase commit protocol for the top-level transaction. Any coordinator that is subsequently created for an existing transaction becomes either a nested coordinator if it is created as the result of the operation *create_subtransaction* on the parent coordinator (as described in Fig. 4), or an interposed or subordinate coordinator if it is created as the result of the *recreate* operation on a *TransactionFactory* object (2)

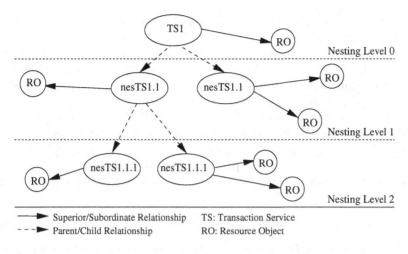

Fig. 5. Transaction Service and *Resource* Objects in a Transaction Tree

(as described in Fig. 6). By registering either a *Resource* object or a *SubtransactionResourceAware* object (3), the interposed coordinator becomes a transaction/subtransaction participant. In the interposed domain the recoverable server can create a nested transaction by invoking the *create_subtransaction* operation on interposed coordinator (4).

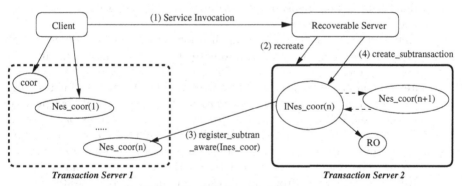

Fig. 6. Nested Transaction and Interposition

Top-Level Root Coordinator Role. As described in [20], the root coordinator initiates the two-phase commit protocol when the client asks to commit the transaction (with *commit* operation invoked either on the with *Current* interface

or the *Terminator* interface). The root coordinator issues the *prepare* request to
all registered resources.

Once at least one registered *Resource* object has replied *VoteCommit* and
all others have replied *VoteCommit* or *VoteReadOnly*, a root coordinator may
decide to commit the transaction by sending a commit request to each registered
Resource object that responded *VoteCommit*.

If any registered *Resource* object replies *VoteRollback* or cannot be reached,
then, the coordinator will decide to rollback and thus inform the registered resources that already replied *VoteCommit*. Once a *VoteRollback* reply is received,
a coordinator need not send a prepare request to the remaining *Resource* objects.
Rollback will be subsequently sent to *Resource* objects that replied *VoteCommit*.

Nested Coordinator Role. A nested transaction can be completed with:

- *Rollback*: The application issues rollback on *Current* or *Terminator*, which
  allows the invocation of the *rollback_subtransaction* operation on each registered *SubtransactionResourceAware* object.
- *Commit with closed semantic*: The application issues a *commit* on *Current* or
  Terminator. The nested coordinator must notify any registered subtransaction aware resources of the subtransaction's commit using the operation *com-
  mit_subtransaction* of the *SubtransactionAwareResource* interface. When the
  subtransaction is committed and after all registered subtransactions aware
  resources have been notified about the commitment, the subtransaction registers any resources registered using *register_resource* with its parent coordinator or it may register a subordinate coordinator to relay any future
  requests to the resources.
- *Commit with open semantic*: The application issues *definite_commit* on *Current* or *Terminator*. As a root coordinator the nested coordinator uses the
  two-phase commit protocol to terminate the subtransaction by issuing prepare and commit messages to all resources or subordinate coordinators registered with it as if it was a top-level transaction. If the commitment protocol
  completes successfully and the *Compensator* object passed as parameter to
  the *definite_commit* operation is not null (meaning that a compensating action is previewed for this open nested transaction), the nested coordinator
  becomes a participant of its parent transaction in such way that it can receive a rollback coming from any ancestor and invokes compensate effects of
  its committed open nested transaction as illustrated in Fig. 7.

In the case of multi-level open nested transactions, the path between the different nested coordinators should be preserved since each of these coordinators is
responsible for saving the object reference of the *Compensator* object needed to
be invoked if an ancestor rolls back. Note that the natural behavior after the
two-phase commit protocol completes is to delete first all branches to subordinates, then all paths to reach them. In order to maintain a branch to reach
a coordinator having to compensate, a particular notification is needed by any
superior in a transaction tree. For this aim, a new vote named *VoteReadyOpen*

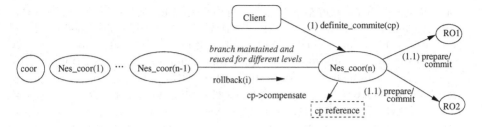

Fig. 7. Open Nested Termination and Compensation Management

has been added in reply to the prepare request used in the commitment of an open nested transaction, to indicate to the superior coordinator that the branch from which this vote has been received need to be kept and to participate to the completion of the parent transaction. Fig. 8 shows how the nested coordinator of the level n can be maintained level by level until the top-level transaction. Note that the vote *VoteReadyOpen* is only used during the two-phase commitment of a nested transaction and never for the top-level commitment. Indeed, there is no sense to ask maintaining a branch beyond the commitment of the top-level.

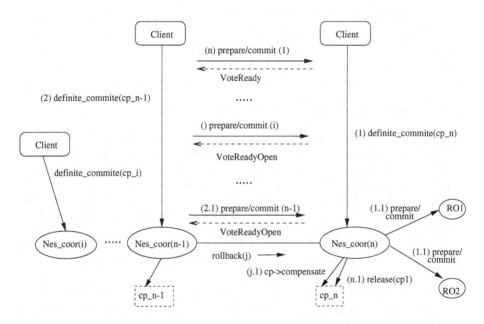

Fig. 8. Open Nested Termination - Compensator Awareness

Interposed Coordinator Role. To keep track of any nested transaction committed with open semantic in the case of interposition, the interposed coordinator will use the vote *VoteReadyOpen*, as illustrated in Fig. 9, to indicate to the superior domain that the path to the interposed need to be maintained until the top-level to trigger an eventual compensation if needed. In fact, *VoteReadyOpen* can be used by any subordinate coordinator within a same transaction level to indicate that a branch need to be maintained, either because this subordinate coordinator manages a *Compensator* object or it propagates this vote coming from its transaction sub-tree.

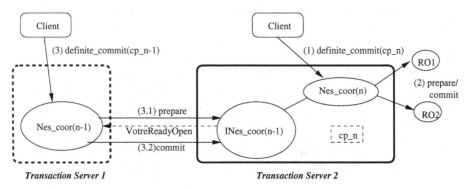

Note: INes_coor(n-1) will partcipate to the completion of (n-2)

Fig. 9. Open Nested Termination and Interposition

4.5   Open Nested Transaction and Recovery

Failures and Logs. The Transaction Service provides atomic outcomes for transactions in the presence of transaction failure, or system/communication failure1. The technique for implementing transactions in presence of failures relies on two-phase commit presumed abort protocol and on the use of logs. The coordinator and participant must log certain changes in their state, so if either of them fails and subsequently recovers, it can tell what it was at the time of failure and take appropriate action. In particular any subordinate should log the prepare decision before acknowledging the prepare request from its superior, and any coordinator must log the commit decision when it gets all acknowledgements (*VoteCommit*) for its prepare requests.

The presumed abort assumption permits efficient implementations to be realized since the root coordinator does not need to log anything before the commit decision and the participants (i.e., resource objects and interposed coordinators) do not need to log anything before they prepare. That is any failure occurring during an ACTIVE state will cause a rollback:

1. A transaction failure occurs when a transaction aborts. The strategy for recovering when a transaction aborts will restore all previous values of all data that the transaction wrote. Within this strategy, known as abort recovery,

- every active nested transaction is aborted and rolled back,
- every committed closed nested transaction is rolled back, and,
- every committed open nested transaction is compensated by invoking the *compensate* operation on the *Compensator* object.

2. Concerning the system or communication failures, two types of failure are relevant: a failure affecting the object itself due to the server crash (local failure) and a failure external to the object (external failure), such as failure of another object or failure in the communication with that object.

An external failure is detected and provided to a calling object when the ORB raises the standard exception COMM_FAILURE. The calling object cannot make the difference if the exception is due to a communication failure or if the invoked object crashed.

MAAO OTS Recovery Procedures. To ensure atomicity and durability in the presence of failure, MAAO OTS provides additional protocols, based on those described by the OTS specification, to ensure that transactions, once begun, always complete. The approach is to continue the completion protocols at the point where the failure occurred, which is referred as recovery.

When restarted each participant adopts a specific behavior according to its position in the transaction tree.

- A *Coordinator* in the COMMITTING state has the responsibility for sending the commit decision to its registered subordinates. If any registered resources exist but cannot be reached, then the *Coordinator* must try again to send the commit decision.
- A *Resource* object in the PREPARED state has the responsibility for finding out its coordinator decision to either commit or rollback, by invoking the *RecoveryCoordinator* with the *replay_completion* operation to get the status of its associated transaction. If the superior coordinator exists but cannot be reached (COMM_FAILURE exception returned), then the subordinate must retry recovery later. If the superior coordinator no longer exists (OBJECT_NOT_EXIST exception returned), then the outcome of the transaction can be presumed to be rollback.
- A *Coordinator* in the COMPENSATING state is responsible for determining the transaction outcome of its parent coordinator. If the parent coordinator no longer exists, the outcome of the parent transaction can be presumed to be rollback, then the compensation action of the committed open nested transaction is triggered.

The compensation action may fail. If the OBJECT_NOT_EXIST exception is returned when the compensate operation is invoked on the *Compensator* object, which means that is does not longer exist, the standard *HeuristicMixed* exception is returned since a sub-tree has committed while an other has rolled back. If the COMM_FAILURE exception returned, the *compensate* operation need to be re-invoked.

In order to avoid the waiting for the completion of the compensation action, an asynchronous invocation of the *compensate* operation could be applied via an message queueing mechanism.

5   The Asynchronous Nested Transactions Model

5.1   Discussion

The current messaging products and specifications reach their limits when they are confronted with the problem of guaranteeing the atomicity of distributed multi-tier transactional applications. To illustrate this problem, let us consider a simple credit/debit application. Assume that a client application would like to make a call to credit an account and debit another on two different banks, using the messaging paradigm. It is usually recommended to execute this work in an atomic manner. However, using the current products or future CORBA messaging products can lead to the following:

A client starts a transaction, makes two asynchronous calls, *credit* and *debit*, then commits the transaction. The messaging system will start two different transactions, one to debit the count and the other to credit another count. If one of them definitely rolls back, the messaging system cannot undo the committed transaction.

Because the client (or the *Reply-Handler*) is "rollback aware", it will be receive a TRANSACTION_ROLLBACK message. The client (or reply-handler) is obliged to take the appropriate compensation action. But it is not always able to do this, particularly if the multi-tier servers' topology is complex. Even if one of them can easily re-establish the atomicity by executing the right compensation action, it is intolerable to bother them with such things.

The problem of atomicity in the building of multi-tier transactional application comes from the fact that when the client wants to send several requests involving several remote servers in a single Unit of Work, the messaging systems execute each request in a separate transaction. Further, the messaging systems are not able to coordinate globally the outcome of these separate transactions.

The independent outcome property destroys the atomicity property. Thus, a high-level transaction control is needed that

1. preserves the asynchronous communication style,
2. respects the queueing transactional principles, and
3. minimizes the clients concerns about compensation actions.

To guarantee these requirements, we propose a new transaction model, called the Asynchronous Nested Transaction model. Before describing this model, we first define a set of transaction queueing principles based on characteristics of the existing products and the coming standards.

The Transaction Queueing Principles. A queueing system (Fig. 10) is interposed between clients and servers. Each server and each client owns an input queue in the queueing system.

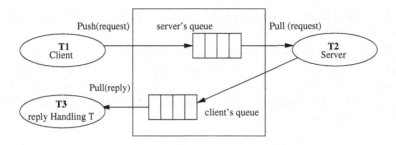

Fig. 10. Transaction Queueing Principles

- Within the scope of a first transaction T1, a client pushes a message (request) to the server queue. The message becomes available, if and only if T1 commits.
- In a second transaction T2, the server pulls its queue and gets a message or it waits the queueing system to push the message to it.
  In the both cases, the server processes the message and enters a reply message in the client-input queue. When T2 commits, the message is removed from the server's queue.
- In a third transaction T3, the client takes the reply message by it own or it can delegate a *Reply-Handler* which picks up the message reply and process it. The *Reply-Handler* can be co-allocated with the client application or it can be in a separate process.

If T2 rolls back, the message is scheduled for a next trial according to a retrying policy. It is possible that after a retry condition is reached the message is moved to an error queue and deleted from the server's pending messages. The originating client or the *Reply-Handler* receives a TRANSANCTION_ROLLBACK message reporting the problem.

With regard to each transaction, the queueing system handles the messages as if it was a database and coordinates the queue manager with the transaction outcome commit/rollback. Such a queueing system is called recoverable queueing system (RQS).

Asynchronous Nested Transaction Model. We define an asynchronous nested transaction (ANT) as follows:

1. An ANT is a tree of transactions. The root transaction is the top-level transaction, the other transactions are open nested transactions.
2. The top-level transaction contains:
   - $QT1$, the request message producing subtransaction
   - $QT2$, the message processing subtransaction, and
   - $QT3$, the reply message subtransaction.
3. The three subtransactions $QT1$, $QT2$, and $QT3$ obey the precedence rule:

$$QT1 > QT2 \text{ and } QT2 > QT3.$$

4. Messages exchanged during the ANT's active phase are hold in a recoverable queueing system.

5. The subtransactions completion are a two-phase commit.

6. Once a subtransaction has committed and if either a top-level or an ancestor in the tree rolls back, a compensating operation is assumed to undo, if necessary, the committed subtransaction effects, due to its lock release at completion time.

The ANT model relies on two main ideas:

- It assumes the existence of a recoverable queueing system that assures the creation of the asynchrony between two consecutive levels.
- The commit and rollback rules of the ANT model are equal to that of the ONT model. This implies that the commit of an asynchronous nested transaction actually is two-phase commit. As in the ONT model, the rollback of a committed subtransaction is performed by a compensation transaction, which semantically reverses the effects of the whole ANT sub-tree.

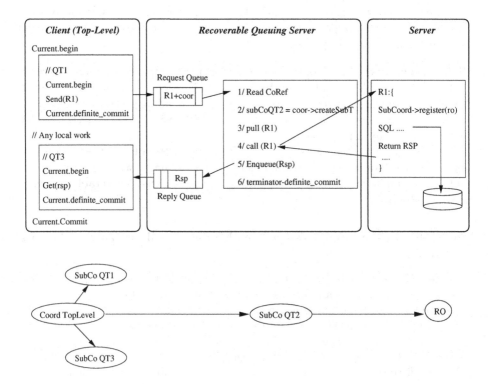

Fig. 11. The Application View and The Tree Expansion and *Control*

Fig. 11 gives an engineering view of the ANT model implementation. Our first example shows the case where a client asynchronously sends a unique request to the server.

The client begins by starting a top-level transaction in which it creates a subtransaction $QT1$ in order to send a request to the server. As a result a co-ordinator $CoordTopL$ and a subcoordinator $SubcoQT1$ objects are created to control the top-level transaction and the subtransaction $QT1$. The coordinator reference as well as the subcoordinator reference are propagated with message request. These references are stored in the RQS's request queue when the $QT1$ commits. The RQS dequeues the coordinator object reference and asks the coordinator to create a subtransaction $QT2$. The subtransaction $QT2$ is then tied to the top level transaction and managed by the subcoordinator object $SubCoQT2$, which may be either located near the top-level coordinator $CoordTopL$ in the same client's OTS service or located in an interposed OTS domain.

After creating $QT2$, RQS dequeues the request and calls the server. The server first registers a resource object, then performs the requested work on behalf of $QT2$. Finally it returns the response and the control to the RQS. The RQS stores the response in a reply queue and commits.

During the propagation and the execution of the request the client can take advantage of the asynchrony to perform other work. When it decides to retrieve the reply, it first starts a subtransaction $QT3$, pulls the RQS's reply queue. and commits $QT3$. Depending on the reply content, the client may commit or abort the top-level transaction.

The model can support a two-tier application if a server in the first tier calls an other server (Server2 in Fig. 12). In this case Server1 in the first tier behaves as a client. It starts the request message producing subtransaction $QT12$ to send the request (Req2), performs any other work, and later gets back the response in the reply message of subtransaction $QT32$. $QT12$ and $QT32$ are enclosed by the subtransaction $QT2^1$ which is started by the RQS1. The RQS2 in the second tier executes the message processing subtransaction $QT2^2$.

The examples given below can be generalized to cover the case where a client wish to send N request toward N different servers which can in their turn calls other servers. The top-Level transaction may contain:

- One $QT1$ subtransaction producing N request messages,
- N message processing subtransactions noted $QT2_i^1$, $i \in [1, N]$, (which should be read $QT2$ number "i" at the level "1"), and,
- N message reply subtransactions noted $QT3_i^1$, $i \in [1, N]$.

Each $QT2_i^1$ can be structured as a top-level transaction and contains one $QT1^2$ (in the level 2) and several $QT2^2$ and/or $QT3^2$.

5.2   Structuring the Asynchronous Nested Transaction Model

Application Level. Let us return to the credit/debit application to illust-rate the use of the Asynchronous Nested Transaction model. In this example,

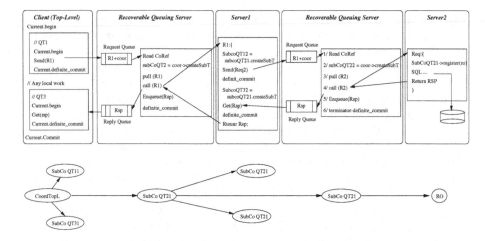

Fig. 12. Two-Tier Application Using the ANT Model

we suppose two servers: bank1 and bank2 that respectively offer the application objects O1 and O2 and the *Compensator* objects C1 and C2. The object O1 possesses the *credit1* operation and the object O2 possesses the *debit2* operation. The *Compensator* objects C1 and C2 implement two compensation operations: *debit1* and *credit2*. A client starts a top-level transaction in which it creates the subtransaction $QT1$. $QT1$ involves the *credit1*(100) and the *debit2*(100) operations.

Transaction Tree Expansion and Control. During the active phase of $QT1$, the coordinator reference is passed to the recoverable queueing system. When it commits, the recoverable queueing system starts two ANTs: $QT2_1^1$ and $QT2_2^1$. $QT2_1^1$ involves the bank1 server and $QT2_2^1$ involves the bank2 server.

To be part of the client's top-level transaction the recoverable queueing system use the top-level coordinator reference to create $QT2_1^1$ and $QT2_2^1$.

The recoverable queueing system commits $QT2_1^1$ and $QT2_2^1$ using the operation *definite_commit* with the *Compensator* objects C1 and C2 and the money amount received from the client. Thus, the ONT-OTS-aware owns the appropriate object references and data to compensate all effects of $QT2_1^1$ and $QT2_2^1$.

When the recoverable queueing system has to return the two reply messages of the *credit1* and *debit2* operations, it creates the subtransactions $QT3_1^1$ and $QT2_2^1$ by using the top-level coordinator object. Thus $QT3_1^1$ and $QT2_2^1$ become part of the top-level transaction.

Application Control and Concerns. Assume that an unrecoverable failure occurs on bank1, leading to a rollback of the subtransaction $QT2_1^1$. On the other hand, if $QT2_2^1$ commits normally. The *Reply-Handler* receives in the $QT3_1^1$ subtransaction the $QT2_1^1$'s reply which is TRANSACTION_ROLLBACK. In this case, the *Reply-Handler* has to rollback the top-level transaction, and then the ONT-OTS-aware will automatically compensate $QT2\frac{1}{2}$ by calling the operation *compensate*(100) on the *Compensator* object C2. The operation *compensate* internally performs the operation $credit2(100)$.

The Asynchronous Nested Transaction Consistency. In order to prove the consistency of the ANT model we propose to analyze the failure cases in a simple topology containing a top-level transaction with $QT1$, $QT2$, and $QT3$ subtransactions. Five potential failure points are examined. They are noted A, B, C, D, E in Fig. 13.

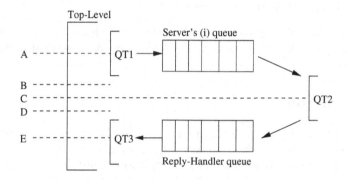

Fig. 13. Failure Cases Analyze

- (A) if the recoverable queueing system tries to create the $QT2$ subtransaction, it will not be able the top-level transaction rollback occurs during the active phase of $QT1$then $QT1$ is forced to abort. Thus, no request messages will be sent.
- (B): If the top-level transaction rollback takes place after the commit of $QT1$ but before the starting of $QT2$, according to the transaction queueing principles, the message will not be immediately removed from the server's queue.
  However, when the recoverable queueing system tries to start $QT2$ the coordinator object reference becomes invalid, since the top-level transaction rolls back. At that moment the recoverable queueing system discards the request message from the server's queue. This can be viewed as the compensation of $QT1$, which is performed by the recoverable queueing system itself.
- (C): If the rollback of the top-level transaction occurs during the active phase of $QT2$, $QT2$ is forced to abort.
  As in the (B) case, the request message is kept in the server's queue and the server connector's trial to create $QT2$ will be unsuccessful. In this case, the recoverable queueing system discards the request message.

- (D): If the rollback of the top-level transaction occurs after the commit of $QT2$ but before the starting of $QT3$, $QT2$ will be compensated by executing the *compensate* operation.
  Later, it will not be possible to start $QT3$ because the coordinator object reference is invalid. Consequently, the reply message is discarded.
- (E): If the rollback occurs during the active phase of $QT3$, the $QT3$ is forced to abort, and the reply message is discarded as in the (D) case.

To summarize, when the top-level transaction rolls back:

- all active subtransactions are forced to roll back,
- all committed subtransactions are compensated, and
- all coming subtransactions that would like to tie-up the rolled back top-level transaction are prohibited to start.

The result is that the atomicity execution semantic wished by the client is achieved, and the announced requirements A1, A2, and A3 described in Section 5.1 are fulfilled.

6   Conclusion

In this paper we have described an extension to OTS to support the open nested transaction model which relaxes the isolation property by releasing locks acquired by a nested transaction at its completion rather than transferring them to the parent transaction as done by the closed nested model, which is already optional in OTS. This relaxation is suitable for certain classes of application, where it is known that resources acquired within a transaction can be "released early", rather than having to wait until the transaction terminates. However certain (typically application specific) compensation activities may be necessary to restore the system to a consistent state, when a parent transaction rolls back.

In terms functionalities and internal mechanisms, we have completely used those already provided by OTS. To terminate a nested transaction with open semantics, we have used the two-phase commit protocol provided by OTS. To structure a transaction into open nested transactions, we use the nested creation and deletion as rules provided by OTS, thereby maintaining a nested coordinator for each. The benefits are that a *Compensator* object is created and its reference maintained by coordinators until top-level commits or any ancestor (including the top-level rolls back). Thus the OTS makes the *compensate* operation invocation guaranteed whenever specified and necessary.

Since open nested transactions has the same tree structure as closed nested transactions, any ancestor rollback is propagated to its subtransactions. This releases the application from handling a mean for rollback signaling and propagation in the case of where a long-lived activity is split into several top-level transactions. At the present time, a new request for proposal recently adopted by Object Management Group [21] addresses the need for providing application structuring mechanisms using OTS transactions to increase concurrency. A service involving the concept of compensation and using an unchanged OTS could be proposed by a set of top-level transactions on top of OTS. However, an additional specific context and protocol specific for this service is needed to maintain a path through top-level coordinators, in the case of interposition, while similar mechanisms are already provided by OTS, as described in this paper.

The atomicity of a unit pf work in a distributed environment remains crucial for multi-tier applications and do not have to be abandoned even if the communication paradigm is asynchronous. In this paper, we have proposed the Asynchronous Nested Transaction model to overcome the limits of the current messaging products and standard specifications when they are confronted with the problem of guaranteeing the atomicity of distributed multi-tier transactional applications. This model is an integration of an open nested transaction model and queueing transaction principles.

We have also proved the feasibility of our model by building a framework that integrates our ONT-OTS-aware prototype MAAO-OTS [12] and our recoverable queueing system ATCS (Asynchronous Transactions Coupling System).

Acknowledgments

We would like to thank Nawal Sabri for her help to establish a latex version of this paper.

References

1. G. Alonso, D. Agrawal, A. El Abbadi, M. Kamath, R. Günthör, and C. Mohan. Advanced Transaction Models in Workflow Context. In S. Y. W. Su, editor, *Proc. of the 12th IEEE Int. Conf. on Data Engineering, ICDE'96, New Orleans, Lousiana, USA*, pages 574–581, IEEE Computer Society Press, 1996.
2. ANSI X3.13561992. American National Standard for Information Systems – Database Language – SQL, November 1992.
3. P. A. Bernstein, V. Hadzilacos, and N. Goodman. *Concurrency Control and Recovery in Database Systems.* Addison-Wesley, 1987.
4. CORBA Messaging Specification. OMG Document orbos/98-05-05, 1998.
5. H. Garcia-Molina and K. Salem. Sagas. In U. Dayal and I. Traiger, editors, *Proc. of the 1987 ACM SIGMOD Int. Conf. on Management of Data, San Franscisco, CA*, ACM SIGMOD Record, Vol. 16, No. 3, pages 249–259, ACM Press, 1987.
6. E. Grasso and N. Perdigues-Charton. Transaction Concepts in Connection Management Applications. TINA'97, November 1997.
7. J. Gray. Notes on Data Base Operating Systems. In R. Bayer, R. M. Graham, and G. Seegmüller, editors, *Operating Systems, An Advanced Course*, Lecture Notes in Computer Science, Vol. 60, pages 393–481, Springer-Verlag, 1978.
8. J. Gray and A. Reuter. *Transaction Processing: Concepts and Techniques.* Morgan Kaufmann Publishers, 1993.
9. IBM corporation. *IBM MQSeries: Message Queue Interface*, 1993.
10. Imprise. Persistence Service. Joint Revised Submission. OMG Document orbos/99.03, 1999.
11. B. Jepson. *JAVA Database Programming.* Wiley Computer, 1996.
12. J.Liang and S.Sedillot and M.Saheb. EEC ACTS ACTranS - The MAAO-OTS White Paper. Deliverable D2aa, http://www.actrans.org/Publications.html, 1998.

13. H. Korth, E. Levy, and A. Silberschatz. A Formal Approach to Recovery by Compensating Transactions. In D. McLeod, R. Sacks-Davis, and H.-J. Schek, editors, *Proc. of the 16th Int. Conf. on Very Large Data Bases, VLDB'90, Brisbane, Australia, August 13–16, 1990*, pages 95–106, Morgan Kaufmann Publishers, 1990.
14. B. Liskov. Distributed Programming in Argus. *Communication of the ACM*, 33(3):300–312, March 1988.
15. B. Liskov, M. Day, M. Herlihy, P. Johnson, G. Leavens, R. Scheifler, and W. Weihl. *Argus Reference Manual*, 1995.
16. C. Mohan and D. Dievendorff. Recent Work on Distributed Commit Protocols, and Recoveralbe Messaging and Quering. *Bulletin of the IEEE Technical Committee on Data Engineering*, 17(1):22–28, March 1994.
17. J. E. B. Moss. *Nested Transactions: An Approach to Reliable Distributed Computing*. PhD thesis, MIT, Cambridge, April 1981.
18. supported by the University of Newcastle upon Tyne Nortel. Submission for the OMG Business Object Domain Task Force (BODTF): Workflow Management Facility. OMG Document bom/98-03-01, 1998.
19. Workflow Management Facility Revised Submission. OMG Document bom/98-06-07, July 1998.
20. The Object Transaction Service, Version 1.1. OMG Document orbos/97-12-17, November 1994.
21. Additional Structuring Mechanisms for the OTS. Request For Proposal. OMG Document: orbos/99-05-17, 1999.
22. Tuxedo/Q Guide. Release 5.0, 1995.
23. H. Wächter and A. Reuter. The ConTract Model. In A. K. Elmagarmid, editor, *Database Transaction Models for Advanced Applications*, pages 219–263, Morgan Kaufmann Publishers, 1992.
24. G. Weikum and H.-J. Schek. Concepts and Applications of Multi-level Transactions and Open Nested Transactions. In A. K. Elmagarmid, editor, *Database Transaction Models for Advanced Applications*, pages 515–553, Morgan Kaufmann Publishers, 1992.
25. The Workflow Reference Model, Version 1.1. WfMC-TC-1003, November 1994.

Execution Guarantees in Electronic Commerce Payments

Heiko Schuldt, Andrei Popovici, and Hans-Jörg Schek

Database Research Group
Institute of Information Systems
ETH Zentrum, 8092 Zürich, Switzerland
{schuldt,popovici,schek}@inf.ethz.ch

Abstract. Electronic Commerce over the Internet is one of the most rapidly growing areas in todays business. However, considering the most important phase of Electronic Commerce, the *payment*, it has to be noted that in most currently exploited approaches support for at least one of the participants is limited. From a general point of view, a couple of requirements for correct payment interactions exist, namely different levels of atomicity in the exchange of money and goods of a single customer with different merchants. Furthermore, as fraudulent behavior of participants in Electronic Commerce has to be considered, the ability to legally prove the processing of a payment transaction is required. In this paper, we identify the different requirements participants demand on Electronic Commerce payment from the point of view of execution guarantees and present how payment interactions can be implemented by transactional processes. Finally, we show how the maximum level of execution guarantees can be provided for payment processes in a natural way by applying transactional process management to an Electronic Commerce *Payment Coordinator*.

1 Introduction

Along with the enormous proliferation of the Internet, Electronic Commerce is continuously gaining importance. The spectrum of applications that are subsumed under the term Electronic Commerce leads from rather simple orders performed by Email to the purchase of shopping baskets consisting of several goods originating from different merchants while electronic cash tokens are spent for payment purposes.

Remarkably, Electronic Commerce is a very interdisciplinary research area. As existing approaches are powered by different communities (i.e., cryptography, networking, etc.), they are very heterogeneous in nature and thus always focus on different special problems. From the point of view of the database community, atomicity properties have been identified as one key requirement for payment protocols in Electronic Commerce [14,15]. The more complex interactions with consumers and merchants become, the more dimensions of atomicity have to be addressed. In the simplest case, only money has to be transferred atomically from

G. Saake, K. Schwarz, and C. Türker (Eds.): TDD '99, LNCS 1773, pp. 193–202, 2000.

the consumer to the merchant. However, considering complex shopping baskets filled with (electronic) goods from several merchants, atomicity may also be required for the purchase of all these goods originating from different possibly independent and autonomous sources, along with the atomic exchange of money and all goods.

Due to their distributed nature, protocols that have been suggested to support payment atomicity in Electronic Commerce impose high requirements on the participating instances (e.g., NetBill [4]). In these approaches, each participant not only has to implement a given set of interfaces. Since the application logic of these payment approaches is not centrally defined but distributed to all participants, they also impose high prerequisites to the participating instances.

However, with a centralized payment coordinator, the complex interactions of the various participants can be embedded within a payment process, thus reducing the prerequisites for merchants and customers to participate in Electronic Commerce. Transactional process management [12] can then be exploited in order to provide the necessary execution guarantees for Electronic Commerce payment processes in a natural way.

This paper is structured as follows: In Section 2, we provide a general framework for Electronic Commerce payment interactions. Based on this framework, we analyze the different atomicity requirements for Electronic Commerce payment (Section 3). Then, in Section 4, we shortly summarize transactional process management and describe how these ideas can be exploited in order to let Electronic Commerce payment process benefit from the execution guarantees provided by a payment process coordinator. Section 5 finally concludes the paper.

2   Schema for Payment Protocols in Electronic Commerce

The description for sales interactions in non-electronic markets [11] encompasses three phases: information, negotiation, and payment. During the information phase, a customer evaluates and compares the offers of several merchants. After selecting the best offer, she negotiates with the chosen merchant the conditions for the deal (negotiation). If they reach an agreement, the last step (the payment) involves the money transfer from customer to merchant and the service (the merchant fulfills his contract).

Most electronic payment systems only focus on the money transfer of the last phase. Our view of an *electronic payment scheme* also considers the systems and protocols for accomplishing both the money transfer and the service.

2.1   Participants

An electronic payment scheme involves participants originating from two distinct worlds: on the Internet side there are the customer, the merchant, and the payment server (also known as payment gateway) as a third entity which coordinates the former ones. The other side is represented by the financial world with its proprietary network infrastructure and protocols. The participants are financial institutes and again the payment server, that has to consistently transform the data flow on the Internet side in corresponding "real world" money flow. The participants are depicted in Figure 1.

2.2 Steps of an Electronic Commerce Transaction

Prior to the payment transaction, the participants are involved in an *initialization* phase, depicted in Figure 1 by dashed arrows. Both customer and merchant have to establish accounts within the financial institutes "issuer" (or "acquirer", resp.). The transformation of the electronic money into real money is performed using these accounts. Also in this phase the customer receives from his bank a *customer secret* which enables him to perform electronic payments. The customer secret is visible only for the customer herself, for the issuing bank and (eventually) for the payment server. The most common form of the customer secret is the credit card number, in electronic cash schemes (such as eCash^{TM} [5]), the customer secret is an E-cash token. Because account operations are rather less often than payments, we can consider them as part of the initialization phase.

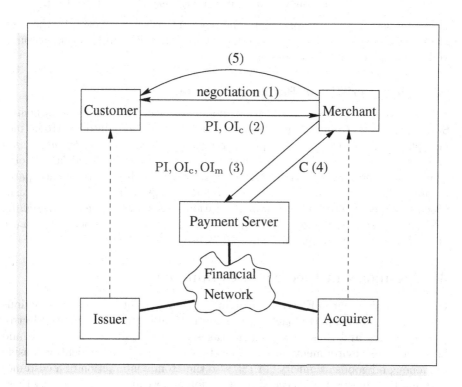

Fig. 1. Generic payment steps

Almost all the payment schemes contain the following steps, marked in Figure 1 with numbers 1 to 5:

- Negotiation (1): the customer selects the desired service or merchandise she wants from the merchant, and negotiates with the merchant the price of the service. The result of this step is the Order Information. The Order Information is a protocol of the negotiation phase, including service (merchandise) and price specification.
- Payment order (2): the customer sends Payment Information (PI) and Order Information (OI_c) to the merchant. The OI_c is the customer's view of the agreement with the merchant.
- Payment authorization (3): the merchant forwards PI, OI_c, OI_m and additional data to the payment server. OI_m is the merchant's view of the agreement with the customer.
  The payment server directly or indirectly verifies the validity of the payment information, the consistency of the payment using OI_c and OI_m. It eventually triggers the real world money transfer using its role on the non-Internet side. At the end of the payment authorization, the merchant receives a confirmation message C from the payment server (4).
- Purchase response (5): The merchant sends himself a confirmation to the customer. In case of electronic (non-tangible) goods, the purchase response can be immediately followed by the merchandise or the service itself.

In most existent payment protocols, the payment server is invoked by the merchant. This is not an intrinsic restriction, and communication between customer and payment server is also possible.

2.3   Characteristics of Payment Protocols

Several criteria serve as classification models of electronic payments schemes. Starting from the moment of transformation of real money into electronic money, payment protocols can be split in *pre-paid systems* and *pay-by-instruction* ones. *Atomicity* is another item, which will be discussed in detail later. Some protocols introduce the notion of *provability*, which is the ability of each party to prove their correct interactions. *Anonymity* is especially addressed by cash-based-systems. There are also implementation issues like *scalability, flexibility, efficiency, ease of use* and *off-line operation*, which are also important because of the large number of persons expected to use these systems.

3   Atomicity in Electronic Commerce

One key requirement in Electronic Commerce is to guarantee atomic interactions between the various participants in Electronic Commerce payment. As Electronic Commerce and thus also payment takes place in a highly distributed and heterogeneous environment, various aspects of atomicity can be identified: aside of money and goods atomicity [14,15], also the atomic interaction of a customer with multiple merchants is needed. In what follows, we analyze and classify these different atomicity requirements in detail.

3.1 Money Atomicity

The basic form of atomicity in Electronic Commerce is associated with the transfer of money from the customer to the merchant. This is denoted by the term *money atomicity* [14]. As no viable Electronic Commerce payment solution can exist without supporting this atomicity property, multiple solutions have been proposed or are already established [8,5]. However, the atomicity property is tightly coupled with the protocol architecture and design.

3.2 Certified Atomic Delivery

Aside of money, also goods have to be transferred. Therefore, a further requirement is that the delivery takes place atomically. This can even be reinforced in that both associated parties —customer and merchant— require the necessary information in order to prove that the goods sent (or received, resp.) are the ones both parties agreed to in the initial negotiation phase (*certified atomic delivery*, encompassing the goods atomicity and the certified delivery described in [14]). This strengthened requirement results from the fact that —in contrast to traditional distributed database transactions where only technical failures have to be addressed— in Electronic Commerce also fraudulent behavior of participants has to be coped with.

Especially when dealing with goods that can be transferred electronically, the combination of money atomicity and certified delivery is an important issue. In [3], this is realized by a customized Two-Phase-Commit protocol (2PC) [6]. To support both dimensions of atomic interactions and to avoid a payment coordinator to deal with the goods to be transferred, cryptographic mechanisms are applied. Prior to the payment process, the merchant sends the ordered goods in an encrypted way to the customer. On successful termination of the payment, the coordinator has both to transfer the money from the customer to the merchant and the key needed for the decryption of the previously received goods to the client in an atomic way.

3.3 Distributed Purchase Atomicity

In many Electronic Commerce applications, interaction of customers is not limited to a single merchant. Consider, for instance, a customer who wants to purchase specialized software from a merchant. In order run this software, she also needs an operating system which is, however, only available from a different merchant. As both goods individually are of no value for the customer, she needs the guarantee to perform the purchase transaction with the two different merchants atomically in order to get both products or none. *Distributed purchase atomicity* addresses the encompassment of interactions with different independent merchants into one single transaction.

This problem is in general reinforced by the fact that different heterogeneous interfaces are involved and different communication protocols are supported by the participating merchants. To this end, in order to support distributed purchase atomicity in very heterogeneous environments with applications using communication protocols for which there are no transactional variants (such as, for instance, HTTP), the Transaction Internet Protocol (TIP) [7] has been proposed. TIP is based on the Two-Phase-Commit protocol (2PC). The main idea of this protocol is to separate communication between transaction managers from the application communication protocol (two-pipe-model). While communication at transaction manager level takes place by the TIP 2PC protocol, arbitrary protocols can independently be exploited at application communication level (such as, for instance, HTTP).

3.4   Summary of Atomicity Requirements

In Figure 2, the three dimensions of atomicity that can be identified in Electronic Commerce applications are depicted. Most currently deployed payment coordinators only support money atomicity while some advanced systems also address distributed purchase atomicity. However, to our best knowledge, all three dimensions are not provided by existing systems and protocols although the highest level of guarantees would be supported and although this is required by a set of real-world applications.

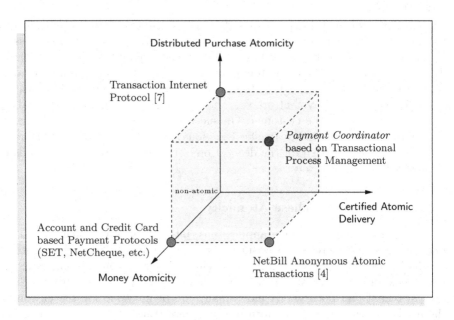

Fig. 2. Classification of Atomicity in Electronic Commerce

This lack of support for full atomicity in Electronic Commerce payment is addressed in this paper where we apply transactional process management (Section 4) to realize an Electronic Commerce payment coordinator.

4   Transactional Process Management

In this Section, we introduce the theory of transactional process management that provides a joint criterion for the correct execution of processes with respect to recovery (when failures of single processes have to be considered) and concurrency control (when multiple parallel processes access shared resources simultaneously) and we point out how this theory can be applied for payments in Electronic Commerce.

4.1   Overview

In conventional databases, concurrency control and recovery are well understood problems. Unfortunately, this is not the case when transactions are grouped into entities with higher level semantics, such as *transactional processes*. Since concurrent processes may access shared resources simultaneously, consistency has to be guaranteed for these executions.

Transactional process management [12] has to enforce consistency for concurrent executions and, at the same time, to cope with the added structure found in processes. In particular, and unlike in traditional transactions, processes introduce flow of control as one of the basic semantic elements. Thus, it has to be taken into consideration that processes already impose ordering constraints among their different operations and among their alternative executions. Similarly, processes integrate invocations to applications with different atomicity properties (e.g., activities may or may not be semantically compensatable).

The main components of transactional process management consist of a coordinator acting as top level scheduler and several transactional coordination agents [13] —one for each subsystem participating in transactional processes— acting as lower level schedulers. Processes encompass *activities* which are invocations in subsystems scheduled by the coordinator. Firstly, the execution guarantees to be provided by the coordinator include guaranteed termination, a more general notion of atomicity than the standard all or nothing semantics which is realized by partial compensation and alternative executions. Secondly, the correct parallelization of concurrent processes is required and thirdly, by applying the ideas of the composite systems theory [1], a high degree of parallelism for concurrent processes is to be provided.

The key aspects of transactional process management can briefly be summarized as follows: The coordinator acts as a kind of transaction scheduler that is more general than a traditional database scheduler in that it

i.) knows about semantic commutativity of activities,
ii.) knows about properties of activities (compensatable, retriable, or pivot, taken from the flex transaction model [9,16]), and
iii.) knows about alternative executions paths in case of failures.

Based on this information, the coordinator ensures global correctness but only under the assumption that the activities within the processes to be scheduled themselves provide transactional functionality (such as atomicity, compensatability, order-preservation, etc.).

4.2 Application of Transactional Process Management in Electronic Commerce

According to [10], trade interactions between customers and merchants can be classified in three phases: pre-sales, sales, and post-sales. While the sales phase has a well-defined structure (especially the payment processing, see Section 2), this is in general not the case for the pre-sales and the post-sales phase.

Due to this well-defined structure, processes are a highly appropriate means to implement the interactions that have to be performed for payment purposes. Furthermore, the atomicity requirements for payments in Electronic Commerce can be realized in an elegant way by applying the ideas of transactional process management in an *Electronic Commerce Payment Coordinator*.

Based on the NetBill protocol guaranteeing both money atomicity and certified atomic delivery, payment processes can be enhanced to additionally provide distributed payment atomicity. To this end, and in contrast to the currently applied payment schemes, the payment has to be initiated by the customer. She has to invoke a payment process at the Payment Coordinator by specifying the payment information PI and all n bilaterally agreed Order Information (and thus also all different merchants) that have to be encompassed within one single payment transaction. Therefore, a tuple $(OI_c, M)_j$ with Order Information OI_c and Merchant Identifier M for each product j with $1 \leq j \leq n$ has to be sent to the Payment Coordinator. Within the payment process invoked, the necessary steps are taken to guarantee all three dimensions of atomicity. The Payment Coordinator first contacts all merchants involved and collects the merchant's views on the Order Information $(OI_m)_j$. Then, in order to determine the success of the payment transactions, $(OI_m)_j$ and $(OI_c)_j$ are compared for each product j. In the case of success, the Payment Coordinator collects all keys from all merchants participating in the transaction, checks the validity and the value of the E-cash token received and atomically delivers all keys to the customer while at the same time initiating the money transfer to the merchants and sends a confirmation C_j to all merchants. In case that $(OI_m)_j$ and $(OI_c)_j$ do not match for some j, some keys are not available, or the E-cash token is not correct, the Payment Coordinator aborts the payment transaction and no exchange will take place.

Electronic Commerce payment can benefit from a Payment Coordinator based on transactional process management ideas in several ways. Firstly, as application logic is centrally defined, the prerequisites for the participants of Electronic Commerce trade (customers, merchants, banks) are minimized. Secondly, with the inherent structure of payment processes invoked by a customer, it is possible to provide all dimensions of atomicity identified as requirements in Electronic Commerce. This is thirdly enhanced by additional properties as, for instance, the possibility to legally prove correct execution of a payment process by persistently logging process execution. This process log is part of the transactional process management and thus, provided by the Payment Coordinator in an elegant and straightforward way. Finally, by executing payment processes by a Payment Coordinator, the monitoring of the state of a payment interaction is facilitated compared with the distribution found in current payment protocols.

5 Conclusion

This paper provides a detailed analysis of requirements participants in Electronic Commerce payment impose with respect to atomicity issues. Different levels of atomicity can be identified which, however, are not simultaneously provided by existing approaches. Using the notion of processes, it has been shown that all payment interactions can be embedded into a single payment process where all possible levels of execution guarantees can be provided while at the same time the prerequisites of the participants are reduced. Finally, by applying the ideas of transactional process management, it has been shown how a Payment Coordinator supporting atomic and provable payment processes can be developed.

This process-based Payment Coordinator is currently being implemented within the WISE system [2]. Based on this implementation, we will in our future work extend the analysis of payment processes to further properties (such as, for instance, anonymity, scalability, or flexibility). Our goal is to decouple these properties, to identify the building blocks needed to realize them and to flexibly generate payment processes with user-defined properties by plugging together the building blocks needed.

References

1. G. Alonso, S. Blott, A. Feßler, and H.-J. Schek. Correctness and Parallelism in Composite Systems. In *Proc. of the 16th ACM SIGACT-SIGMOD-SIGART Symposium on Principles of Database Systems, PODS'97, Tuscon, Arizona, USA*, pages 197–208, ACM Press, 1997.
2. G. Alonso, U. Fiedler, C. Hagen, A. Lazcano, H. Schuldt, and N. Weiler. WISE: Business to Business E-Commerce. In *Proc. of the 9th Int. Workshop on Research Issues in Data Engineering, Information Technology for Virtual Enterprises, RIDE-VE'99, March 1999, Sydney, Australia*, pages 132–139, IEEE Computer Society Press, 1999.
3. J. Camp, M. Harkavy, D. Tygar, and B. Yee. Anonymous Atomic Transactions. In *Proc. of the 2nd Usenix Workshop on Electronic Commerce*, pages 123–133, 1996.
4. B. Cox, D. Tygar, and M. Sirbu. NetBill Security and Transaction Protocol. In *Proc. of the 1st USENIX Workshop on Electronic Commerce*, pages 77–88, 1995.
5. DigiCash, 1999. http://www.digicash.com/.
6. J. Gray and A. Reuter. *Transaction Processing: Concepts and Techniques*. Morgan Kaufmann, 1993.
7. J. Lyon, K. Evans, and J. Klein. Transaction Internet Protocol Version 3.0. Network Working Group, Request for Comments (RFC 2371), July 1998. http://www.ietf.org/html.charters/tip-charter.html.
8. MasterCard and Visa. *Secure Electronic Transaction Specification*. MasterCard and Visa, draft edition, June 1996. Book 1: Business Description, Book 2: Programmer's Guide, Book 3: Formal Protocol Specification (Slightly revised version of Book 3 appeared August 1, 1997).
9. S. Mehrotra, R. Rastogi, H. F. Korth, and A. Silberschatz. A Transaction Model for Multidatabase Systems. In *Proc. of the 12th Int. Conf. on Distributed Computing Systems, ICDCS'92, June 1992, Yokohama, Japan*, pages 56–63, IEEE Computer Society Press, 1992.

10. P. Muth, J. Weissenfels, and G. Weikum. What Workflow Technology can do for Electronic Commerce. In *Proc. of the EURO-MED NET Conference, March 1998, Nicosia, Cyprus,* 1998.

11. B. Schmidt. Electronic Markets – Characteristics, Organization, and Potentials. In A. Hermanns and M. Sauter, editors, *Management Handbook Electronic Commerce,* Vahlen, 1998. (In German).

12. H. Schuldt, G. Alonso, and H.-J. Schek. Concurrency Control and Recovery in Transactional Process Management. In *Proc. of the 18th ACM SIGACT-SIGMOD-SIGART Symposium on Principles of Database Systems, PODS'99, May 31–June 2, 1999, Philadelphia, Pennsylvania,* pages 316–326, ACM Press, 1999.

13. H. Schuldt, H.-J. Schek, and G. Alonso. Transactional Coordination Agents for Composite Systems. In *Proc. of the 3rd Int. Database Engineering and Applications Symposium, IDEAS'99, August 1999, Montréal, Canada,* pages 321–331, 1999.

14. D. Tygar. Atomicity in Electronic Commerce. In *Proc. of the 15th Annual ACM Symposium on Principles of Distributed Computing, May 23–26, 1996, Philadelphia, PA, USA,* pages 8–26, ACM Press, 1996.

15. D. Tygar. Atomicity versus Anonymity: Distributed Transactions for Electronic Commerce. In A. Gupta, O. Shmueli, and J. Widom, editors, *Proc. of the 24st Int. Conf. on Very Large Data Bases, VLDB'98, Ney York City, August 24–27, 1998,* pages 1–12, Morgan Kaufmann Publishers, 1998.

16. A. Zhang, M. Nodine, B. Bhargava, and O. Bukhres. Ensuring Relaxed Atomicity for Flexible Transactions in Multidatabase Systems. In *Proc. of the 1994 ACM SIGMOD Int. Conf. on Management of Data, Minneapolis,* ACM SIGMOD Record, Vol. 23, No. 2, pages 67–78, ACM Press, 1994.

Transactions in Mobile Electronic Commerce

Jari Veijalainen

University of Jyväskylä
Dept. of Computer Science and Information Systems
P.O.Box 35, FIN-40351 Jyväskylä, Finland
veijalai@cs.jyu.fi

Abstract. With the development of global networking, invention of WWW, and proliferation of Internet-enabled computer hardware and software into homes and pockets, a huge customer base has been created for electronic commerce. It is rapidly expanding in USA and Europe and Japan are following the trend. So far, the development of E-commerce has happened in a rather unregulated way especially in USA, whereas in Europe the European Commission has been developing a regulatory basis mainly in form of directives. Currently (12/1999) they have not yet all been accepted and a major restructuring of the regulatory framework has also been planned. Another technological development is the rapid growth of mobile computing, especially through WAP technology, which makes also mobile E-commerce possible.

In this article we review the need of a transaction model and the corresponding transactional mechanism and its usefulness for E-commerce in general and for mobile E-commerce in particular. We tackle the issue both theoretically and empirically. In the theoretical part we review some of the earlier work, and discuss especially money atomicity, goods atomicity and certified delivery. The empirical part consists of trials at three E-commerce sites, two in Finland and one in USA and reveal important differences in the structure of E-commerce transactions in different cases. These must be taken into consideration when transactional support is developed further.

Using the emerging technology both customer and merchant can now become mobile, although it is more probable that a customer is mobile but a merchant stationary. Communication autonomy and other autonomy aspects and miniature size of the terminals aggravate the problems of achieving the various levels of atomicity. Security, privacy, authentication, and authorization are of paramount importance in an open network environment. One important conclusion is that the transactional mechanism must be closely related with these aspects and that the main goal of using the transactional mechanism is actually to support security, privacy, authentication and authorization — and vice versa.

1 Introduction

With the development of global networking, invention of WWW, and proliferation of Internet-enabled computer hardware and software into homes, a huge

G. Saake, K. Schwarz, and C. Türker (Eds.): TDD '99, LNCS 1773, pp. 203–224, 2000.

private customer base has been created for electronic commerce. E-commerce is rapidly expanding in USA and Europe and Japan are following the trend.

So far, the development of E-commerce has happened in a rather unregulated way especially in USA, where the philosophy has been to let the market find the best practices. In Europe, the European Commission has been developing a regulatory basis in form of directives. Many of the directives regulating E-commerce are still in a proposal stage, unfortunately.

A difference between USA and Europe is that in Europe more emphasis is put on the consumer protection aspects and this is believed to be achieved by writing down the necessary requirements into the directives and later into national legislation [30]. The regulative tool set in EU is thus a bunch of directives where the principles applicable are laid down. They should then be incorporated into the national legislation in the member countries. Japan seems to be behind USA and EU in this development but their initial ideas concerning regulation seem to be close to the European ones [28].

Unfortunately, there are currently over twenty directives or directive proposals that regulate or will regulate different aspects of electronic commerce (see [4,6,5,18,16,17,15,10,11,9,29,13,7,8,14]).

Currently, this makes the environment rather difficult for the players in the field, until the issues have been settled. From technical point of view, there is the risk that merchants in different countries set up E-Commerce servers that impose different protocols between the customer and the server. This makes automation of the services cumbersome at the customer end and the differences might deter the customers from E-Commerce.

The European Commission has now decided to restructure the regulatory framework. After that, it should only consist of about five to six directives that cover usage and licensing of both telecommunication networks, broadcast-oriented terrestrial and satellite TV networks, and computer networks, especially IP networks [24]. So far, the directive proposal [29] is rather central from our point of view, because it regulates to some extent the structure of the business processes at the merchant and customer. Third parties are not really addressed (intermediary is defined, but it concerns network operator and similar instances providing the infrastructure). Another important one is [15] that lays down the principles for electronic signatures.

The legislators in EU consider Information Society Services (ISS) as a major innovation. These are services provided at distance through a communication network using some form of electro-magnetic carrier. The service is always requested by a customer, i.e. the interaction is not started by the merchant [29], Art.2. Contracts can be made electronically, except contracts that require notary, registration by a public authority, concern family law, or law of succession [29], Art.9.

The above directive proposal [29], Art.5 states that merchant must give necessary information in order to be identified. The information includes also the physical address that determines which legislation is applied concerning the (mobile) E-commerce transaction (origin of source issues). The E-commerce taxation directive [11] says that the indirect taxes should be paid according to the law of the country, where the merchant has the residence (taxation of origin principle). Electronic goods are considered as services in EU and treated accordingly in respect of taxation.

GSM and other wireless networks and especially Wireless Application Protocol technology designed for GSM and subsequent mobile networks [21] have now opened access to Internet for hand-held mobile terminals. Bluetooth technology [20] will further enhance the sphere of mobility. Both facilitate also mobile E-commerce. Using these technologies, both customer and merchant can now be mobile, although it is probable that a customer is more mobile than a merchant.

In this article we review the need of a transaction model and corresponding transactional mechanisms and their usefulness for E-commerce in general and for mobile E-commerce in particular. We tackle the issue both theoretically and empirically. In Section 2 we review the work done so-far in the field. Section 3 consists of trials of three E-commerce sites, two in Finland and one in USA. The trials show important differences in the structure of E-commerce transactions in different cases that must be taken into consideration when transactional support is developed further. In Section 4 we discuss the transactional requirements for "fixed" E-commerce. In Section 5 we analyze the transactional and other related requirements in the mobile environment. Section 6 concludes the paper.

2   Related Work

The work in the transaction field started at the beginning of the seventies. In the eighties new application areas emerged and new transactional issues were confronted. The book [19] is a rather good overview on the work done during eighties in the field.

Electronic commerce is a new application area needing transactional support. One of first well-known analyzes in this application context is [34]. In it, the author concentrates on the atomicity aspects of E-commerce transactions, introducing *money atomicity, goods atomicity*, and *certified delivery*. Money atomicity states that funds transfers must be implemented in such a way that the money is either moved from one party to another or not moved at all, i.e. the money is not "lost"[1]. It is worth noticing that the Semantic transaction model aiming mainly at money atomicity in distributed, highly autonomous international banking environment was introduced already in the eighties and analyzed thoroughly in [35,36]. The term semantic atomicity was used, because the meaning of atomicity can be semantically specified and enforced in the S-transaction model.

Goods atomicity guarantees money atomicity and in addition to it the semantic constraint: "The customer will get the goods if and only if the money is transferred from her to the merchant". Finally, certified delivery guarantees goods atomicity and additionally that both customer and merchant are able

---

[1] The author speaks about creation or destruction of money in this context, but this aspect is in reality orthogonal to the funds transfer atomicity requirement.

to prove exactly which goods were delivered. The latter protects the customer against a fraudulent merchant (who might cheat by delivering wrong or defect goods or delivering nothing) and the merchant against a dishonest customer, who would claim that the goods delivered deviated in some sense from those ordered. Tygar continues the work in [33], where he discusses whether and how anonymity and atomicity could be combined.

The above considerations do primarily target digital goods and a three-party structure for the transactions (customer- merchant - bank/credit card company). Delivery of physical (or tangible) goods poses further complications, because e.g. digital signatures cannot be used to certify the goods themselves.

Three parties can also be a too small number; the customer might want to buy e.g. software X that requires some other software Y to run. Y is, however, not obtainable from the merchant of X and thus the customer has to buy either both X and Y or none of them. This kind of scenario requires a further transactional property called Distributed Purchase Atomicity in [31] that guarantees money atomicity and goods atomicity for a set of dependent purchases at different merchants.

Secure Electronic Transactions (SET) is probably the best known commercially developed standard [25]. It is aimed at three-party E-commerce transactions (customer-merchant-credit card company). From transactional point of view it mainly addresses money atomicity, i.e., it guarantees that the payment is performed if and only if the customer (credit card holder) authorizes it and the sum debited to the customer card is the correct one. The mechanism assumes a sophisticated certificate infrastructure that guarantees the correct identity of the participants.

Pioneering work considering the secure payment protocols has been performed by Michael Waidner and his group at IBM Zurich. A recent overview of the so-called iKP family of protocols, closely related to SET, can be found at [3]. The work done in part by the above laboratory and other partners in the European Semper project (AC026) is also of pioneering nature in the field [32].

The above work mainly concentrate on business-to-customer transactions. Requirements for transactions in business-to-business E-commerce with emphasis on value chains have been discussed e.g. in [27] and general requirements, regulatory frameworks and their relevance for mobility aspects have been dealt with in [22].

3   Some Experiences in Current E-Commerce Systems

We took a closer look at the following three sites:

- www.keltainenporssi.fi (a Finnish WWW-based customer-to-customer market place),
- www.amazon.com (a famous electronic bookstore in USA), and
- www.bokus.com (a Nordic book store).

3.1   Keltainen Pörssi: A Finnish Electronic Market Place

We will look at the site from service ordering angle. It is interesting, because it is possible to pay for the service (reading the announcements of other customers) also by Internet banking using one's own account. This is our main interest in this case. The interactions are presented in Fig. 1.

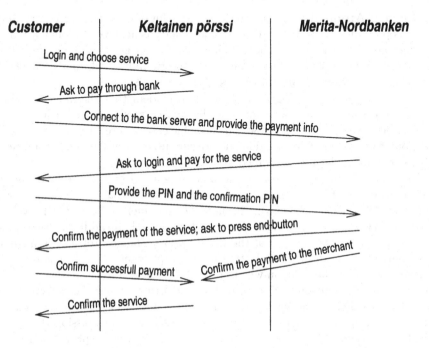

Fig. 1. The exchange of messages between the customer, service provider and a bank

It is worth noticing that the control and data both flow through the customer site, in practice through the customer browser. Thus, the service provider sends the data concerning the customer service order to the customer who can check it through the browser. Some of the fields contain information to the bank, such as the transaction id. It also contains the URI at the bank through which these kind of services at the bank can be used by the customer and the merchant.

From communication security point of view, all communication happens using HTTPS, the encrypted form of HTTP. While dealing with the bank the customer uses his or her PINs, in a similar way as when the bank services are used in a peer-to-peer fashion. Thus, the security risk does not increase in this case as compared to direct usage of Internet banking services.

The bank and the service provider guard against malicious customers by providing an information flow directly between them. Thus a customer who would try to fake the payment should do it in his or her machine and, additionally, he or she should make the service provider side (in this case Keltainen Pörssi) to believe that the bank has sent the direct confirmation about the payment, even if the customer faked it in a way or the other. Depending on how well the system at the service provider is designed and how secure is the authentication between the bank and service provider, this might or might not require direct penetration to the system of the service provider. Of course, the penetration might be tried at the bank, too, but there is evidently less hope of breaking into their systems than to those of a service provider.

Achieving Atomicity? From transactional point of view, the three-party interactions pose questions. Which degree of atomicity is achieved? Money atomicity is guaranteed to the degree the banking system can perform it in general; the accounts might be in different banks, so domestic inter-bank funds transfer, or even an international bank transfer might be needed.

Goods atomicity is a bigger problem. It is evident that the money might be taken from the customer account, but the service provider does still not grant the service. We discuss this below. The possible case, where the service is granted without the customer to pay does not occur, unless the customer could cheat the merchant in the way described above.

The weak point from the goods atomicity point of view is the following: the information about the payment (control flow) from the bank to service provider must arrive via two paths, both through the customer and directly. If even one control flow brakes the service is (evidently) denied. In addition to technical problems like failures at any of the three parties, the control flow is mediated manually at the customer site. In the current implementation, the customer gets a form back from the bank on which he or she is advised to close the transaction by pressing the "end-button" provided on the form. Behind the button there is an URI provided by the service provider and the identification of the payment transaction, along the notice that it was successful. Upon pressing the button, the browser sends a HTTP request to the server of the service provider, using the URI meant for confirmations, along the parameter values. It probably also sends the previous URI visited that in the normal case should be that of the bank. The final confirmation of the granted service comes from the service provider server as a response to the request above.

Thus, the goods atomicity of the combined payment and service provision transaction is achieved manually. There are several places where it is threatened. Maybe the most evident one is crash of the customer workstation or the critical software (browser or the communication software) after he or she has confirmed the payment and the bank has done it, but the "end-button" has not been pushed. In this case the customer either does not at all get the critical confirmation information from the bank or fails to press the end button and thus fails to convey the confirmation to the server. Trying later to convince the service provider of the payment will be rather difficult, because the necessary information has evidently been lost.

Another thing is that even if there was no crash at the customer site, confirmation for the payment is based on actions of people who do not necessarily understand the necessity of following the instructions. Should the customer ignore the advice and not press the "end-button", it is likely that the service is denied by the service provider, because it does not get the other necessary confirmation for the payment. It is currently unclear, whether the customer can be made liable for loosing money in the case he or she does not follow instructions given on the form returned by the bank.

Certified delivery is achieved, provided the user can use the service in the specified way and for the paid time. The latter property can only be verified after the entire subscription period has elapsed.

3.2   A Bookstore in USA: Amazon.com

This company has its headquarter in Seattle, USA and activity in several places in USA and Europe.

Taxation and Legislative Framework Affecting the Customer. The applicable law for E-commerce transactions for the address amazon.com is that of State of Washington[2]. The site gives the following information on what they record of the customer: "When you order, we need to know your name, e-mail address, mailing address, credit card number, and expiration date. This allows us to process and fulfill your order and to notify you of your order status"[23].

Sales tax is only levied for shipments where the destination address is State of Washington or Nevada in USA. Other shipments are tax free. The duties possibly levied are left for the customer. Notice that from sales tax point of view the residence of the customer is decisive, whereas the applicable law with respect to disputes is that of Washington. In addition, the customs laws of the customer's country of residence may play a role in the shipment. Thus, the customer should know the legislation of two or three countries/states in order to master properly the purchase transactions in this environment - at least, if something goes wrong.

The Overall Process at Amazon. The whole overall process is described in Fig. 2. The customer can first pick up the items into the shopping cart and register at the merchant as part of the payment procedure. The information mentioned above is collected. A returning customer is identified when he or she enters the site (based on cookies). If the customer has chosen the One-Click service mode, further identification is not necessary. When the customer gives final ok for the transaction, the card information is checked (if changed) and the value of the items in the shopping cart debited to the credit card account.[3]

---

[2] APPLICABLE LAW: "This site is created and controlled by Amazon.com in the State of Washington, USA. As such, the laws of the State of Washington will govern these disclaimers, terms, and conditions, without giving effect to any principles of conflicts of laws. We reserve the right to make changes to our site and these disclaimers, terms, and conditions at any time"[2].

[3] In addition to a credit card other payment methods can be used, too, but credit card is the most convenient one.

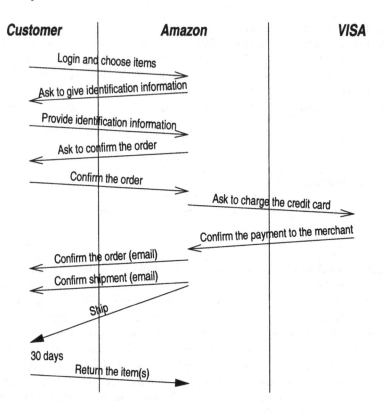

Fig. 2. The overall process at amazon.com in a successful case

After the customer has accepted the purchase transaction, the information (and material) flow is one-directional, from the merchant to the customer. First, a message is sent by the merchant to the email-address of the customer when the order is placed. It usually arrives within a minute after placing the order. This message looks as follows:

From: orders@amazon.com
Date sent: Thu, 23 Sep 1999 05:50:45 -0700 (PDT)
To: veijalainenj@acm.org
Subject: Your Order with Amazon.com (Nr. 002-4352468-0391217)

Thank you for ordering from Amazon.com! Your order information appears below. If you need to get in touch with us about your order, send an e-mail message to orders@amazon.com (or just reply to this message).

– Amazon.com Customer Service

Your order reads as follows:
E-mail address: veijalainenj@acm.org
Ship to: ...
"Memoirs of a Geisha" Arthur S. Golden; Paperback; $7.00 each (Usually ships in 24 hours) ...

The next piece of information sent by the merchant is the announcement that the items have been shipped and the statement that this completes the order.

From: orders@amazon.com
To: veijalainenj@acm.org
Subject: Your Amazon.com order (Nr.002-4352468-0391217)
Date sent: Thu, 23 Sep 1999 19:04:50 -0700 (PDT)

We thought you'd like to know that the following item has been shipped to: Jari Veijalainen ... using DHL WorldMail (Averages 7-21 business days). Please note that these shipments do not have tracking numbers. Your order Nr.002-4352468-0391217 (received September 23 1999 05:50 PDT)

Ordered Item	Price	Shipped	Subtotal
Memoirs of a Geisha	$7.00		$7.00

Subtotal:	$7.00
Shipping & Handling:	$12.95
Total:	$19.95

This completes your order. If you have any questions, please contact us via e-mail (orders@amazon.com), FAX (1-206-266-2950) or phone (1-800-201-7575 for US customers or 1-206-266-2992 for international customers). Thank you for shopping at Amazon.com. ...

After that, the items should arrive to the address specified.

If the customer is not satisfied with the product(s), he or she can return the items back to the merchant within 30 days of receiving the items.

RETURN POLICY: "Our returns policy is simple. Within 30 days of receipt of your order, you may return any of the following items for a full refund: any book in its original condition, or any book we recommended (but you didn't enjoy) in any condition any unopened music CD, DVD, VHS tape, or software toys, electronics, tools, home-improvement items, and any other merchandise in new condition, with its original packaging and accessories Please note that we can process returns and refunds only for items purchased from Amazon.com. You can also cancel unshipped items. Find out more about how to cancel..." [1].

Security Considerations. Is the security high enough and authentication proper in this kind of trading system and could they be improved by transactional means? If the returning customer is recognized based on cookies, the http server at Amazon asks whether it has resolved the identity correctly (of course, a fraudulent person would not say no). This makes possible the "One-click service"[4], where the customer does not need to type in any identification information, provided he or she is coming from a machine where the old cookies are stored.

---

[4] The service has been lately even patented by Amazon.

Rather, he or she can collect books and other items into the shopping cart and just acknowledge the bought items at the end of the session.

This opens up the possibility at the customer site to use the same machine to buy books and other items, even if the actual customer would not want it. A further danger is that the service at Amazon offers possibility to send gifts to other persons. A fraudulent person could use this possibility to send books to him- or herself or to a third person, if he or she gets access to the machine of a customer and/or gets somehow hold of the relevant cookie file. The gifts are sent to a person only after he or she has responded to an email sent from the merchant and subsequently revealed the delivery address, but this does not reduce the risk much.

3.3   Bokus: A Nordic Book Store

This case is rather similar to the Amazon. The difference is mainly that the bookstore operates in Scandinavian countries and applies the local mail-order business rules. Thus, instead of charging the customer before or upon shipping, the store sends the book, along the invoice. The customer can then either pay the bill or return the book without paying. The risk is thus more at the merchant side, because the customer will not pay, before the items ordered have arrived and they satisfy the customer.

From structural point of view, the difference to Amazon is that this is a genuine two-party ordering transaction between the customer and merchant. Third party might be needed later if the payment happens through the banking system, but it is conceptually not necessary.

A difference to Amazon is that the order is confirmed by email within three days after the order is placed through a WWW interface at the server. Thus, the customer might be three days in doubt, whether the order will be accepted or not. Another interesting difference is that the bookstore wants to know the birth date of the customer. They do not tell why, but evidently they do not necessary want to sell to minors. Maybe they also have in mind advertising aspects and security aspects, because knowing the birth date makes the address check in Nordic countries easier.

From process point of view, there is a slight difference to Amazon allowing the customer to cancel the order also by email. In this case it remains a bit unclear from the instructions, when the book itself should be returned. It is neither said very clearly, what will happen if the book is returned and it is not in an acceptable condition.

The bookstore does not tell openly what information they will collect. For instance, if I pay the invoice through a bank, they will get the account information and could add it into the customer record. This reduces the risk of having customers with a faked identity.

4   What Kind of Transactional Issues are Relevant in E-Commerce in General

4.1   The Lower Level: The Business Process View

When looking at Fig. 2 one notices that there is a business process performing at the merchant site and that this business process has a fairly standard form (the business process has a fairly similar form also at the Bokus):

1. Let the customer fill the cart.
2. After a new customer provides the identification information, along the credit card information, process the customer order: debit the sum to the credit card; if ok send confirmation by email otherwise send negative response.
3. If the customer cancels the order before the items have been shipped, acknowledge this and cancel the payment at the credit card company; cancel the order from the database; stop the process instance at the state "customer cancelled before shipment".
4. Send the items to the address given; send the delivery report to the customer by email.
5. Wait until the time to return the items has expired or the items have been returned.
6. If the return time has expired, close the process instance in a state "books delivered and paid, not returned".
7. The customer returns the items during the 30 days period: process the returned items; announce to the customer the possible expenditures by email; adjust the costs at the credit card company.
8. Close the order processing process instance in a state "customer returned the items; costs adjusted".

Looking at Fig. 2 we also see that the business process at the merchant runs a rather long time, over 30 days (21 days at Bokus), at least conceptually. It is thus a long-lasting process instance. The business process in Fig. 1 normally runs only a couple of minutes. This has certain implications for the implementation of the processes. They both have, however, a rather similar overall goal: "The customer pays if and only if exactly the ordered service/items are delivered". This is another formulation for the certified delivery.

4.2   Jeopardizing the Certified Delivery

When could the customer loose money, but not get the items in a case obeying the business process structure exemplified by Amazon? This happens if something goes wrong at the merchant site, at the credit card company site, or during the delivery, after the merchant has asked the credit card company to charge the ordered items and this has been performed. The transaction that causes to charge the credit card of the customer at the credit card company is a typical business-to-business E-commerce transaction that guarantees money atomicity and coherent view of the both sides on the outcome. There is as such nothing new; the participants must carefully log the various states of this E-commerce transaction and use basic ACID transactions at database to implement it.

The interaction between the merchant and credit card company is completely out of the control of the customer, in contrast to service provision case where the customer was responsible for the atomicity. The errors at that stage are not very probable, because the problems are rather well understood and standards like SET [25] have been developed to tackle this problem.

Another point, where things can go wrong is the shipment after the book has been charged. First, the customer might not get the email that notifies about the successful order. The reason might be e.g. wrong email address which again can be customer's fault, or could be caused by the problems at the merchant system or at some other part in the network. If the message does not leave the merchant site it is again an atomicity problem of the implementation of the business process step that notifies about the success. Other delivery problems are more communication-related.

Should somebody want to misuse one's credit card, the email confirmations should actually be directed to an address not belonging to the card owner. This could be done rather easily by delivering an abstract email address that is mapped to another one in a server that does not tell the mapping to outside, when the customer identification is given. If somebody found out the password of the customer at the merchant, then of course address and other information can be temporarily changed so that the credit card owner does not get confirmation about the items purchased behind his or her back.

Further, the logistics might fail in delivering the items. This is mostly outside the control of both the merchant and customer and although transactional mechanisms might help in keeping track of the status of the delivery process, they are outside the scope of this paper.

Transactional Requirements for the Business Processes and Distribution Aspects. Analyzing the abstract goal of certified delivery and possible problems above, one easily sees that one needs to guarantee several sub-goals at the lower level of abstraction, namely at the business process level and at the distributed system level. The following two requirements should be satisfied:

1. The business processes involved run until some acceptable end state. Intuitively this means that none of them stops in the middle, but each of them runs either to a full success or complete cancellation.
2. The end states of different processes are semantically coherent with each other. This means that if for instance the customer paid for the items or service and did nor cancel the order in due time, then the business process ends in the state "service/items delivered". Otherwise it should end in the state "not delivered" or "items returned", depending on when and how the customer decided to cancel the order.

The first requirement above forces to guarantee (semantic) atomicity for the business processes. A part of guaranteeing this is to guarantee atomicity of the steps by a lower level mechanisms, like usual database transactions. An important subproblem is to guarantee that the states of the business process are stored permanently and that steps involving state changes and messages sent between sites are implemented in an atomic way.

The second requirement can only be achieved by distributed transactions means. Abstractly speaking, it is the question of guaranteeing in a distributed system that a set of nodes agrees on the same value. The usual problems (processing errors, lost messages etc.) must be handled. The peculiarity of the environment is that it is hostile in the sense that the nodes can not necessarily be trusted (there might be malicious customers or merchants). Therefore, the possible hostility must be taken into consideration while designing these mechanisms. For instance, Keltainen Pöorssi does not rely on the customer as a coordinator of the transaction, because the customer might fake the other part (funds transfer) to have happened, even if it had not. Therefore, there is the direct information flow between the bank and the service provider. This makes the structure different from e.g. 2PC protocol, where the coordinator is assumed to be benevolent, respecting the decisions of the subordinates and asking really their votes, instead of faking or guessing votes.

One remedy to the above problems would be that ack or nack would be required from the customer to the shipment announcement. Thus, the merchant would be able to check that the real customer knows about the shipment and really wants it. The customer could also confirm the reception of the items to the merchant. This would alleviate the uncertainty about the success of the delivery to the right customer and thus confirm the goods atomicity aspect. But even the above two additional confirmations would not help very much in the cases where a person would just take another person's credit card information and use it to purchase items. The only information Amazon can easily check is namely the credit card number, the name on it, as well as the expiration date. Everything else can be fabricated. Thus, there is nowhere a real authentication of the person in the current Amazon system.[5]

To guard against these kinds of misuses, an end-to-end authentication feature should be incorporated into the system. A person should be able to identify him- or herself to the merchant, before the orders could be placed and delivery issued. One solution would be to use public and private keys and an infrastructure (Certification Authority) to guarantee the allocation of the keys to persons.

Using both strong authentication mechanisms and distributed transactional mechanisms, security, authentication, and non-repudiation level can be raised much higher than what they are today. On the other hand, authentication combined with distributed transactional mechanism that guarantees distributed atomicity can also be a problem for the smooth running of the business process at the merchant. The degree of autonomy of running the process is reduced, because the customer can stop it by not confirming a step. Confirmations also

---

[5] Basically, the customer address is obtainable from the credit card company, but the delivery address could still deviate from it for many acceptable reasons, like a recent change of residence

reduce the autonomy of the customer, because he or she must issue them. Thus, there is clearly a trade-off between the desired level of security and authentication and the reduction of the degree of autonomy at both sides. How much are the customer and merchants ready to pay for the increased security?

An evident requirement in this context seems to be that the customer should be able to choose the security level and at the same time accept the consequences. It is reasonable to think that the more valuable items are purchased, the higher the need for security and proper authentication. It is much less a problem for a customer if a 10 dollar book is not delivered, but it is a rather big problem if a 100000 dollar car gets charged but never arrives.

Cancelling an Order. Cancellation is a natural part of the business we have been dealing with above. For the (Information Society) services it is not so important, because the service is delivered at the same instance as it is paid. There might be, however, good reasons to entitle a customer to cancel an order for digital goods, too. If a piece of software does not function, the customer should have means to cancel the order.

The cancellation of the delivery of goods is interesting from transactional point of view. The often used term is *compensation* for such a case. In Amazon case the customer is entitled to cancel the order as long as the order has not been moved to the state "shipped". A book can also be returned to the merchant, in which case the merchant should pay back the price — or at least a part of it.

It is worth on noticing that cancelling the order before shipment and after the delivery have significant differences from practical point of view, although in abstract terms the end state of the process would be the same: "The item was not sold and the customer did not pay (almost) anything".

It is mainly the problem of the merchant to organize the cancelling in a smooth way into the business process.

5   Transactional Mechanisms in Mobile E-Commerce Environment

5.1   Relating the Mobile Environment with the Fixed One

What is the difference between a mobile environment and a more traditional network environment? Mobility can be understood in several ways. One can think that a person moves from one physical place to another, but does not carry any mobile equipment with him or her. In this case he or she uses the locally available (fixed) network infrastructure to take actions in the network, including issuing E-commerce transactions.

Assuming that the above mobile person does carry with him or her a piece of personal equipment that facilitates the access to the network resources we come closer to the concept of mobile E-commerce. The most general idea is that a customer can conduct E-commerce at any time at any place using the miniature devices.

Overall, our view is that mobile hand-held devices and the supporting networks are a special access technology to Internet or another backbone network facilitating many services, including E-commerce.

5.2 Authentication and Authorization Issues

The perception of mobility of a person makes evident that authentication and authorization are of paramount importance in the mobile environment. By nature of mobility, authentication of a customer cannot be based in any respect on the physical location or similar criteria. Considering from this perspective the mobile authentication and authorization problem, it does not really change radically whether or not a person carries a piece of equipment or not. The reason is that the current small hand-held devices are rather vulnerable to theft. Thus, basing authentication of a person on the equipment identity or data stored therein is less secure than in the case of a fixed network and fixed workstations (cf. the cookies in the case of Amazon) and should be avoided. For the same reason, authorization of mobile E-commerce transactions should not be blindly and solely based on the device identity of any kind; stealing the device after a proper authentication of the correct user would open a full access to all services for a wrong person. This has also certain ramifications for the transactional services we have been discussing.

We discussed above in Section 4 the need to combine end-to-end authorization of a customer and the merchant in different phases of the E-commerce transaction in order to minimize the probability of undetected failures and fraudulent orders. Authentication of a person should be based on something personal, like finger prints, eyes, etc. Currently, however, the approach is to use some piece of information that is only known by the person to be identified and the system, like Personal Identification Number (PIN) or password. Another approach is to base the identification on something the person possesses and controls, typically a smart card. The latter are typically used together with PINs, because steeling a smart card is not difficult and the mere possession of it must thus not be enough for identification.

Authorization in mobile environment is a more tricky issue than within a fixed environment. Typical general solution is to use private and public key and the corresponding infrastructure (cf. [25]). There are several reasons, why the private key should be kept in the terminal or at least on a device from which it can be automatically read by the terminal: it is a long bit sequence and thus impossible to remember by heart; keeping it on paper would expose it rather easily to other people; typing it in every time it is needed would be very error prone and tedious. In practice, the key should be protected by a much shorter PIN that is only known by the person the secret key is attached to. Thus, using the authorization key would happen in a tight symbiosis with authentication of the user.

One solution to the latter problem is to store the secret key to a SIM card [26]. The operator would be responsible for establishing the link between a person and his or her private and public keys and delivering the SIM card to the right person. This would solve the key distribution problem. Storing the private key on a smart card readable by hand-held terminal makes it possible to generate the digital signatures on which the authentication and non-repudiation can be based. The weak point is that at least currently the access to the SIM card is protected by a PIN of four digits only. The PIN cannot be much longer, because the people could not remember it any more and would use PINs like 1111111.., or paper or other means to memorize it. Thus, too long a PIN would be more vulnerable than a shorter PIN. It remains to be seen, whether there will be more reliable authentication methods that are not based on PINs in the future.

5.3 Mobility versus Legal Basis

The legal basis for dispute handling in ISS case seems to be a bit problematic thing in EU, because it should be based on the applicable law of the customer's residence. The rational behind this is that the customer needs to know only one legislation and can be expected to know best the legislation of his own country. As long as the customer is a citizen of the EU member country, this is not a big issue, because one can easily determine where the customer's permanent residence is. Mobility does not change this consideration.

For non-EU customers coming from abroad, this approach becomes a problem. Especially in the mobile E-commerce performed by non-EU citizens within Europe it is not evident which legislation should be used in dispute handling. It would be very difficult to apply legislation of an arbitrary non-EU country within EU. One solution would be to apply the legislation of that member country, where the order was placed. This is also rather problematic, because the customer might move from one country to another within Europe, while placing an order.

Another evident solution to determine the applicable legislation for mobile non-EU customers trading within the borders would be to use that applicable to the merchant. This would be sound in the sense that all non-EU customers could be treated in the similar manner, no matter whether they are inside or outside of EU while trading with a merchant. This would correspond to the current practice in USA (cf. the Amazon example).

How about taxation? At Amazon the taxes can always be determined, because the delivery address is decisive, no matter where the customer was when the order was placed. Still problems might arise if the Amazon begins to sell digital goods that are delivered to a mobile terminal. The duties are a problem of the customer in Amazon's view. The same view is shared by EU.

In EU, VAT should be paid in some country, if the service or product is consumed within EU. If it is paid in the country of origin, then it does not need to be paid second time. The current approach is that the service provider or merchant is primarily responsible for paying the VAT, an individual customer is not. Individual customers need not pay VAT, if they purchase goods from abroad for their personal use, with some minor exceptions [12]. This also applies to E-commerce.

In general, European Commission pursues a simple, clear and neutral taxation framework, as is stated in [12]:

> Legal certainty enables commerce to be conducted in an environment where the rules are clear and consistent reducing the risks of unforeseen tax liabilities and disputes. Simplicity is necessary to keep the burdens of compliance to a minimum. In that respect the Commission continues to be fully committed to the introduction of the future common VAT system based on taxation at origin and providing for a single country of registration where an operator would both account for and deduct tax in respect of all his EU VAT transactions.
>
> Neutrality means that:
>
> - The consequences of taxation should be the same for transactions in goods and services, regardless of the mode of commerce used or whether delivery is effected on-line or off-line.
>
> - The consequences of taxation should be the same for services and goods whether they are purchased from within or from outside the EU.

Although not likely, there might be states or groups of states where the location of a customer or merchant while placing an order would have implications for the legislative framework applicable to the corresponding transaction. Currently, this would be a problem, because there are no standardized technical means to expose the customer location to applications (although the information about the location at the base station resolution level is known by the network infrastructure). Location determination would be actually a new dimension or level in the atomicity discussed earlier, because it presupposes atomic decision about the applicable legislation framework based on spatial information and its recording, while placing an order. Should the actual location while placing on order - or using a service - have some legal consequences in some part of the world, this would require a rather heavy technical infrastructure to be supported.

5.4   Technical Problems in Supporting Mobile E-Commerce Transactions

We take here the view that the dominant form of mobile E-commerce will be based on miniature, hand-held devices. Keeping this in mind, one can argue that the same or similar E-commerce services as discussed above in Section 3 can be offered to mobile terminals, e.g. to WAP terminals. There is a strong pressure to go into this direction among the banks, mobile equipment manufacturers, and other service providers.

What are the problems? We have discussed the basic problems above, as concerns the security, authentication, authorization etc., and suggested certain transaction-oriented solutions. Mobility does not solve any of the problems discussed above, on the contrary. Mobile environment poses rather a question, how could even the current mechanisms be implemented in the environment.

Currently the hand-held terminals are still more error-prone than stationary work stations. In addition, it is rather common that a mobile terminal looses the network connection. This happens, because the terminals are effectively C-autonomous [35]; the user decides to turn-off the the radio transceiver, the terminal runs out of battery, or simply because the user moves during the transaction processing to a place where there is no coverage. Should the connection be lost during the a service ordering provision transaction, e.g. at Keltainen Pörssi at the critical places described above, it is likely that the customer will loose money. This is because, currently, there is no mechanism guaranteeing delivery atomicity either at the terminal or at the bank server in the case of crash.

It is evident that the states of e.g. such a service provision transaction as discussed above should be logged more carefully at the three sites. Based on the logs, it should be possible to continue the transaction after the terminal has been possibly re-charged and rebooted and the communication capability has been re-established. It is also evident that providing a more resilient service provision than what is offered now at the example bank and service provider requires changes to the current implementation of the services, especially at the bank site. Also, the terminal must store more information about the status of the transaction in order to be able to continue it after a terminal crash or communication failure. This requires some kind of distributed recovery protocol, the exact form of which needs to be investigated.

One evident technical requirement in this context is that the amount of information stored for recovery purposes at the terminal must not be large. Otherwise, the current smallest hand-held terminals could not cope with it. Another requirement is that the algorithms needed to support the transactional mechanism, security and authentication at the terminal should not be overly complicated, i.e. their time and space complexity should be modest.

Which requirements would the above business process-oriented approach discussed in Section 4 pose in the mobile environment? From a mobile device point of view, it might be hard to persistently store the entire state of several long-running transactions. This would, however, be required in practice should the customer want to have several common checkpoints with the merchant's process (confirming the start of the delivery, acknowledging the delivery of the goods). Remembering by heart many pending orders and their status would be too tedious.

How many process variants should be supported at the terminal? For both Amazon and Bokus cases a rather similar mechanism between the terminal and merchant site would be of help when the order is placed. Storing the state of the E-commerce transaction (like ordered/non-shipped, shipped, cancelled) at the terminal would be of benefit, especially if confirmations were used. How this could be technically done in a WAP environment, for instance, is not clear for the moment.[6] Further, whether it is possible to develop only a small set of typical process specifications for the terminals remains to be seen. They should be so

---

[6] The first WAP services are now (11/1999) in use in Finland. The first complaints have also been issued: the operator has charged for the service based on the connection

simple that programming them using WMLScript in WAP environment would be feasible.

Implementing end-to-end authentication and authorization at different phases of the transaction would raise the security level of the mobile E-commerce. It is for further study, whether the SIM card-based authorization technology can easily be used in the context of advanced transactions.

6   Conclusions

In this paper we have analyzed a few real examples and discussed what kinds of problems there are in the current E-commerce. It turned out that from structural point one can distinguish between two-party (customer-merchant) or three-party (customer-merchant-bank/credit card company) E-commerce transactions. It is probable that there might be even more parties involved in the future, when the contents providers step into the stage or the customer has to buy several products from different merchants in order to compile a functioning system.

One of the findings is that the regulatory frameworks seem to be different in Europe and USA and this has certain ramifications for the technology and transactional mechanism that might be considered reasonable in this context. The regulatory frameworks and emerging de-facto standards must be studied further. Depending on how they evolve, it might or might not be possible to design a more or less homogeneous transactional support for mobile E-commerce.

Another conclusion is that transactional mechanism must be closely related with the authentication and authorization mechanism and that the main benefit of using them together is actually to guarantee security and other related properties in the mobile environment. Further, the transactional mechanism and authentication and authorization mechanisms and their combination should be applicable in a flexible way. If the customer does not want to use them, he does not need to. The current systems we reviewed here are more or less lacking these kind of features, but the mobile E-commerce seems to need them.

An important conclusion of this study is that transactional mechanisms are needed in two rather orthogonal directions. On the one hand, the individual workflows implementing the business processes at the merchant and customer (and possibly at the third party like credit card company or bank) should exhibit certain transactional properties, especially (semantic) atomicity and durability. This guarantees that the workflows reach an acceptable end-state in spite of failures. On the other hand, in order to ascertain that both customer, merchant, and possible further parties have the same view on the state of a E-commerce transaction, one needs distributed transaction guarantees, especially distribution atomicity. Based on these lower level goals the more higher goals, like goods atomicity and certified delivery coined in [34], can be achieved.

Mobility seems to pose one genuinely new problem. The location of the terminal at the point of time the order is placed might play a role as concerns the

_____

time, but the customer never got the contents he/she asked for; a typical violation of the above goods atomicity requirement legislation to be applied. It is still open, how this issue will be put aside or solved within the forthcoming regulatory framework(s).

Apart from the above peculiarity, mobile E-commerce is similar to the "fixed" E-commerce. The new issues to be solved are mainly caused by the communication autonomy and miniature size of the hand-held terminals used to facilitate the E-commerce. Authentication and authorization require, for instance, a more careful treatment, because the hand-held terminals can be stolen at any point of time. Authorization should not be based on device identity, session, or similar concepts only, but genuine end-to-end user authentication should be enforced at critical moments.

An important implementation level issue is how to achieve failure resilience in mobile terminals. Another issue is, how the authentication and authorization can be organized in a such a way that stealing a hand-held device would not jeopardize them. At least partial solution to this seems to be a special SIM card containing the private key of a person.

Many aspect are still open in this field. More research and experiments are still needed to find out whether transactional mechanisms are really needed and how they should exactly look in the mobile E-commerce environment. Bluetooth technology[20] will evidently cause again new kind of considerations in this respect while allowing terminals and cash registers to talk directly to each other, also for the purpose of mobile E-commerce.

Acknowledgments

The author wishes to thank the editors of this book for valuable comments on the earlier drafts of the manuscript. The comments, practical findings, and insights gained while compiling other papers with the members of the Multimeetmobile project groups at University of Jyväskylä and Helsinki are highly appreciated. This research was supported by the grant 330/401/99 of the Finnish National Technology Agency.

References

1. Amazon.com. Cancelling Policy. WWW page at:
   www.amazon.com/exec/obidos/subst/help/self-service-cancel-howto.html, 1999.
2. Amazon.com. Legal Notices. WWW page at:
   www.amazon.com/exec/obidos/subst/misc/copyright.html, 1999.
3. M. Bellare, J. A. Garay, R. Hauser, A. Herzberg, H. Krawczyk, M. Steiner, G. Tsudik, E. Van Herreweghen, and M. Waidner. Design, Implementation and Deployment of iKP A Secure Account-based Electronic Payment System. Technical Report 3137, IBM Zurich Laboratory, http://www.zurich.ibm.com/publications/, 1999.
4. European Commission. The Data Protection Directive. Directive 95/46/ec, European Commission, 1995.
5. European Commission. Data Protection in Telecoms. Directive 97/66/ec, European Commission, 1997.
6. European Commission. Distances Selling. Directive 97/7/EC, European Commission, 1997.

7. European Commission. Proposal for a European Parliament and Council Directive on the Harmonization of Certain Aspects of Copyright and Related Rights in the Information Society. Technical Report COM1997:628, European Commission, 1997.
http://158.169.50.70/eur-lex/en/com/reg/en_register_1720.html.

8. European Commission. (Commission Proposal - COM(98)784 final) Amended Proposal – Proposal for a Community Action Plan on Promoting Safer Use of the Internet by Combating Illegal and Harmful Content on Global Networks. Directive Proposal COM(98)784, European Commission, 1998.
http://158.169.50.70/eur-lex/en/com/reg/en_register_132060.html.

9. European Commission. Directive 98/48/EC of the European Parliament and of the Council of 20 July 1998 Amending Directive 98/34/EC Laying Down a Procedure for the Provision of Information in the Field of Technical Standards and Regulations. Directive 98/48/EC, European Union, 1998.
http://158.169.50.70/eur-lex/en/lif/dat/1998/en_398L0048.html.

10. European Commission. Directive on Legal Protection of Services Based on/Consisting of Conditional Access. Directive 98/84/EC, European Commission, 1998.

11. European Commission. E-Commerce and Indirect Taxation. Directive 98/374/ec, European Commission, 1998.

12. European Commission. E-Commerce and Indirect Taxation: Communication by the Commission to the Council of Ministers, the European Parliament and to the Economic And Social Committee: COM(98)374final; 17/6/98. Communication of the commission, European Commission, 1998.
http://158.169.51.200/ecommerce/legal/taxation.html.

13. European Commission. Proposal for a Council Decision on the Approval, on Behalf of the European Community, of the WIPO Copyright Treaty and the WIPO Performances and Phonograms Treaty. Proposal 598PC0249, European Union, 1998.
http://158.169.50.70/eurlex/en/com/reg/en_register_1720.html.

14. European Commission. COM(1999)/427 Final. Amended Proposal for a European Parliament and Council Directive on Certain Legal Aspects of E-Commerce in the Internal Market. Technical Report COM(99)427, European Commission, 1999.
http://158.169.50.70/eurlex/en/com/reg/en_register_132060.html.

15. European Commission. Directive on a Community Framework for Electronic Signatures. Draft directive, European Commission, 1999.
http://europa.eu.int/eur-lex/en/com/pdf/1999/com1999_0626en01.pdf.

16. European Commission. Directive on Copyright and Related Rights in the Information Society. Draft directive, European Commission, 1999.

17. European Commission. Directive on Electronic Money. Draft directive, European Commission, 1999.
http://europa.eu.int/eur-lex/en/com/dat/1998/en_598PC0461_01.html.

18. European Commission. Regulatory Framework for Distances Selling of Financial Services. Draft directive, European Commission, 1999.

19. A. K. Elmagarmid, editor. *Database Transaction Models For Advanced Applications*. Morgan Kaufmann Publishers, 1992.

20. Bluetooth Forum. Bluetooth Overview. www.bluetooth.com, 1999.

21. Wireless Application Protocol Forum. WAP Overview. www.wapforum.com, 1999.

22. J. Heikkilä, A. Tsalgatidou, J. Veijalainen, and J. Laine. Requirements for Electronic Commerce Transactions in a Mobile Computing Environment. Manuscript, Submitted for Publication, 1999.

23. Amazon.com Inc. Your Privacy. WWW page at:
www.amazon.com/exec/obidos/subst/misc/policy/privacy.html, 1999.
24. E. Liikanen and R. Verrue. Sessions on Regulation in a Liberalized and Converging Environment and on Scenarios for Business in the Digital Economy. Sessions at IST'99 Conference, Helsinki, Nov. 22–24, 1999; http://www.ist99.fi, 1999.
25. L. Loeb. *Secure Electronic Transactions; Introduction and Technical Reference.* Artech House Publishers, 1998.
26. Sonera Oyj. Mobile Commerce.
http://www.sonera.fi/smarttrust/mobile_commerce/our_vision.html, 1999.
27. M. Papazoglou, P. Ribbers, and A. Tsalgatidou. Integrated Value Chains and their Implications from a Business and Technology Standpoint. *DSS journal — Special Issue on E-commerce*, 2000. To appear.
28. European Parliament. Opinion of the Economic and Social Committee on the Communication from the Commission on Electronic commerce and indirect taxation (COM(1998) 374 final); adopted at the plenary session of 9-10/09/98, OJ C 407 of 28/12/98. Opinion of the european parliament on directive ec/98/374, European Parliament, 1998.
http://158.169.51.200/ecommerce/OJ/1998/1998C407/pe223_962_en.pdf.
29. European Parliament and Council. Report on the Proposal for a European Parliament and Council Directive on Certain Legal Aspects of Electronic Commerce in the Internal Market. Report DOC-EN/RR/377/377189, European Commission, 1998.
30. B. Salmelin. Electronic Commerce:Europe at the Forefront of the Global Digital Economy. Transparencies, 1999.
http://e-conomy.berkeley.edu/pubs/conf/deip/salmelin/.
31. H. Schuldt, A. Popovici, and H.-J. Schek. Execution Guarantees in Electronic Commerce Payments. In *this volume*, pages 198–207, 1999.
32. Semper. Secure Electronic Marketplace for Europe. http://www.semper.org, October 1999.
33. D. Tygar. Atomicity versus Anonymity: Distributed Transactions for Electronic Commerce. In A. Gupta, O. Shmueli, and J. Widom, editors, *Proc. of the 24st Int. Conf. on Very Large Data Bases, VLDB'98, Ney York City, August 24–27, 1998*, pages 1–12, Morgan Kaufmann Publishers, 1998.
34. J. D. Tygar. Atomicity in Electronic Commerce. In *Proc. of the 15th Annual ACM Symposium on Principles of Distributed Computing, May 23–26, 1996, Philadelphia, PA, USA*, pages 8–26, ACM Press, 1996.
35. J. Veijalainen. *Transaction Concepts in Autonomous Database Environments.* R. Oldenbourg Verlag/GMD, 1990.
36. J. Veijalainen, F. Eliassen, and B. Holtkamp. The S-transaction Model. In A. K. Elmagarmid, editor, *Database Transaction Models for Advanced Applications*, pages 467–513, Morgan Kaufmann Publishers, 1992.

Transactions and Electronic Commerce

Heiko Schuldt and Andrei Popovici

Database Research Group
Institute of Information Systems
ETH Zentrum, 8092 Zürich, Switzerland
{schuldt,popovici}@inf.ethz.ch

Abstract. Electronic Commerce is a rapidly growing area that is gaining more and more importance not only in the interrelation of businesses (business–to–business Electronic Commerce) but also in the everyday consumption of individuals performed via the Internet (business–to–customer Electronic Commerce). Since Electronic Commerce is a very interdisciplinary area, it has a lot of impacts to various communities. The goal of this paper is to identify and to summarize the impact of Electronic Commerce from a database transaction point of view and to highlight open problems in transaction management arising in Electronic Commerce applications by reflecting the discussions of the working group "Transactions and Electronic Commerce" held at the TDD Workshop.

1 Motivation

The exchange of electronic data between companies has been an important issue in business interactions for quite a while. However, the recent proliferation of the Internet together with the rapid propagation of personal computers led to an enormous diversification and an ubiquity of businesses performed electronically.

Since various participants, all having different requirements, operating in different, distributed and heterogeneous environments, etc., are encompassed in Electronic Commerce interactions, a couple of problems arise in this context. This affects communication infrastructures as well as business models and cryptography but also aspects of information management, information integration, and transaction processing. In the latter case, fair interactions between all participants in the presence of potentially malicious parties, or the enforcement of complex business processes with certain transactional execution guarantees, all to be supported in an holistic way by an appropriate Electronic Commerce infrastructure are examples of problems to be dealt with in order to provide feasible solutions.

The paper summarizes the working group "Transactions and Electronic Commerce" held at the TDD'99 workshop[1] and points out the benefits transactions

---

[1] The participants of this working group were (in alphabetical order): N. Aoumeur, H. Balsters, A. Berztiss, B. de Brock, A. Fent, S. Gançarski, G. Guerrini, E. Kindler, C. León, K. Nagi, J. Pinto, A. Popovici, E. Rodriguez, G. Saake, M. Saheb, R. Schenkel, K.-D. Schewe, H. Schuldt, K. Schwarz, C. Türker, J. Veijalainen, and C.-A. Wichert.

G. Saake, K. Schwarz, and C. Türker (Eds.): TDD '99, LNCS 1773, pp. 225–230, 2000.

can offer protocols and applications in Electronic Commerce but also the open problems that still exist in this area. In Section 2, the impact of the Internet for Electronic Commerce is discussed. Section 3 generalizes the idea of distributed transactions by addressing transactional workflows. In order to cope with the special requirements of Electronic Commerce, agent-based systems and architectures (Section 4), secure transactions (Section 5), and legal issues (Section 6) are discussed. Finally, a summary and conclusion is given in Section 7.

2 Internet Transactions

One important characteristics of most Electronic Commerce interactions is that they take place via the Internet. Therefore, atomic commitment is an important requirement for distributed Electronic Commerce transactions. When executing transactions over the Internet, heterogeneity and the lack of transactional communication protocols have to be considered. Unlike traditional two phase commit (2PC) [3] solutions, this limits the applicability of common approaches such as the XA application programming interface of the X/Open standard [3] and necessitates further efforts.

The Transaction Internet Protocol (TIP) [4] proposed by Tandem and Microsoft aims to overcome the above mentioned problems in Internet transactions. Therefore, it is also highly appropriate for Electronic Commerce applications. The main idea of the TIP is the *Two Pipe Model*, the separation of application communication (which can take place, for instance, via non–transactional protocols such as HTTP) and communication at transaction manager level.

Although atomic commitment is an important building block in Electronic Commerce transactions, it is considered not to be sufficient. Additionally, dynamic aspects and more flexible mechanisms for ensuring the correctness of complete Electronic Commerce workflow processes (transactional workflows) are required.

3 Transactional Workflows

Interactions in Electronic Commerce can be characterized by their well-defined structure but also by their inherent complexity and their long duration. Workflow processes are thus an appropriate means to encompass all dependencies within Electronic Commerce interactions. As identified in [11], transactional properties are crucial requirements in order to make these processes viable for Electronic Commerce applications. These transactional properties have to consider both the correctness of single processes but also the correctness of concurrent executions of processes when accessing shared resources (e.g., as addressed in the transactional process management approach [7] which is also exploited for business-to-business Electronic Commerce applications [1]). Important aspects in this area are the exploitation of the flexibility offered by workflow technology with respect to failure handling by alternative executions but also the ability to be able to prove the correctness of processes specified.

Payment processes are an important application of transactional workflows in Electronic Commerce [8]. However, more general approaches covering further phases of trade interactions such as post-sales or negotiation are required in order to provide complete and holistic solutions [5].

4 Agents and Transactions

Agent–based systems are widely considered to be an appropriate means to cope with the ever–growing complexity of large information systems by decoupling them into small and easily manageable components, the so-called *agents*. Especially in Electronic Commerce applications, agents are seen as an important means to support the different participants such as customers or (information) brokers.

However, although agent–based systems may be characterized by the mobility of single components and the dynamics emerging by continuously adding and removing components, transactional properties for agent interactions are crucial. To this end, some problems in the intersection of agent technology and transaction management have to be addressed:

- The correctness of single agents —in spite of their hierarchical structure where decisions and plans are made at different levels of abstraction— is a basic prerequisite for the correctness of agent–based systems. Agent architectures and agent implementations therefore have to be enhanced by appropriate transactional support (*intra–agent* transactions) such as the multilevel transaction approach presented in [6].
- Additionally, concurrency in agent interactions has to be dealt with. Therefore, *inter–agent* transactions are required in order to ensure the overall correctness in agent–based systems while considering at the same time the dynamics of these systems.
- Finally, in the context of transaction management, agent technology may be useful to "databaseify" components and applications [12,9].

5 Secure Transactions

According to the discussion of the previous sections, all Electronic Commerce application scenarios encompass transactional interactions implemented either by pre-defined (and eventually dynamically modified) processes or, in some cases, on an ad-hoc basis (according to the needs of the respective business-case, eventually implemented by appropriate agents, or to the local legislation). Firstly, cryptographic mechanisms have to be tightly coupled to all kinds of information exchange in Electronic Commerce transactions in order to to integrate authorization and authentication in a seamless way (see, for instance, the SEMPER project [10]). Secondly, higher guarantees then just atomicity and isolation are required: it is necessary to protect sensible information and to ensure that no participant can cheat the others.

For the latter purpose, an extended notion of transaction would be needed. This transaction model should use non-repudiable protocol messages in order to prove (in case of failure) which parties corrupted the protocol. Moreover, additional information should be added to the protocol to enable certain trusted participants to check the correctness of a commit decision.

By using such a model, scenarios like the ones mentioned above can be implemented and tested much easier. Additionally, since the security of the customer is moved into the transactional protocol, a much wider area of applications can profit of using such a model.

Of course, there are several (justified) questions which arise in such an extended model:

- Which should be the right formalism to describe such *secure* transactions? Without a formal description for a secure transaction, automatic checking of correctness and security requirements would not be possible.
- If trusted parties are encompassed in the secure transactions, which participants, and under what conditions, are to act as such parties.
- Is it possible to ensure anonymity of certain participants in secure transactions?

6   Legal Issues

There is no secret that the laws and business regulations are not the same in different countries or national communities. Such differences, as for instance between the USA and Europe, sometimes seem to be negligible. However, they may have a strong impact on the Electronic Commerce software developed on both sides of the Atlantic. In Europe, for instance, customers have to pay *after* they receive their service, in USA they have to pay *prior* to the receipt. This leads to customer-centric Electronic Commerce scenarios in Europe and merchant-centric ones in the USA.

The solution in these area would be Electronic Commerce frameworks, with hot-spots reflecting the legislation differences. This would permit homogenize the landscape of Electronic Commerce solutions and would lead to a higher degree of integration of companies on the two continents. However, in order to be able to do this, a better understanding of the concrete legislation differences as well as a clear classification of such scenarios is needed.

In addition to the different business models exploited, varying taxes applied in different countries or states also reinforce the heterogeneity problem encountered in Electronic Commerce applications and necessitate appropriate support in coherent solutions.

In certain cases, persistence of data gathered during Electronic Commerce transactions is required in order to fulfill legal regulations associated with the requirement to a posteriori verify the fairness of transactions. However, in this context, persistence also raises ethical problems in terms of privacy and the extent this data can subsequently be exploited for.

7   Conclusion

Taking a close look at Electronic Commerce applications, it becomes clear that transactional execution guarantees for the diverse interactions of all involved participants are an important prerequisite.

The following topics have been identified as key properties of Electronic Commerce solutions form a transaction point of view:

Language Support (Specification):
An appropriate higher-order specification language (e.g., like transaction logic [2]) is needed to model the interactions and dependencies in Electronic Commerce transactions as well as to add the additional properties these transactions are supposed to have (for instance w.r.t. security), thus integrating all essential aspects of Electronic Commerce transactions at specification level.

Validation:
Based on the specification of Electronic Commerce transactions, validation mechanisms should be added to the modeling environment in order to be able to formally prove the overall correctness, the absence of contradictions, or to validate certain properties of whatever transaction has been specified.

Electronic Commerce Infrastructure:
Aside of specification tools, support for the execution of Electronic Commerce transactions, enforcing all specified properties, is required. In order to support different business models, different interaction paradigms, etc., a modular, framework–oriented infrastructure for the generation of Electronic Commerce transactions should be provided. This would offer the possibility to plug together pre-defined building blocks; the advantage of this approach is that already validated ("certified") components could extensively be reused. Additionally, a tight link to the modeling environment by automatically transforming a specification into an executable Electronic Commerce transaction would complete this effort.

All viable Electronic Commerce systems should offer the above mentioned characteristics in some way. However, in order to provide feasible and coherent systems and tools for Electronic Commerce applications being fit for commercial use, collaboration with other communities is required since —aside of transactional properties— a variety of other aspects not discussed in this paper have also to be considered.

Acknowledgments

The authors would like to thank Can Türker for his comments on an early draft of this working group summary and all active participants of the working group "Transactions and Electronic Commerce" for their contributions.

References

1. G. Alonso, U. Fiedler, C. Hagen, A. Lazcano, H. Schuldt, and N. Weiler. WISE: Business to Business E-Commerce. In *Proc. of the 9th Int. Workshop on Research Issues in Data Engineering, Information Technology for Virtual Enterprises, RIDE-VE'99, March 1999, Sydney, Australia*, pages 132–139, IEEE Computer Society Press, 1999.
2. A. Bonner and M. Kifer. *Logic Programming for Database Transactions*, chapter 5, pages 117–166. Kluwer Academic Publishers, 1998.
3. J. Gray and A. Reuter. *Transaction Processing: Concepts and Techniques*. Morgan Kaufmann, 1993.
4. J. Lyon, K. Evans, and J. Klein. Transaction Internet Protocol Version 3.0. Network Working Group, Request for Comments (RFC 2371), July 1998. http://www.ietf.org/html.charters/tip-charter.html.
5. P. Muth, J. Weissenfels, and G. Weikum. What Workflow Technology can do for Electronic Commerce. In *Proc. of the EURO-MED NET Conference, March 1998, Nicosia, Cyprus*, 1998.
6. K. Nagi and P. Lockemann. An Implementation Model for Agents with Layered Architecture in a Transactional Database Environment. In *Proc. of the 1st Int. Bi-Conference Workshop on Agent-Oriented Information Systems, AOIS'99, June 1999, Heidelberg, Germany*, 1999.
7. H. Schuldt, G. Alonso, and H.-J. Schek. Concurrency Control and Recovery in Transactional Process Management. In *Proc. of the 18th ACM SIGACT-SIGMOD-SIGART Symposium on Principles of Database Systems, PODS'99, May 31–June 2, 1999, Philadelphia, Pennsylvania*, pages 316–326, ACM Press, 1999.
8. H. Schuldt, A. Popovici, and H.-J. Schek. Execution Guarantees in Electronic Commerce Payments. In *this volume*, pages 198–207, 1999.
9. H. Schuldt, H.-J. Schek, and G. Alonso. Transactional Coordination Agents for Composite Systems. In *Proc. of the 3rd Int. Database Engineering and Applications Symposium, IDEAS'99, August 1999, Montréal, Canada*, pages 321–331, 1999.
10. SEMPER. SEMPER: Secure Electronic Market Place for Europe, 1999. http://www.semper.org.
11. J. Veijalainen. Transactions in Mobile Electronic Commerce. In *this volume*, pages 208–229, 1999.
12. A. Wolski and J. Veijalainen. 2PC Agent Method: Achieving Serializability in Presence of Failures in a Heterogeneous Multidatabase. In N. Rishe, S. Navathe, and D. Tal, editors, *Proc. of the Int. Conf. on Databases, Parallel Architectures, and Their Applications (PARBASE-90), Miami Beach, Florida*, pages 321–330, IEEE Computer Society Press, 1990.

Transactional Computation: Overview and Discussion

Alfs T. Berztiss[1,2]

[1] University of Pittsburgh, Pittsburgh PA 15260, USA
[2] SYSLAB, University of Stockholm, Sweden

Abstract. The concept of a transaction, highly significant in the context of data bases, is broadened to make it refer to any atomic operation that changes the state of a software system or its environment, or initiates a control action. This leads us to consider software systems as composed of transactional and procedural computations. We discuss the specification of transactional software, and introduce a mechanism for linking transactions into processes. We also raise several issues relating to transactional computing that were the basis for discussion at the workshop, and include comments by participants.

1 Introduction

For some time there has been a realization that some computations are fundamentally different from others. For example, Harel [10] talks of reactive systems and transformational systems, where reactive systems are driven, at least to some extent, by external events. Wegner [27] distinguishes between interactive and algorithmic computation, and interactive computation is investigated in some detail by Kurki-Suonio and Mikkonen [14]. It is also being understood that different modes of computation may be needed for a single application. Thus, Stonebraker *et al* [24] suggested quite a while back that procedures should be introduced into data bases. This suggestion has evolved into the active data base concept (see, e.g., [16]). The role that transactions play in information systems is studied in [25,2]. Workflow systems are particularly dependent on transactions [18,11]. Our purpose here is to explore these developments.

We propose to group computations into two classes, transactional and procedural, where a software system is likely to contain components belonging to both classes. In so doing we shall arrive at an interpretation of a transaction that is both broader and narrower than the one given to it by the data base community. By introducing the two-way partition we identify transactional and procedural computation as two distinct foci for research. However, our primary purpose is to investigate the nature of transactional computation, and to define a number of discussion topics. We hope that this will contribute to a closer interaction and cooperation of researchers, particularly those studying information systems and data bases.

G. Saake, K. Schwarz, and C. Türker (Eds.): TDD '99, LNCS 1773, pp. 231–245, 2000.

Section 2 is an examination of the differences between transactional and procedural computation. In Section 3 we introduce our interpretation of a transaction, and discuss how queries fit into our framework. Sections 4 and 5 describe an approach to the specification of transactions. In Section 6 we introduce a number of topics that were the basis for a discussion session at Schloss Dagstuhl, and comments by participants form the main contribution of this section.

2   Two Modes of Computation

Looking back at the history of computing, the earliest computations were simple transformations of inputs into outputs. Soon there arose the realization that data files could be preserved from one instance of a computation to another, and that different applications could make use of the same file. Operating systems were soon providing file management systems, and separate data base management systems arose. What characterizes this trend is the evolution of persistent memory: from no persistent memory at all, to rather rigid data files, to highly complex data bases. Persistent memory is one characteristic of transactional computation, but the more important characteristic is that transactional computation brings about changes in this persistent memory.

Persistent memory is irrelevant for procedural computation. There the concern is with a transformation of an input into an output. Let the transformation be effected by a device F that accepts an input x and produces an output $f(x)$. One example is the cosine function, which, given angle x, produces $cos(x)$. Of course, both x and $f(x)$ can be composite data elements. Now, quite often the input x will be picked up from a data base, and the result $f(x)$ deposited in a data base, but as concerns F, it is immaterial where the inputs come from, or what happens to outputs. Procedural computation obeys what we shall call I/O semantics, i.e., the specification of such a computation has to describe the output, and indicate how the output is related to the input. Time is irrelevant.

Transactional computation obeys state-transition semantics. Invariants describe valid states of a system. They may also indicate impermissible state transitions. For example, we may have a situation in which borrowers are not permitted to borrow books from a library if they owe money to the library. Then a state in which a borrower holds four books and owes money is valid, and so is the state in which the borrower holds five books and owes money, but not a transition from the first state to the second. In such a case the borrowing transaction can be equipped with a precondition, which, if not satisfied, stops further borrowing: $Owes(borr) = 0$. An alternative view, adapted from [9], considers a state space U, and defines a transaction to be a member of a state change relation $R \subseteq U \times U$, i.e., the pair $< S, S' >$, where S and S' are members of U. A constraint on transactions can then be defined as an invariant:

$$\forall < S, S' > \in R : S.Owes(borr) \rightarrow S'.HasOut(borr) \leq S.HasOut(borr),$$

where $HasOut(borr)$ returns the number of books being held by $borr$. Still another approach is to define an invariant in terms of temporal logic, which introduces a further difference between the two modes of computation: time can be important in transactional computation.

Temporal logic has been used extensively in specification (see, e.g., [13,17,23]), and it is well suited when there is no need to introduce real time, such as for precedence ordering of tasks. It has even been claimed that real time has no place in specifications [26]. However, sometimes it is necessary to deal with real time even in early requirements stages, such as when government regulations set strict time limits on reporting obligations by banks. Temporal logic, despite its elegance, need not then be the best approach.

A problem can in general be addressed in different ways. The simplest solution is usually purely transactional, from which we can advance to solutions in which there is an increasing dependence on procedures. We illustrate this by a simple example: a date and place are to be selected for a meeting, and participants are to be registered for the meeting.

At the lowest level a steering committee selects a date and place for the meeting, and an information system merely performs registration transactions. At the next higher level the steering committee selects a date, but now considers several places for the meeting. A procedure selects the place for which the travel costs of the participants are minimized. A third solution is obtained in stages. In the first stage the steering committee polls prospective participants, asking for preferred dates and places, with the preferences ranked or given numerical weights. An algorithm then selects a time and place that maximizes an objective function. Our example shows that an information system may have to allow both transactional and procedural computations.

Such refinement of a design is not limited to information systems. Consider a controller for a set of elevators in a large building. Suppose that a person on floor 5 requests service by pressing the UP-button. The simplest, purely transactional design puts floor 5 on the up-section of the pick-up agenda of every elevator, and all elevators will stop at this floor. The next design, although more complex, is still purely transactional: once an upward moving elevator stops at floor 5, this floor is removed from the relevant agenda of every elevator. The design becomes more elaborate and partly procedural when scheduling algorithms are added in — they are to improve efficiency by moving empty elevators to strategically selected holding floors and by selecting specific elevators for the pick-up of riders. Efficiency is improved still further by fine tuning of this design when the actual usage history of the elevators becomes available.

3   Transactions Redefined

In traditional data base applications a transaction is a data base update or a query evaluation. We shall both broaden this interpretation and make it narrower. The broadening allows "updates" to relate not just to a data base, but also to the environment in which a software system may be embedded. The narrowing excludes query processing.

We regard the processing of a query as a typical procedural task. First, it does not bring about a state change of the system. Second, it obeys I/O semantics — the input is a data base and a predicate defining a result the user is interested in, the output is the result, and the computation consists of operations applied to the data base to produce the result. Moreover, at a sufficiently high level of abstraction, there are cases in which it is immaterial whether a query will refer to a data base or be evaluated by an algorithmic procedure. Suppose one is interested in the times of sunrise for Magdeburg in the year 2000. One approach would be to list the 366 entries in a table, and to look up the table. The other would be to evaluate the sunrises by means of an algorithm.

The difference between updates and queries is fundamental. In updating, i.e., changing the state of a system, there must be a system to update, and it must be possible to describe states of the system. Thus, if I am adding sunrises for the year 2001 to my year-2000 system, I must point to a specific system that is to be augmented, and I must know how this system determines its responses. However, when a user puts a query to this system, there should be no need for the user to know whether the response is obtained by means of look-up or algorithm. Indeed, if I need the sunrise time for Magdeburg for September 18, 2000, I do not necessarily have to go to my system. I could also try to get this information by means of Internet search. Of course, with existing query systems, such as SQL, a detailed knowledge of a data base is needed.

Thus, query evaluation follows precisely the procedural model: input x (the query)is processed by device F (the query processing system), resulting in $f(x)$ (the answer to the query). A control action seems to be conceptually similar: the system receives an input x from a sensor; a device F determines a response $f(x)$, which is conveyed to an actuator. The point here is that a dynamic response, i.e., a change imposed on a controlled system, is to be made only if F detects a change in the controlled system. This means that F must be able to refer to earlier sensor readings, which means in turn that some kind of data base, however rudimentary, must be maintained, and that the data in this data base undergo changes. It should be kept in mind that differences between information systems and control systems are vanishing — in which category would one put programmed stock market trading by a mutual fund?

This effect suggests that the interpretation of the concept of transaction should be quite broad. A control system is embedded in a host environment, and its purpose is to change the state of this environment. Just as a transaction of an information system changes the state of a data base, so a transaction of a control system affects the state of the device or system of devices under its control, and a transaction executed by a programmed trading system affects the state of the portfolio held by the mutual fund. But there are differences. Most transformations of information systems are initiated by users, and most transactions of systems that control devices are initiated by the systems themselves in response to sensor inputs. Such differences will be discussed in greater detail in the next section.

Note also that research on active data bases deals with the introduction of aspects of information systems into data bases, thus reducing the distinction between the two. There remain concerns that relate purely to data bases, such as query optimization and data base locking, and concerns that relate purely to information systems, such as enterprise analysis. However, the two fields have much in common, and an in-depth study of the two modes of computation as they relate to information systems should be a joint undertaking of data base and information systems researchers and developers.

4   Specification of Transactions

Let us now take a closer look at transactions. We consider a transaction to be an atomic operation that is initiated by a user, initiated by the system itself, or initiated by a user after being prompted by the system to do so. Let us call the three types user transactions, system transactions, and prompted transactions, respectively. The withdrawal of money from a bank account by a customer is a user transaction, but an automatic monthly salary deposit into the account, because it requires no intervention by people, is a system transaction. For an example of a prompted transaction we turn to the refereeing of conference papers. The system should have the knowledge that a paper needs referees. Hence, after the details of a submitted paper are entered into the conference data base, the system is able to prompt the chairperson of the program committee that referees are needed, but the actual referee selection is left to the chairperson.

An important concern in defining specifications relates to constraints. In Section 2 we discussed the example of a library that stops further borrowing when money is owed. This can be expressed as a system invariant or as a precondition attached to the borrowing transaction. Our preference is for the latter because such preconditions are nearly always easier to write and to understand than system invariants. The format of the specification of a transaction is thus to allow for preconditions. It also has to allow for data base changes ("data conditions"), and, as we shall discuss in the next section, there has to be a mechanism for chaining transactions together into a process ("signals"). Note that there are two types of signals: N-signals are raised in the normal case, i.e., when the preconditions are true; E-signals are raised when preconditions are false. In the latter case the data conditions are ignored, and the signals invoke an exception handler. A schematic format for the specification of a transaction is thus:

```
TRANSACTION Name(Inputs) ;
    PRECONDITIONS Predicates ;
    DATACONDITIONS Predicates ;
    N-SIGNALS ;
    E-SIGNALS ;
ENDTRANSACTION;
```

Let us return to the library example. The specification of the borrowing transaction under this format is

TRANSACTION $Borrowing(borr, book)$;
   PRECONDITIONS $HasOut(borr) < 6$; $Owes(borr) = 0$;
   DATACONDITIONS $Borrower'(book) = borr$;
     $HasOut'(borr) = HasOut(borr) + 1$;
     $State'(book) = $ borrowed;
     $ReturnDate'(book) = DateNow + BorrPeriod$;
   E-SIGNALS
     $HasOut(borr) \geq 6 \rightarrow (LimitExceeded)$ON;
     $Owes(borr) > 0 \rightarrow (MoneyOwed)$ON;
ENDTRANSACTION;

For simplicity we assume all data to be in the form of sets or functions. This allows great flexibility in defining preconditions: a function value may come from a data base, it may be computed by means of an algorithm, or it can be obtained from an external Internet site. Here there are two preconditions. The function $HasOut$ tells, for each borrower, how many books are currently out to this borrower. This number may not exceed 6. The function $Owes$ returns, for each borrower, the amount of money the borrower owes to the library. The functions of the data conditions are necessarily mutable. Hence they have to be stored as entries in a data base, and data conditions define data base changes: the value of function $Borrower$ for $book$ after this transaction (indicated by a prime) will be $borr$; the value of function $HasOut$ for $borr$ after the transaction will be its value before the transaction increased by 1. The state of the book will be "borrowed", and the book is to be returned a certain number of days after today's date. Signals are used to send out messages that facilitate the combination of transactions into processes. Here we are dealing with an isolated transaction, so that there are no normal-case signals.

5   Transactions and Processes

Nearly every computer program implements some process, but there is great variety in the interpretation of what is meant by a process. A fairly extensive search through software engineering textbooks revealed that most did not have process in the index. Where they did, process was interpreted as something that converts an input into an output, or as a bubble in a data flow diagram, or as something that results in a software system. In [7] we define a business process as an ordered collection of tasks that is to achieve a value-adding objective within a finite time interval. To allow for control processes as well, particularly continuous processes, this definition should be generalized: a process is an ordered collection of tasks that is to achieve some objective. This basic definition can be expanded and elaborated — for one such elaboration see p.19 of [18].

   A definition is important because organizations such as business enterprises are increasingly being defined in terms of processes rather than their organizational structures. Davenport [8] among others, considers this a basic characteristic of business reengineering. Moreover, Davenport argues convincingly that the management of the data on which a process is based should be the responsibility of the manager of the process. This seems to go against the philosophy of enterprise-wide data bases, but does not really do so. There can still be a central data base, but the transactions that effect changes in this data base are to be defined by the designers of the software systems supporting the individual business processes.

A very simple instance of a process arises with the library example of Section 4. For all borrowed books that have become overdue, i.e., with yesterday's return date, the book is to be marked overdue, and a message is to be sent to the delinquent borrower.

ACTION;
    @(08:15:)::FORALL($b \in State^{-1}$(borrowed)):
        $ReturnDate(b) < DateNow \rightarrow$
        ($MarkOverdue(b)$, REMIND("Send out late notice": b));
ENDACTION;

TRANSACTION $MarkOverdue(book)$;
    DATACONDITIONS $State'(book)$ = overdue;
ENDTRANSACTION;

At 8:15 every morning (the bare colon after the 15 tells that the clock to be used here is to have a resolution of one minute; 08:15:00 would require a clock with resolution of one second) every element of the set defined by the inverse of *State* with respect to "borrowed", i.e., the set of all books that are currently borrowed, is to be examined. If the return date shows that the book is overdue, then a system transaction is invoked that is to change the state of the book to "overdue", and a reminder is issued telling that a late notice regarding the book is to be sent out. Knowing b, a librarian can find out the name and address of the delinquent borrower, and the librarian is expected to send out the notice. This step could, of course, be easily automated.

It is important to note that an action cannot define a data base change. Conversely, all time-related effects are confined to actions, and so is everything relating to task coordination.

Our transaction-action model was first introduced in our specification language SF — for a brief introduction and earlier references see [7], but there a transaction is called an event, and the actions of this paper are called transactions. Actions can be started by a signal, or by a calendar or clock, and the initiation of a transaction by an action may be delayed. It is also possible to perform periodic monitoring of a system, and to initiate a transaction when the system is found to be in a particular state.

An entire process composed of our transactions and actions can be represented by a Petri net (actually a slightly modified time Petri net — for time Petri nets see [4]). In this net a transaction is represented by a place, a signal by a token, and an action by a subnet composed of places and transitions. This provides actions with formal semantics.

Space limitations prevent the presentation of the full SF syntax, but we are including the productions that relate to actions. Many formalisms for connecting transactions have been devised; two based on finite state machines are discussed in [10,2]. However, the partitioning of transactions into user, system, and prompted transactions, where system and prompted transactions are the responsibility of actions, is unique to our approach. So is the introduction of time constraints and delays, which can be expressed as time intervals rather than sharp values, with this feature having sound semantics based on time Petri nets.

<Action>::=	ACTION [<ActionId>];
	<Activator>::[<ActPart>]*
	ENDACTION;
<Activator>::=	<SigConstr>[<Delay>] ⋄ <TConstr>
<SigConstr>::=	ON(<Signal> [,<Signal>]*)OFF
<Signal>::=	<SigId>[(Exp [,<Exp>]*)]
<Delay>::=	DELAY (<TimeExp> [,<TimeExp>])
<TConstr>::=	@ (<TimeExp> [,<TimeExp>]) [: <SigConst>]
<ActPart>::=	[<BoolExp>: ⋄ <Delay>: ⋄ <SigConstr>: ⋄ <Iterator>:]*
	<PrimAct> ⋄ (<PrimAct> [,<PrimAct>]*)]+;
<Iterator>::=	FORALL(<Id>∈ <SetExp>)
<PrimAct>::=	<TransInvoc> ⋄ <Prompt> ⋄ <Reminder>
<TransInvoc>::=	<TransId> [(<Exp> [,<Exp>]*)]
<Prompt>::=	PROMPT(<TransId> [(<Exp> [,<Exp>]*)])
<Reminder>::=	REMIND(" <Textexpr>" [:<Exp> [,<Exp>]*])

Notation: Square brackets indicate that the item enclosed in the brackets is optional. If square brackets are followed by the symbol *, then the enclosed item may be present zero or more times. The symbol ⋄ indicates alternation, e.g., production A ::= B ⋄ C indicates that A may be rewritten as B or as C, and [B ⋄ C]* stands for any number of Bs and any number of Cs, written in any order. All syntactic categories whose names end with Id (for Identifier) or Exp (for Expression) are left undefined. The vocabulary consists of terminals denoted by these syntactic categories, those symbols in the productions that consist of capital letters alone (e.g., ACTION, OFF), and the nine symbols in the braces: { ( ) , : ; ∈ @ " " }. Time expressions are discussed in detail in [5].

We explain the structure of actions by means of an example. In order to bring in nearly all the features of the language, the example is much more complex than any action one will ever need to define in practice.

```
ACTION Sample;
    @(8:00:, 9:00:): ON(SigA, SigB(Switch, SetX))OFF::
        Switch: DELAY(*15*, *30*): ON(SigA)OFF: (TransA, TransB);
        FORALL(x ∈ SetX): PROMPT(TransC (x, _));
        REMIND(" Send out papers to reviewers ");
        DELAY(4*0*): REMIND(" Have papers been sent to reviewers? ");
ENDACTION;
```

Action *Sample* is initiated by a clock (with resolution of one minute) between 8:00 and 9:00 in the morning. If at this time signals *SigA* and *SigB* are both on, they are switched off, and four ActParts are considered. If the signals are not both on, nothing further happens, and, if one of the signals is on, it remains in this state. If the boolean *Switch*, which has been brought in by *SigB*, is true, then, after a delay of between 15 and 30 minutes, but only if at that time *SigA* has again been raised, *SigA* is switched off and transactions *TransA* and *TransB* are initiated.

The FORALL on the next line is an iterator over all elements of the set *SetX*. Here, for each such element, transaction *TransC* is to be initiated. One of the arguments of this transaction is to be supplied by a user — this argument is represented by an underscore. Note that *SetX* has been brought in by *SigB*. The next two lines define reminders, one to be issued immediately, and the other after a delay of four hours.

The components of an action are interpreted in terms of time Petri nets [5]. Then an entire action of arbitrary complexity can be represented by a time Petri net, as we show in [5]. Since UML activity diagrams are just streamlined basic Petri nets, SF process specifications can be represented by UML activity diagrams, but with time-related annotations added. Also, since Petri nets are considered well suited for specification of workflows (see p.119 of [18], and p.368 of [29]), SF can be used as a workflow specification language, which we already noted in [7].

6 Discussion Topics

By identifying transactional and procedural computations as the two principal modes of computing we have tried to give a basis for the examination of some recent trends in information systems and data base research. For example, active data bases can be regarded as transactional systems in which the triggers correspond to our actions. However, there are numerous unresolved questions regarding transactional computation. We introduce some of them in what follows. These questions were the basis for a discussion session. Following each topic, comments by participants are given in full or in summary. Particularly thoughtful comments were submitted after the workshop by E.O. De Brock, G. Saake, H. Schuldt, and K.-D. Schewe.

1. What is the best way of combining specifications of transactions and procedures? How suitable are our actions for this purpose?

Comments: (a) For each system specification it is interesting to know what are the needs of the application area in terms of expressiveness. Then a certain language may be chosen according to individual preferences and understandability. In general, I do not believe that there is one overall "best" solution for all application scenarios. (b) This question can only be answered after making precise the difference between transactions and procedures. I prefer to speak about atomic actions (comparable to a method invocation or an SQL update) and transactions composed of these actions as units of integrity preservation.

(c) It depends on the extent to which one wants to combine transactions and procedures. When a procedure forms the basis that is enhanced so as to make it transactional, then it is ok. (ATB: This comment is based on a view of procedures and transactions that differs somewhat from that advanced above, where we consider transactions to be more primitive than procedures. Of course, sooner or later, transactions have to be implemented, and then they become procedural.)

2. Should the specification of transactions be explicit or implicit? Implicit specification means that not every transaction that will be needed is specified. Instead, a set of predicates defines permissible system states and state transitions. When, for example, a transaction puts the system into an impermissible state, the system is to be restored to a permissible state, but how this is done is left unspecified.

Comments: (a) In the paper by de Brock in this volume the set of permissible system states is simply captured by a database universe U and the set of state transitions by a transition relation R on U. Under this approach it can be clearly and neatly specified what should happen in case a transaction leads into an impermissible state — see the discussion following Theorem 1 of that paper. (b) Note that in traditional database systems in general you have to specify only your transaction; recovery is performed by the database management system transparently. (c) It is well known that there is no algorithmic solution for the transformation of an implicit specification with lots of static and dynamic constraints into an (executable) explicit specification — see, e.g., [1]. This implies that whenever an implicit application appears to be suitable in terms of an intended application, there is a need for pragmatically driven refinement process. I would prefer to provide application-specific refinement calculi for that purpose, consisting of certain predefined and a priori correct refinement rules — such a system of rules for relational reification can be found in [19]. On the related issue of consistency enforcement, we have defined greatest consistent specifications and variants thereof. This work includes a characterization of desirable properties in consistency enforcement and contains results on commutativity and compositionality [22,21]. On the other hand it shows the non-computability of any reasonable approach and the non-suitability of triggers. (d) If there are many types of transactions, then invariants may be a better solution. (e) Complete specification of all possible transactions is only possible in very restricted application areas, and is feasible only for safety-critical systems. However, in some scenarios it may be feasible to specify a set of a few generic transaction patterns that are to guarantee integrity instead of all transactions. A sound mix of those alternatives will enhance the reliability and performance of information systems even if it is not a 100 percent solution. Implicitly specified transactions require expensive monitoring of constraints.

3. System transactions are candidates for implicit specification, but, since prompted and user specifications relate to the user interface, is it not essential that they be specified explicitly?

Comments: (a) Yes, it is our experience that it is essential that they be specified explicitly: a lot of misunderstandings will otherwise be left unnoticed. (b) In most cases, user transactions have to be specified explicitly (e.g. by some application program linked to a database). But what if some user sitting on a SQL GUI types in his/her update, insert, etc. statements in an ad-hoc way? This suggests that it is not necessary to have a complete specification of a transaction in all cases. (c) It is my true belief that only a holistic view of an information system will lead to well designed information systems. This means that all aspects of a system are to be specified at the same time, taking care of interdependencies. In particular, the user interface is not something to be added on later or to be derived automatically. A strategy which emphasizes "do first this, then that" is not adequate. (ATB: Comment c emphasizes that the traditional separation between specification, the "what", and design, the "how", may not be productive.)

4. A dialogue system is transactional, but it consists of a very large number of very simple transactions. What is the best way of specifying such a system? Is a separate specification step even needed in the development of such a system?

Comments: (a) The best way to develop dialogue systems is to use an integrated approach, as covered in, for example, our work on dialogue objects [20]. (b) A straightforward way is to specify all transactions independently (in fact, they are independent; otherwise there would be no separation) and have a (database) system enforce correctness. To this end, allowed system states (or, more easily, forbidden system states) have to be specified and have to be enforced (=invariants). (c) For large systems we need a modularized approach, such as proposed in object-oriented specification languages for information systems (see, for example, the language TROLL [12]). This approach allows the separate specification of small composable parts of an information system, called objects, which can be handled as small reactive and communicating systems.

5. Generalizing the implicitness-explicitness issue, are there "best" models and notations, or is the acceptance of a particular model or notation determined by the personality of a user? This may depend on deep-seated traits such a left-brain or right-brain dominance. It has long been recognized that users have different attitudes to the form of a query language (see, e.g., [28]). Is one form really better than another, or is it merely more appropriate for a particular user?

Comments: (a) What is relevant in specification is expressiveness and semantics. Which specific language (or graphical formalism, which is also a language) is used may then become a matter of taste and general conventions within a company or development project. If effective transformations are at hand, different formalisms may be combined. Usage is a matter of pragmatics. (b) There is no "best" model well-suited for all application scenarios.

6. Is it necessary to take special steps to assist communication across "personality gaps"? In other words, should we develop tool support for a transformation between textual (e.g., SF) and graphical (e.g., UML) representations at the specification level?

Comments: (a) UML is nothing, because it is just syntax and pictures without clearly defined semantics. The same applies to OMT, Booch method and the other predecessors of UML. Usually, system design is organized within projects, and, with respect to a project, representation means are fixed. Then it is important to emphasize the perspective of the user, i.e., to ask, how people will work with a system. (b) I agree that such special steps are needed.

7. Does explicit specification of all transactions necessarily mean that system integrity is to be maintained by preconditions? The invariants that specify permissible states and state transitions under implicitness constitute an equivalent mode of integrity control. However, one of the reasons for giving control over process data to the manager of the process is that this allows some preconditions of some transactions to be sometimes ignored at the discretion of the manager of the process. This raises two questions. First, how are such exceptions to be reconciled with corresponding invariants, should such invariants exist? Second, should we introduce a notation for preconditions that explicitly allows overrides for certain transactions, and, in case an override is to be effective for just a limited time interval, indicates the length of this time interval?

Comments: (a) My answer to the first question is No, and I agree with the next sentence — see again the discussion following Theorem 1 in the paper by de Brock in this volume. My answer to the rest of the discussion is that there should be two transactions in such cases, one for managers and one for ordinary employees, or that the specification of the transaction contains a case analysis (for managers and non-managers). This avoids a lot of problems, including the ones mentioned. (b) In general, you may want to consider static, transition and dynamic constraints. In the first two cases there exist well known proof obligations for consistency. Then the task is either to verify these conditions or to use consistency enforcement (see comments on 2). Exception handling is related to overspecification: (transition) constraints are too strong. In most case it is preferably to leave a certain decision latitude to the user and to specify not what must be done, but instead, what is not allowed. In some sense this is exactly the spirit of Wegner's co-inductive view on interaction. To my true belief this approach is best captured by dialogue objects (see comments on 4). The issue of "weak constraints", possibly to be specified in deontic logic, is still a challenging research issue. (c) In my opinion, preconditions are too weak. When transactions have to transfer one allowed system state into another one, some kind of invariant has to exist that may be temporarily violated within one transaction but that has to be re-established at least at the end of a transaction. (d) No. That is just one approach to do the job. Other approaches are monitoring, query and update rewriting, active rules, etc.

8. How are we to assist unsophisticated users in the definition of preconditions? Although preconditions are in general easier to write than "global" invariants, even people with a good understanding of formal logic are known to make errors in writing logical expressions. In [6] we consider a visual approach to defining the answer to a query, and we indicate that, in parallel with the construction of this answer, the system could generate a predicate. Could this approach be used to construct preconditions? A broader question relates to our ability to convert global invariants into preconditions, and vice versa.

Comments: (a) My answer to the first question is that we (as analysts) have to do it and not, e.g., the librarians in your example. My reaction to the second sentence is that it turns out to be a good check to translate your resulting logical expression back again to the natural language of the user. (b) In fact, communication with users in unavoidable and specifications have to be explained (see comments on 6). (c) Unsophisticated users should deliver examples and counter-examples that are to be transformed into logical expressions by analysts. Then we can start an iterative process of refinement/validation. The first step can even be supported by learning or data mining tools.

9. Is there a difference between active data bases and information systems, and, if so, what is it? What, if any, difference is there between information systems and control systems? Medina-Mora *et al* [15] distinguish between material, information, and business process perspectives. To what extent can this classification assist in the specification of transactions?

Comments: (a) I see information systems as covering a much broader ground than active databases. The latter are just one way of implementing an information system. (b) There is a significant difference between ADBs and ISs. The latter do not just comprise databases, but also application programs, constraints, user interfaces, etc. What is important is the purpose and the usage of a system including ergonomic aspects, preservation of user skills, etc. When we are talking about information systems we also mean their environment, which brings us to the consideration of aspects that are not computable, e.g. the human work with an IS. ADBs, on the other hand, merely capture a very limited amount of system dynamics, represented in the form of rules. There are significant limitations even w.r.t. problems that are being claimed as major applications, such as consistency enforcement. (c) There is no user interaction with ADBs; the qualifier "active" is therefore somewhat misleading.

10. Do existing workflow management systems provide sufficiently effective mechanisms for the sequencing, coordination, and synchronization of transactions?

Comments: (a) Commercial workflow management systems definitely not! They support some limited kind of failure handling and persistence, but, to the best of my knowledge, concurrency is not properly addressed by any of the commercial products. Within the WISE project of ETH at Zürich, we developed a process management system that is aware of concurrency, thus offering not only the persistent storage of process states and sophisticated failure handling mechanisms, but also the correct scheduling of processes accessing shared resources. (b) Workflow systems ignore the differences pointed out under 9. Human work, especially how it differs from computable processes, is ignored. Wegner [27] shows the difference between interaction and computation. Stated differently, workflow systems lead to a completely wrong view of information systems.

11. How relevant is speech/act and language/act research to the specification of transactions? It appears that speech acts have a very similar structure to our transaction/action patterns (see, e.g., [3]).

12. What exactly is a transaction?

Comments: (a) In my opinion a transaction on a state space U is simply a function from U into U — see Definition 1 in the paper by de Brock in this volume. (b) In my traditional thinking, transactions are atomic and isolated state changes (encompassing a set of basic operations), bringing a system from one consistent state to another (not necessarily different) one. The actions as described in the paper are in my opinion much more: they correspond to ECA rules of active databases. Therefore, they are not only actions but do also indicate when these actions are to be executed. (c) The standard use of the notion "transaction" is an execution of a database program reduced to database-relevant operations. In the paper the term is used more or less in the sense of an atomic database program. (d) There does not appear to be a clear understanding of how a transaction differs from an event. (e) A transaction is any operation that depends on a system state, which would include query processing. Procedures are state-independent. (f) A transaction is an explicitly specified transformation of the database state that preserves integrity.

References

1. S. Abiteboul and V. Vianu. A Transaction-based Approach to Relational Database Specification. *Journal of the ACM*, 36:758–789, 1989.
2. B. Babin, F. Lustman, and P. Shoval. Specification and Design of Transactions in Information Systems: A Formal Approach. *ACM Transactions on Information Systems*, 17:814–829, 1991.
3. M. D. Beer, T. J. M. Bench-Capon, and A. Sixsmith. Dialogue Management in a Virtual College. In *Database and Expert System Applications, Proc. of the 10th Int. Conf., DEXA'99*, pages 521–530, Lecture Notes in Computer Science, Vol. 1677, Springer-Verlag, 1999.
4. B. Berthomieu and M. Diaz. Modeling and Verification of Time Dependent Systems Using Time Petri Nets. *IEEE Transaction on Software Engineering*, 17:259–273, 1991.
5. A. T. Berztiss. A Linkage Mechanism for Transactions. Available from the author.
6. A. T. Berztiss. The Query Language Vizla. *IEEE Transactions on Knowledge and Data Engineering*, 5:813–825, 1993.
7. A. T. Berztiss. *Software Methods for Business Reengineering*. Springer-Verlag, 1995.
8. T. H. Davenport. *Process Innovation: Reengineering Work through Information Technology*. Harvard Business School Press, 1993.
9. B. de Brock. *Foundations of Semantic Databases*. Prentice Hall, 1995.
10. D. Harel. Statecharts: a Visual Formalism for Complex Systems. *Science of Computer Programming*, 8:231–274, 1987.
11. M. Jackson and G. Twaddle. *Business Process Implementation: Building Workflow Systems*. Addison-Wesley, 1997.
12. R. Jungclaus, G. Saake, T. Hartmann, and C. Sernadas. TROLL – A Language for Object-Oriented Specification of Information Systems. *ACM Transactions on Information Systems*, 14(2):175–211, April 1996.
13. F. Kroger. *Temporal Logic of Programs*. Springer-Verlag, 1987.
14. R. Kurki-Suonio and R. Mikkonen. Harnessing the Power of Interaction. In H. Jaakkola, H. Kangassalo, and H. Kawaguchi, editors, *Information Modelling and Knowledge Bases X*, pages 1–11, IOS Press, 1999.

15. P. Medina-Mora, T. Winograd, R. Flores, and C. F. Flores. The Action Workflow Approach to Workflow Management Technology. In J. Turner and R. Kraut, editors, *Proc. 4th Conf. Computer-Supported Cooperative Work*, pages 281–288, ACM Press, 1992.

16. T. A. Mueck. Active Databases: Concepts and Design Support. In *Advances in Computers*, pages 107–189, Vol. 39, Academic Press, 1994.

17. G. Saake. Descriptive Specification of Database Object Behaviour. *Data & Knowledge Engineering*, 6(1):47–74, 1991.

18. T. Schael. *Workflow Management Systems for Process Organization*, Lecture Notes in Computer Science, Vol. 1096. Springer-Verlag, 2 edition, 1998.

19. K.-D. Schewe. Specification and Development of Correct Relational Database Programs. Technical report, TU Clausthal, 1995.

20. K.-D. Schewe and B. Schewe. Integrating Database and Dialogue Design. To appear in Knowledge & Information Systems.

21. K.-D. Schewe and B. Thalheim. Limits of Rule Triggering Systems for Integrity Maintenance in the Context of Transition Specifications. *Acta Cybernetica*, 13:277–304, 1998.

22. K.-D. Schewe and B. Thalheim. Towards a Theory of Consistency Enforcement. *Acta Informatica*, 36:97–141, 1999.

23. A. P. Sistla and O. Wolfson. Temporal Triggers in Active Databases. *IEEE Transactions on Knowledge and Data Engineering*, 7:471–486, 1995.

24. M. Stonebraker, J. Anton, and E. Hanson. Extending a Database System with Procedures. *ACM Transactions on Database Systems*, 12(3):350–376, September 1987.

25. M. Thorin. *Real-time Transaction Processing*. Macmillan, 1992.

26. W. M. Turski. Time Considered Irrelevant for Real-time Systems. *BIT*, 28:473–486, 1988.

27. P. Wegner. Why Interaction is more Powerful than Algorithms. *Communications of the ACM*, 40(5):80–91, May 1997.

28. C. Welty and D. W. Stemple. Human Factors Comparison of a Procedural and a Nonprocedural Query Language. *ACM Transactions on Database System*, 6:626–649, 1981.

29. M. Weske and G. Vossen. Workflow Languages. In P. Bernus, K. Mertins, and G. Schmidt, editors, *Handbook on Architectures of Information Systems*, pages 359–379, Springer-Verlag, 1998.

Author Index

Lecture Notes in Computer Science

For information about Vols. 1–1697
please contact your bookseller or Springer-Verlag